Lifestyle

English for work, socializing & travel

Intermediate Coursebook

Iwonna Dubicka & Margaret O'Keeffe

PEARSON

Longman

Contents

180514 Language pack (1 book + 3 CDs) Intermediate. 31 LS CB

1

A Tense review
B Present tense question forms
C Free-time activities
D **Communication strategies** Making suggestions
E **Interaction** Life coaching

Quality time

Tense review

Reading: Got things to do

1 Is your life busy at the moment or do you have plenty of free time?

2 Look at the to-do list. Do you have any similar jobs to do? What other jobs are on your to-do list? Which jobs on your list will you enjoy doing and which will you dislike? Why?

to do

Complete tax form ✔

Reply to emails ✔

Take clothes to cleaners

Submit expenses ✔

Make dentist's appointment

Plan trip to Athens ✔

Look for cheaper car insurance ✔

Sell the old printer on eBay

Buy Jim and Jenny's wedding present ✔

Pay gas bill ✔

Clean out garage

3 Read the website. Would you like to use its services? Why?/Why not?

Have you got too much to do and no time to do it?

Gottajobtodo.com helps thousands of people like you every month. It's as easy as one, two, three. Here's how it works.

1 **Post a job ad on our site**
It doesn't matter what it is – no job's too big or too small. You can give all your boring chores to our assistants.

2 **Choose your assistant**
Individuals and companies reply to your ad and bid a price. You just select the one you want to do your job.

3 **Sit back and relax**
Let someone else get on with it. You can put your time and energy into more important projects instead.

In the past our assistants have done everything you can imagine. They've painted houses, filled in tax forms, researched better rates for car insurance, taught kids English, built websites, and even bought Aunty Freda's birthday gift. Last year more than 100,000 people found the help they needed at **Gottajobtodo.com**.

So tell your friends and family you're going to have a lot more time to spend together. We have thousands of assistants waiting to bid on your jobs, so you'll have time to begin those projects you've always wanted to do. You're going to love **Gottajobtodo.com**

4 Find words and phrases in the website text which match these definitions.

1 it's not important
2 routine boring tasks
3 advertisement
4 an offer made at a stated price
5 do something on your own without help
6 searched carefully for facts for a thing or person

5 Look at the three numbered paragraphs in the website. Which tenses are used? Past, present, future or a mixture?

Listening: Assistants

6 What do you think the people in these photos are thinking? What kind of assistant do you think they'd like to have?

7))) **1.1** Listen to the people in exercise 6. Find out if you are right.

8))) Listen again and complete the sentences.

1 It always _____ longer to get home on Tuesdays.

2 I'm _____ exhausted but I'd better go.

3 I'm _____ the minutes this evening.

4 I think _____ _____ these ones … or the other ones.

5 No, the other ones _____ _____ my toes.

6 I'm _____ _____ _____ him at home next time.

7 Well, that new diet _____ _____ .

8 I've _____ _____ good at dieting.

Grammar: Tense review

9 Look at the sentences in exercise 8. Which tenses are they talking about?

a past time   **c** future time

b present time   **d** mixture

It always takes longer to get home on Tuesdays.
– They are talking about present time.

10 Compare your answers with a partner. Do you agree? Then find examples of these verb forms in the sentences in exercise 8.

Grammar: Tense review

a the present simple	**e** the present continuous for future
b the present continuous	**f** the past simple
c the *will* future	**g** the past continuous
d the *going to* future	**h** the present perfect

>> **For more information on the English tense system, see page 160.**

Speaking: Past, present and future

11 Write an example of each of these things in the sections of the circle below.

- a routine job you do every day
- a job you didn't have time to do yesterday
- a project you're working on at the moment
- what you were doing at 6 p.m. last night
- a job you think you will do tomorrow
- something you've wanted to do for ages, but you haven't had time
- the name of a place where you've never been to but you've always wanted to go
- something you plan to do this weekend
- something you're going to do as soon as you get home
- something you hate doing but have to do

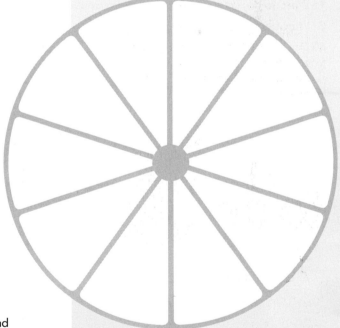

12 Work in pairs. Show each other your circles. Take it in turns to ask questions about the things you have written and develop conversations.

A: Why have you written 'fix door bell'?

B: That's a job I plan to do this weekend. My front doorbell isn't working.

A: Is it broken then?

B: I'm not sure. I'm going to replace the batteries and see.

TALKING POINT
- Are you good at organizing your time? Do you use any kind of planner?
- Do you think modern technology has helped people organize themselves better? Why?/Why not?

Listening: Commuting

1 How do you get to work or school in the mornings? How long does your journey take? Is it generally stressful or peaceful? Why?

2))) **1.2** Listen to a radio interview with some commuters on a train. Make notes on the activities they mention.

Name	What they usually do	What they are doing now
Mario		
Alissa		
Steve		
Wanda		

3 Look at the questions the interviewer asked the commuters. Underline the present simple and present continuous forms. Which questions include both forms? Ask and answer the questions with a partner.

1 What do you usually do while you're commuting?
2 What book are you reading at the moment?
3 Does it take you long to get to work?
4 Do you listen to music while you're commuting?
5 What are you daydreaming about at the moment?
6 Are you studying for any exams at the moment?

Grammar: Present tense question forms

4 Look at the table and answer the questions.

Present tense question forms	
Present simple	
(yes/no questions)	(Wh- questions)
Do you usually **take** the train? **Does** he usually **take** the train?	What **do** you usually **do**? What **does** he usually **do**?
Present continuous	
(yes/no questions)	(Wh- questions)
Is he/she **studying** for exams at the moment? **Are** you **studying** for exams at the moment?	What **is** he **doing** now? What **are** you **doing** now?

Which tense do we use to talk about:

a short-term or temporary activities?

b long-term situations?

>> For more information on the present simple and present continuous, see page 161.

5 Here are some things commuters sometimes do to pass the time on trains. Think of five more to add to the list.

- think about the day ahead
- eat snacks
- draw pictures
- study a language
- do crosswords and puzzles
- look out of the window at the scenery
- sleep
- chat with other travellers
- brush or comb their hair

6 Work in groups. What do you normally do on long journeys? Which are the best ways to pass the time and why?

7 Sometimes we just have to wait for things to happen. In your groups, discuss the best way to pass the time in these situations.

1 While you're standing in a long queue at the airport.

2 While you're waiting for red lights to turn green.

3 While you're listening to recorded music on the phone, waiting for someone to answer.

4 While you're waiting for your dentist to see you.

5 While you're waiting for your computer to boot up.

A: What do you usually do when you are standing in a queue at the airport?

B: I usually watch the other people in the queue.

A: What about you?

B: I sometimes close my eyes and meditate or I read something.

Speaking: Making changes

8 Look at the list below. Which of these aspects of your life would you like to change?

- get more sleep
- lose weight or get fitter
- save money
- find a new job or place to live
- study more English
- learn something new
- become a better parent / husband / wife / boss / employee
- something else (what?)

9 Work in groups. You are going to discuss making changes to your life. Follow the instructions below. Then report back to the class. Which people are making the most changes to their lives?

1 Tell one another what you want to do and why.

2 Explain what you're doing to try to change the situation.

A: Are you trying to find a new job?

B: Yes. I work for a bank at the moment but I have a degree in journalism. I want to be a reporter.

A: Are you looking for jobs in television or radio?

B: I'm answering ads for both. And I'm networking more so I make more contacts.

Writing: Responding to a radio show

10 You are on a daily commute to work and you see the radio's website about commuting. The radio station has invited listeners to email them about what they do while they commute. Send an email to the radio station. Include information about what you usually do and what you are doing now.

TALKING POINT
- Are you generally a patient person? Why?/Why not?
- Do you think things like doing breathing exercises or yoga could improve your life? Why?/Why not?

Reading: Activity Superstore

1 Look at the photos of some activities that are advertised on a website. Match the photos with the name of the sport or activity.

> flying lessons   aqua sphering   spy academy   fashion shoot

2 Work in pairs. Student A: Read the first two adverts. Student B: Read the last two adverts. Match the name of the activity in exercise 1 to the adverts.

3 Try to remember the essential information about the activities and explain them to your partner.

A Dream Come True

1 _____

Ever wondered what it's like inside a washing machine? Then aqua sphering is just the thing for you! It's the latest extreme activity where you roll down a hill in a huge plastic bubble with thirty litres of water. The ball can reach speeds of up to 50km per hour. It's exhilarating and terrifying at the same time. You'll love it!

Price €73.

2 _____

If you fancy yourself as the next James Bond then our Spy Academy is for you! You'll learn how to use specialist spy gadgets* such as hidden cameras and listening devices*. You'll play with some of the famous Bond vehicles such as the moon buggy, and you'll also receive expert advice on how to escape the enemy. Note: No weapons used.

Price €112.

3 _____

This activity will leave you looking and feeling truly amazing. Relax as top professionals create your new look. Your day will start with an interview with a top stylist, followed by stunning make-up and then an incredible up-to-date hairstyle. Then enjoy a fashion photo shoot capturing your fabulous look.

Price €157.

4 _____

We offer you a great range of flying activities to choose from. You can experience the thrill* of taking the controls yourself in a flying lesson, enjoy spectacular views from a balloon, or keep your feet firmly on the ground with a flight simulator*. We have something for everyone.

Price €123–€337.

gadgets: small, useful machines or tools
devices: machines or tools that do a special job
thrill: sense of excitement
flight simulator: a machine that tries to copy the experience of flying an aircraft, used to train pilots

Word focus: Free-time activities

4 Name something you like doing in your free time. Did you like doing this when you were younger? In what ways have your leisure activities changed over time?

5 What do you think most young Europeans aged 15–30 do in their free time? Read the text and find out if you are right.

Young Europeans are still reading books

The two most common leisure activities among young Europeans are taking exercise (45% – going for a walk, a bike ride, practising sports, etc.) and meeting friends (40% – eating, dancing, having a drink, hanging out, etc.).

Roughly one in five (21%) young adults say using the internet or playing video games is one of their preferred activities. Watching television is mentioned by 19%, listening to music by 17% and going to the cinema, theatre or concerts by 16%. Perhaps it's surprising these days, but more young people (one in four) mention reading a book.

6 Do you think the statistics would be similar in your country? Why?/Why not?

7 Complete the notes on -ing forms in the table with the examples from the text. Then find more examples of -ing forms in the text.

-ing forms
-ing forms can be:
1 parts of a continuous verb form
Young Europeans are still _____ books.
2 adjectives
Perhaps it's _____ .
3 used like a noun
_____ television is mentioned by 19%.
When -ing forms are used like nouns, we call them gerunds.
>> For more information on -ing forms, see page 172.

8 Tick (✓) the leisure activities you like doing. Are there any you have never tried? Add some more activities that you like doing to the list.

running   playing chess   skiing   cycling   swimming
yoga   playing computer games   climbing
making jewellery   singing   doing puzzles
visiting museums/art galleries   gardening   diving
photography   shopping   birdwatching
going for a walk   doing up old cars

Speaking: Choosing an activity

9 How do you and your family relax in your free time? Do you have a specific hobby or interest?

- One of my/our free-time interests is …
- I'm/We're into …
- I/We like / enjoy … ing.
- I am/We are keen on …
- I/We spend a lot of time …

10 Discuss these statements. Which ones are true for you and why?

1 I try to find new ways to relax in my free time.

2 I'm bored with the traditional hobbies and activities.

3 I'd like to try a new sport or activity.

4 I'd like to do as many new things as possible before I retire/die.

11 Work in pairs. Look at the adverts in exercise 2 and choose the most appropriate activity for each of these people. Give your reasons. What other activities do you think they might like?

1 Your friend Helena loves adventure sports. She's really into skiing and diving.

2 Baz works with you. He's a shy person who likes computer games. It's his 30th birthday and you and your colleagues want to organize a group activity.

3 It's your parents' wedding anniversary and you want to find an activity they would like to do together. Your mother is keen on photography. Your father likes doing up old cars.

4 Your younger sister passed all her exams and you want to give her something special to celebrate. She loves clothes and shopping.

5 Your brother works in Research & Development for a pharmaceutical company. He enjoys gardening in his free time.

6 Nigel loves gadgets and finding out how machines work. You want to give him a surprise present.

Writing: Giving a dream

12 Write an email to a friend or family member who has something to celebrate and say you want to give them a *Live the Dream!* activity. Tell them what it is and why you think they'd like it.

TALKING POINT
- What other activities or sports would you like to do in your lifetime?
- What dream activity would you like to receive as a present from someone?

Listening: Issues with a project

1 A deadline is a date or time by which you have to do or complete something. Do you ever have deadlines at work? What for? Do you or your colleagues ever have problems meeting deadlines? Why?

2 Read an email about a deadline. What is the deadline for?

☐ **Subject: Project status**

Hi Valerie
I'm just writing to warn you that we're running about two weeks behind schedule with the new website. I know we wanted it by 1 May, but it won't be ready in time. I propose we delay the site launch by another month. What do you think?
All the best
Jay

---

3 Find words and phrases in the email which mean the following.

1 be prepared before the deadline

2 tell someone about something before it happens so they are not worried or surprised

3 later than planned

4 wait until a later time to do something

5 when a new product or service becomes available

4))) 1.3 Valerie talks to Jay about his email. Listen to their conversation. Who says what? Write *V* for Valerie and *J* for Jay.

1 Who says why the project is behind schedule?

2 Who wants to launch the site on 1 May?

3 Who wants to recruit an expert to work on the project?

4 Who doesn't want to pay someone to help?

5 Do you think Jay's suggestion was a good one? Why?/Why not?

6))) Try to remember the missing words from this part of the conversation. Then listen again and check your answers.

Valerie: Is there any way we can have the site ready for the first of May? It's very important.

Jay: ^{1}_____ _____ _____ someone to help us? What do you think?

Valerie: Well, it's an ^{2}_____ idea. Do you ^{3}_____ getting someone from another department?

Jay: No, I mean hiring an external contractor. We could have the site ready in time then.

Valerie: Oh, I see.

Jay: My brother-in-law's a very good web designer. ^{4}_____ _____ _____ _____ him?

Valerie: Um, I ^{5}_____ _____ . It sounds expensive.

Jay: I ^{6}_____ _____ to him today if you like.

Valerie: ^{7}_____ _____ at some other options first.

Jay: Oh, OK.

Valerie: ^{8}_____ _____ _____ a bit later to discuss this again?

Speaking: Making suggestions

7 Find five expressions for making suggestions in exercise 6.

8 Complete these suggestions in the table by putting the verbs in brackets in the correct form.

Making suggestions

1 *What about _____ (delay) the launch date by a month?*
2 *Let's _____ (add) adverts to the site.*
3 *We could _____ (get) a contractor to do the work.*
4 *How about _____ (meet) after lunch?*
5 *Why don't we _____ (look) at some more options?*

! *propose, recommend, suggest* are all verbs that are formal and more common in written than spoken English.

*I **propose** we delay the site launch by another month.* (written)

What about delaying the site launch by another month? (spoken)

9 Read about some more written suggestions. What do you think these people actually said? Use the spoken expressions in exercise 8.

1 Sally proposed we introduce a blog on the website.
2 Tom recommended adding staff photos to the site.
3 Juan suggested we work late to finish the project in time.
4 Anna recommended web training for the whole department.
5 Jean-Philippe proposed ending the meeting earlier than planned.
6 Gudrun suggested we cancel next week's meeting.

10 Valerie tries to reject Jay's suggestions politely. Look at what Valerie thinks in the table and match it to what she says in exercise 6.

Responding to suggestions

Valerie thinks ...	Valerie says ...
I don't like that idea.	_____
No, we're not going to pay for a contractor.	_____
I don't want Jay to talk to his brother-in-law.	_____

11 Do people say similar things in your language when they want to be polite? Think of examples when you have to reject other people's suggestions politely.

12 Work in pairs or small groups. Take it in turns to present one of these problems.

1 Read your problem and then explain it to your partner(s). Ask *Have you got any suggestions?* and try to collect as many ideas as you can.

2 If you like an idea, respond positively and say things like *Good suggestion!* or *Great idea!* If you don't like it, be polite.

The hospital you work for is hosting ten visiting doctors from Australia next month. You're responsible for arranging their weekend activities. You need to plan things to do with them on Friday night, Saturday and Sunday.

You're organizing a 'Bring your child to work day'. It's a day when employees' children will accompany their mum or dad to work, and learn a little about what they do. You need to plan eight hours of entertaining and safe activities for 25 children aged 6–10 and 35 children aged 11–16.

You've noticed your colleagues are putting on weight and in need of exercise. They all work long hours and spend far too long sitting at their desks. How can you encourage everyone to take more exercise?

One of your colleagues spends a lot of time stopping by people's desks for long social conversations that interrupt your work and the work of others nearby. When you complain, he just laughs. You've also complained to your boss, but she doesn't seem to care.

Reminder

Grammar reference
pages **161** and **162**

In the present simple we use *do* or *does* to form questions.

Does it take long to commute to the office?

In the present continuous we change the word order to form questions.

Are you doing anything to change the way you work?

When we respond to suggestions that we don't like or aren't sure about, we try to sound polite.

A: How about asking your boss for help?

B: Well, it's an interesting idea.

Listening: Interview with a life coach

1 What would you most like to change about a) your job and b) your life?

2))) **1.4** Listen to an interview with a life coach, Nancy Bailey. Are these statements true (T) or false (F)?

What is coaching?

1 Life coaches help people to identify life issues that they want to change.

2 Our clients are mainly company executives.

3 We can help people with their career choices.

4 We usually meet clients for an hour every week.

5 The client has to be in the same country as the coach.

6 It takes about a year to get results from coaching.

3))) Listen again and correct the false statements in exercise 2.

4))) **1.5** Listen to phone conversations with two of Nancy's clients. What life changes is she helping them with?

Joe
Sales Manager
Manages a team of 30 staff
Life issue:

_____

Kim
Assistant in an
import-export firm
Life issue:

_____

5 'Time stealers' are common things that waste time at work. Tell your partner two things you do that waste time at work. Make some suggestions to help each other stop wasting time.

6 Nancy sent Joe information on 'time stealers' to help him manage his time better. Read the text. With a partner make suggestions to help Joe manage his time.

TIME STEALERS

These are the most common things that waste time at work. Tick (✔) the top five which are the major obstacles to your own time management – your 'time stealers'.

1 Interruptions – telephone, email and visitors

2 Meetings

3 Tasks you should delegate

4 Procrastination* and indecision

5 Dealing with team members

6 Crisis management

7 Lack of* information or technical knowledge

8 Unclear communication, objectives and priorities

9 Lack of planning

10 Stress and fatigue

11 Inability to say 'No'

12 Desk management and personal disorganization

Fortunately, there are strategies you can use to manage your time, be more in control and reduce stress.

procrastination: delaying doing things you have to do
lack of: when there isn't enough of something

7 Work in pairs. Prepare a short talk for the rest of the class with strategies and suggestions to help people manage their time better.

Speaking: Change we need

8 Read these comments from two of Nancy's clients. What aspect of their lives do they want to change or plan?

Vikram

My catering business is doing really well and I'd like to expand it. But I waste a lot of time doing lots of little jobs that I did when the company was smaller. My business is very important to me but at the same time I'm always busy and I just want to see more of my wife and kids. I also have a very long commute to work.

Ruth

I work for an advertising agency as an admin. assistant. It's not very well-paid or interesting work. I left school at 18 and I don't have a degree. I'd like to get a better job but I'm not well-qualified. I really think I could be doing more creative work.

9 Look at the completed forms for Vikram and Ruth. Read the information and roleplay the telephone conversations between the client and the life coach.

Name: *Vikram Singh*

1 **For each of the following life areas, how would you rate your life out of 10? (10 being you can't imagine it could possibly be any better)**

Health & stress *6*
Money *8*
Own business or career *10*
Family & relationships *5*
Learning and growth *7*
Confidence *5*

2 **Which two areas are you prepared to improve over the next 6 months?**
time management, stress relief

3 **Please write down one thing you would like to have or achieve, but are not sure if or how you can have it?**
more family time

Name: *Ruth De Jesu*

1 **For each of the following life areas, how would you rate your life out of 10? (10 being you can't imagine it could possibly be any better)**

Health & stress *6*
Money *8*
Own business or career *3*
Family & relationships *5*
Learning and growth *3*
Confidence *4*

2 **Which two areas are you prepared to improve over the next 6 months?**
learning, career opportunities

3 **Please write down one thing you would like to have or achieve, but are not sure if or how you can have it?**
A more interesting creative job

Student A:

You are Vikram, one of Nancy's clients. Your life coach, Nancy, phones to talk about your situation. Respond to Nancy's questions and suggestions and make some suggestions of your own.

You are Nancy, the life coach. Phone your client, Ruth and ask questions about the form she has completed. Make suggestions for ways to improve your client's life.

Student B:

You are Nancy, the life coach. Phone your client Vikram and ask questions about the form he has completed. Make suggestions for ways to improve your client's life.

You are Ruth, one of Nancy's clients. Your life coach, Nancy, phones to talk about your situation. Respond to Nancy's questions and suggestions and make some suggestions of your own.

10))) **1.6** Listen to Vikram and Ruth. What has changed in their lives? How could Nancy help them now?

Writing: A way forward

11 Imagine you are Nancy. Write an email to either Vikram or Ruth and suggest a way forward.

Interaction

2

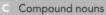
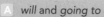

A will and going to
B Present continuous for future plans
C Compound nouns
D **Communication strategies** Agreeing and disagreeing
E **Interaction** Five days in Dubai

Globetrotters

will and going to

Listening: Hong Kong Airport

1 Discuss these questions.

1 How often do you travel for work or holidays?

2 Where do you usually go?

3 What are your plans for your next holiday/business trip?

2)) **1.7** Listen to two travellers taking part in a passenger survey at Hong Kong Airport. What does the interviewer give to each traveller?

3)) Read the interviewer's questions in the survey. Listen again and take notes to answer the questions.

Grammar: will and going to

4 Look at the sentences in the table from the first conversation and answer the questions.

Talking about the future

a I'm **going to** meet the sales and marketing managers.

b I'**ll** probably check my email.

c Then, I'm **going to** charge my cellphone.

d I think I'**ll** get a head and shoulder massage.

Which sentences are about:

1 firm intentions and plans that have already been made?

2 decisions that have just been made or are being made now?

>> For more information on the future, see page 166.

5 Look at the audio script of conversation 2 on page 143. How many times does the second passenger use *will* or *going to*? How certain does he sound about each plan or decision?

	Traveller 1	Traveller 2
1 Where are you travelling to today?		
2 What are you going to do there?		
3 Where are you going to stay?		
4 What are you going to do at the airport today?		
5 Will you buy anything special for yourself? What will you buy?		

Speaking: Plans and intentions

6 Work in pairs. Look at the information for two more travellers that Hong Li interviews. Look back at the questions in exercise 3. What other questions could you ask?

Zhi Peng

Definite plans:
Holiday with wife in Vancouver for three weeks
Go to a family wedding there
Stay with daughter and son-in-law
Take ferry to Vancouver Island
Do Tai Chi in Stanley Park

Possibilities:
Try rafting
Play golf

What he plans to do at the airport:
Watch CNN in the TV lounge
Possibly visit the duty-free shops

Tyler

Definite plans:
Go to Thailand
Travel round South East Asia with friends
Spend a year there
Ride an elephant in Thailand
Learn to dive in Indonesia

Possibilities:
Learn some Thai and Indonesian
Go trekking in the jungle

What she plans to do at the airport:
Update her travel blog in the internet café
Possibly buy some good sunglasses

> **!** *Travel* is most often used as a verb but can also be an uncountable noun. We don't say 'a travel'.
> Where are you **travelling** to today? (verb)
> Is business **travel** important for your job? (noun)
> A **trip** is a short journey or a short period of time in a place.
> And what is the purpose of your **trip**?

7 Work with a different partner. Roleplay the two interviews in exercise 6. Take it in turns to be Hong Li and the traveller.

8 Work in pairs. Look at these travel situations and decide what to do.

- You arrive at the check-in desk with ten kilos of excess baggage and no money to pay for it.

- Your flight is delayed until tomorrow morning. Your budget airline won't provide you with a hotel and you don't want to pay for accommodation yourself.

- You are in airport departures and someone has stolen your ticket, passport, wallet and mobile phone.

- You are stuck in a taxi in traffic getting to the airport and you're going to miss your flight home.

- You have won a competition. You have five minutes to fill a shopping basket with anything you want from the duty-free store.

- You are waiting at the carousel for your luggage and it doesn't appear. All the other passengers have their luggage.

9 Compare your plans with the rest of the class. Who has the best plan?

> **TALKING POINT**
> - What do you like/dislike about travelling?
> - What was your most memorable trip?

Reading: Home exchange stories

1 Discuss these questions.

1 Have you ever rented a room or apartment? When? What was it like?

2 Have you ever rented a holiday home?

3 Have you ever thought about exchanging homes with someone else for a holiday in a different town or country?

4 Can you think of any advantages and disadvantages in exchanging homes with someone else?

2 Read two readers' stories about home exchange in the *LA Times*. Who has had more positive experiences?

My wife, Shannon, and I have done three home swaps*. As we don't have any children it is fairly easy to arrange. The first, in London, was not so good. The house was cold and uncomfortable and there wasn't much furniture. Because of this first experience, we always ask for lots of photos of the home interior. In future, we will also make sure we're in the center of town, or a short bus ride to the center. I really don't want to use a car, because I have to drive so much in Los Angeles.

Carl, Ventura

We have exchanged homes 15 times and it has always been wonderful. We always exchange cars as well, which has saved us quite a bit of money. Having a base* makes it possible to plan short trips.

We like exchanges with families that also have children. It's great to arrive and have books, toys, bicycles, snow gear, etc., to borrow. And we love not having to eat out all the time. It's fun to experience life in a different country.

Sandra, Indian Wells

swap: exchange
base: main place to stay

3 Look at the readers' stories again. What advantages and disadvantages are mentioned?

4 Carl in Ventura reads Nicole's advert. Do you think Carl and his wife Shannon will like it? Give your reasons. What questions do you think the couple would ask Nicole and how would she reply?

Our home is located in Paris in the eleventh district – a perfect location to visit the city! We are planning a holiday in LA this spring. We are two adults and one child (three years old). The apartment is 70 sq m. It's on the seventh floor and there is a balcony with a great view of the neighbourhood. There are two bedrooms, a large living room, a shower room, and a well-equipped kitchen.

Nicole

Grammar: Present continuous for future plans

5 Look at Carl's email about his holiday arrangements. Complete the table and find examples in the email.

Hi Nicole

Guess what? It's all organized! Shannon and I are flying to London on May 23rd – it's cheaper than going direct to Paris and we want to see the city anyway. We're staying in a hotel in Piccadilly for three nights. We got a good deal through the airline.

Then we're taking the Eurostar to Paris. I got the train tickets online. So we're not arriving in Paris until about noon on May 26th and we're leaving on the morning of June 6th.

We'll probably take a few day trips from Paris. Is there anywhere you'd recommend? What time will you be home this evening? I'll phone you for some first-hand advice if you don't mind.

All the best

Carl

Future forms: Present continuous or *will*?

1 We use a) _____ to talk about plans and arrangements that are already decided and organized. We often use it with a definite place or time.
*Shannon and I **are flying** to London on May 23rd.*
We're ¹ _____ .
We're ² _____ .
We're not ³ _____ .
We're ⁴ _____ .

2 When there is no specific plan or arrangement we generally use
b) _____ .
We'll probably ⁵ _____ .
What time ⁶ _____ .

3 We also use c) _____ to talk about decisions that have just, or only recently, been made.
I'll ⁷ _____ .

>> For more information on future forms, see page 166.

6 Complete Nicole's email to Carl about her arrangements. Use the present continuous form of the verbs in brackets or *will*. Sometimes both are possible.

Hi Carl

We ¹ _____ (catch) our flight on 24 May, so we ² _____ (not/see) you in Paris. But don't worry, I ³ _____ (leave) the keys with our neighbour in apartment 5, and she ⁴ _____ (be) here to meet you. I ⁵ _____ (explain) some more things about our apartment nearer the time.

We've hired a car in the end and we ⁶ _____ (collect) it at LA Airport. We've bought tickets for Disneyland and we ⁷ _____ (go) there for two days. We ⁸ _____ (spend) a night in a motel so we don't have to drive back. We ⁹ _____ (probably/visit) Universal Studios, too, but we don't know when. I think we ¹⁰ _____ (eat in) most evenings because we ¹¹ _____ (be) out all day.

Warm regards

Nicole

Speaking: Choosing a home exchange

7 Choose one of the home exchanges from the website and plan a holiday. Think about these points:

- Where are you going and for how long?
- Who are you going with?
- What travel arrangements have you made?
- Where are you staying?
- What will you probably do when you are on holiday?

8 Work in pairs. Ask each other about your holiday arrangements and find out why your partner made his/her choices.

New York – Trendy Manhattan Apartment, New York, USA

FUN, FUN, FUN – Spectacular harbor and downtown view, Times Square location, floor to ceiling windows, sunny apartment in a luxurious new building

BEDROOMS: 1 BATHROOMS: 1 CHILDREN IN OUR PARTY: NO

Venezia, Italy

Romantic house in the heart of Venice. 10-minute walk to San Marco Square and the main shopping street

BEDROOMS: 2 BATHROOMS: 2 CHILDREN IN OUR PARTY: NO

Ho Chi Minh City, Vietnam

Luxurious villa with big garden & pool in most upscale part of Saigon

BEDROOMS: 5 BATHROOMS: 4 CHILDREN IN OUR PARTY: YES

Cusco, Peru

House close to Machu Picchu, incredible views

BEDROOMS: 5 BATHROOMS: 4 CHILDREN IN OUR PARTY: YES

Writing: Describing holiday plans

9 Write an email to a friend telling them about your holiday arrangements. Ask your friend about his/her plans.

TALKING POINT
- Would home exchange be a good way for you to have a holiday? Why?/Why not?
- Where would you like to go?

Reading: Unusual hotels

1 Look at these photos of hotels around the world. What do you think they were used for before they became hotels? Match the hotel to the description.

a

The 747 Jumbo Hostel, Sweden

Swedish businessman, Oscar Dios has converted a jumbo jet into an airport hostel. The newly opened Jumbo Hostel is only a ten-minute walk away from the check-in counters at Stockholm's Arlanda Airport. Ideal for travellers on a budget* who have an early flight and don't want to sleep at the airport, a room starts at 350 Swedish krona (€31.86), which is a lot less than hotel rooms outside major airports. Hotel staff wear flight attendant uniforms and all rooms are equipped with a flat screen TV and wi-fi. You can even get married on the wing of the plane! The only room that has its own bathroom is the honeymoon* suite situated in the cockpit.

on a budget: with not much money to spend
honeymoon: holiday for a couple who have just got married

2

c

Propeller Island City Lodge hotel, Germany

This former prison in Berlin offers a jailhouse experience. It looks like a prison with barred windows and some rooms even have a hole in the wall as an escape route. But what kind of guests pay to have bars outside the windows of a three-star hotel? According to the hotel manager, guests appreciate modern rooms and usually have a sense of humour. You get a traditional prison breakfast (a coffee and some bread with strawberry jam) and can sleep in striped pyjamas for an extra €5. Bathroom facilities are not separate from the rest of the room and there are no double beds, but rooms have two characteristics that previous inhabitants didn't enjoy – a mini-bar and power shower! One night will only cost you €45.

2 Read the hotel listings and match the hotels to this information.

1 These hotels are the cheapest. _____ and _____

2 This one has a suite for recently married couples. _____

3 This one has bathroom facilities in the room which are not private. _____

4 This hotel is near a good restaurant. _____

5 This hotel has rooms with flat screen TVs. _____

6 These hotels offer guests something to wear. _____ and _____

3 Which hotel would/wouldn't you like to stay in? Why?

Word focus: Compound nouns

4 Look at the information in the table about compound nouns.

Compound nouns

A compound noun is made up of two or more words. We can form compound nouns using different combinations:
noun + noun, e.g. *businessman, airport, hairdryer*
adjective + noun, e.g. *Swedish krona, double bed*

1 We sometimes write two words together, e.g. *honey + moon = honeymoon, bath + robe = bathrobe, sea + food = seafood.*
2 We sometimes use a hyphen, e.g. *ten-minute walk, check-in, 24-hour room service, three-star hotel.*
3 They can also appear as two separate words, e.g. *hotel guest, room service, power shower.*

>> For more information on compound nouns, see page 171.

b Molja Fyr lighthouse hotel, Norway

Molja Fyr is situated in a charming harbour. The interior of this 150-year-old lighthouse 'hotel' is completely round, only three metres in diameter, and it only has one bedroom upstairs and a bathroom downstairs. Room facilities include hairdryer, bathrobes, tea and coffee. The lighthouse hotel consists of just one room but full hotel facilities are available from the nearby Hotel Brosundet, including a concierge service, 24-hour room service and a superb seafood restaurant. (€315 p/nt)

5 Match the words in box A with those in box B to make compound nouns. Then find more compound nouns in the texts.

A	bath tooth honey news hair lap light sea

B	moon house top paper food robe brush dryer

6 Look at these combinations of nouns related to hotels. Underline the one that is not possible. Use a good dictionary to help you.

1	three-star / economics / budget / four-star	hotel
2	conference / spa / bed / coffee	facilities
3	walk-in / power / en suite / bath	shower
4	business / hotel / reception / restaurant	guest
5	air-conditioning / heat / entertainment / wi-fi	system
6	flat screen / cable / DVD / satellite	TV
7	honeymoon / executive / luxury / manager	suite
8	room / concierge / facility / laundry	service
9	double / single / three / family	room
10	queen-size / single / double / two	bed

Speaking: Guessing hotel facilities

7 Work in pairs. Write definitions for four compound nouns from exercise 6.
A: What do we call the service when you can send your clothes to be washed?
B: laundry service

8 Read your definitions to another pair and see if they can guess the compound.

9 Work in pairs.
a) Think of one compound noun connected to these places. Write definitions for them.

restaurant airport modern office shopping mall

b) Read your definitions to another pair. They should guess the compound noun.

TALKING POINT
- What's the most unusual place you have ever stayed in?
- What facilities do you expect to find in a modern city?

Reading: Low-cost travel

1 Discuss these questions.

1 When was the last time you flew? Where did you go?

2 What did you think of the service?

3 Will you fly with this airline again? Why?/Why not?

2 Read these postings on a blog about low-cost air travel. Which extra charges do they mention?

3 Who do you agree with most? Why?

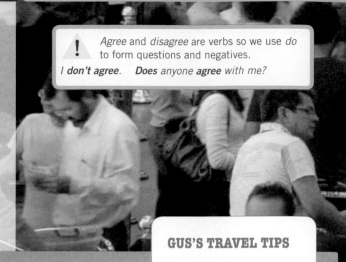

> ! *Agree* and *disagree* are verbs so we use *do* to form questions and negatives.
> *I don't agree.* *Does anyone agree with me?*

GUS'S TRAVEL TIPS

Low-cost airlines

I think low-cost airlines are not as cheap as they seem. I've just booked a flight to Vancouver. When you book with Fly High, you have to pay for checking in your luggage, with additional charges for sports/skiing gear, not to mention the food and drink on the flight. So, sorry, I just don't agree that these airlines are doing us a favour by seeming to be low-priced. What are they going to charge us for next? The flight attendants' uniforms?

POSTED BY GUS AT 12.13) COMMENTS

I agree with you about those additional charges, Gus. But I've never had any problems with Smooth Jets, except for the occasional delay. I think you'll find their flights aren't that expensive if you book in advance. And I think it's great that families with young kids can board first.

POSTED BY KERRY AT 12.19) COMMENTS

You've got a point there*, Gus. Budget airlines aren't that cheap. We're flying to Bucharest next month with Whoosh Air and the airline's charging me for checking in each bag and for boarding first – I'm travelling with my elderly mother. Then there's travel insurance, as well as the credit card charge. And another thing: the airports that low-cost airlines fly to are usually out of the way* and you end up paying for an expensive cab* ride to the hotel. I'm going to fly with a regular airline next vacation. Definitely. Does anyone else agree with me?

POSTED BY MO AT 12.43) COMMENTS

you've got a point there: you're right
out of the way: area where there are few people
cab: taxi

4 Look at these words related to flying. Which words are compound nouns? What do each group have in common?

1 baggage claim, lounge, departures _____

2 cabin crew, ground staff, flight attendant _____

3 board, take off, land _____

4 passport, boarding card, ID _____

5 suitcase, backpack, hold-all _____

6 delay, miss a flight, lost luggage _____

5 Add some more words to each group in exercise 4.

Listening: I don't think so

6 🔊 **1.8** Listen to two friends at an airport. Who says what? Write *B* for Beatrice or *K* for Keith. More than one answer is possible.

1 Who says they are not going to get a good seat?

2 Who thinks you get what you pay for?

3 Who says the flights were cheap?

4 Who thinks they paid a lot of additional charges?

5 Who thinks airlines should provide a better service?

6 Who is going to get a sandwich?

7 The verbs *agree* and *disagree* are more common in written than spoken English. In spoken English we generally agree or disagree in different ways. Read the examples in the table and complete the sentence.

Agreeing and disagreeing
Agreeing
Yes. Absolutely. That's right. That's true. Good point. Good idea.
Disagreeing
Well … maybe. But, is it really cheaper?   *There are all those extras we have to pay for.*
We often use single words or short phrases when we are _____ .

8 🔊 **1.9** Listen to two managers discussing ways to reduce their organization's flight costs. What do they disagree about?

9 🔊 Read the notes in the table on disagreeing. Try to remember the missing words from the conversation. Listen again and check your answers.

Disagreeing
People are often slow to say they disagree. They might:
1 hesitate and sound uncertain   *Well erm, _____ _____ sure.*
2 ask challenging questions   *Yes, but _____ _____ it takes ten hours instead of three?*
3 say they partly agree   *That's _____, _____ productivity is important, too.*
4 suggest alternatives   *How _____ _____ a limit?*
5 When the disagreement is clear, they generally state their opinions more directly and forcefully.   *I'm _____, but I think this rule could cost us more money _____ _____ _____ _____.*   *Yes, but _____ _____ _____ _____ it won't always save us money.*   *I _____ _____ _____ true.*

Speaking: Hidden airline costs

10 Work in pairs. Read your situation and instructions below.

> **Student A:**
> You work for Smooth Jets, an airline that wants to reduce its costs to be more competitive. Look at the possible extra charges. Decide which five things you are going to charge for.

> **Student B:**
> You represent a consumer group. You have received complaints about Smooth Jets, a low-cost airline that is planning to introduce extra costs. Look at the possible extra charges. Decide which five charges they shouldn't charge for.

Smooth Jets
Proposed extra charges

1 checking in luggage
2 in-flight food and drink
3 changing the name of the passenger on the ticket
4 changing the dates of a flight
5 sports and musical equipment
6 use of the overhead locker
7 oxygen for those with medical conditions
8 speedy boarding (boarding first)
9 carbon emissions
10 in-flight magazine

11 Discuss your ideas with your partner. It is not necessary to reach an agreement. Use expressions for disagreeing from exercise 9.

12 How could the airline present these new charges without losing its customers?

Reminder

Grammar reference page 166

We use *going to* when a plan or intention has already been decided.
Are you going to come with me?
We use *will*, often with *probably*, to express decisions when there is no special plan.
I think I'll (probably) go sightseeing on Friday.
We use the present continuous to talk about plans and arrangements that have already been decided and organized.
We're leaving on 16 January.

We often show agreement with short words and phrases.
Yes, that's true.
Absolutely!
When we disagree, we're often hesitant at first and we provide explanations.
Erm, I'm not sure because it might cost a lot.

Listening: Change of plan

1 What do you know about Dubai in the UAE (United Arab Emirates)? Read the information and check your ideas.

Doing business in Dubai

Situated on the Persian Gulf, looking out at Iran, Iraq and Saudi Arabia, Dubai was little more than a desert village 20 years ago. But since then its trade barriers have gone, skyscrapers have risen out of the sand and it has become an international business hub*. Dubai is just three hours from India and six hours from the UK. Dubai's glamorous shopping malls, glorious beaches and towering buildings give it an unreal quality. Tourism and leisure are growing well and Dubai has a number of luxurious hotels, including the seven-star, Burj Al Arab hotel.

hub: centre

2 Fay and Martin are a husband and wife team. Fay is a travel writer and Martin is a professional photographer. Look at Fay's itinerary for their trip to Dubai and answer the questions.

1 When will they arrive at the Novotel hotel?

2 What is Fay going to do on Tuesday and Wednesday?

3 What does Martin plan to do on Tuesday and Wednesday?

4 What are they both going to do on Thursday?

5 How much free time do you think they will both have?

3)) 1.10 Listen to Fay and Martin talking about their trip. What has changed? Correct the itinerary.

4)) Listen again. Why doesn't Martin want to go on the desert trip with Fay? Why doesn't he want to have dinner at the Burj Al Arab hotel?

5 Martin says, *Well, all right then* and *I suppose so*. But is he happy to agree? When do we use these expressions? With people you know very well or with people you don't know very well?

January

10 Monday
8.45 p.m. Arrive in Dubai;
Novotel hotel 9.30–10.00?

11 Tuesday
Tourism Fair;
Martin taking photos of city

12 Wednesday
Interview business contacts;
Martin – desert trip? (sandboarding/dune bashing?)

13 Thursday
Sightseeing together

14 Friday
More sightseeing?
Martin – taking photos inside Burj Al Arab.

15 Saturday
Airport for 11.30 a.m. –
plane leaves 1.30 p.m.

16 Sunday

Speaking: What to do in Dubai

6 Which of these activities do you normally associate with a country like Dubai?

river cruise   snowboarding   desert safari   shopping in a mall   belly dancing   camel ride
ice-skating   sandboarding   hot air ballooning   bus tour   going to the beach

7 Look at the *What's On* guide for Dubai. Which of these activities would/wouldn't you like to do? Why?

6 things to do in Dubai

Desert safaris in UAE

Full day desert safari offers a splendid chance to live the desert experience. Enjoy a typical Arabian welcome at our Bedouin campsite followed by a camel ride, sandboarding, dune bashing and belly dancing. Book online. US$90 per person.

Hot air ballooning

Glide gently in a hot air balloon over giant sand dunes, camels, oases and mountains, while enjoying breathtaking views of the desert. Visit our website. US$245 pp.

Dubai Mall

With more than 1,200 stores and a variety of attractions, the Dubai Mall is the ultimate shopping and entertainment experience, and a place where you will find a gold souk (market) next to a world class aquarium. Do adventure sports or ice-skating, have brunch* and see the latest Hollywood film! The Dubai Mall has something for everyone!

The Big Bus Company

From the towering sail-shaped Burj Al Arab hotel to the gold and spice souks*, what better way is there to see Dubai's breathtaking views and attractions than from an open-top, double-decker* Big Bus. Book online. 24-hour ticket: US$55.

Ski Dubai

Ski Dubai is the first indoor ski resort* in the Arab world and offers an amazing setting for snow sports such as skiing, snowboarding and tobogganing, or just playing in the snow. Call 04 409 8000 for enquiries. Admission Price: US$14. Two-hour ski pass: US$35.

Dinner cruise

Cruise along the Dubai river on traditional Arabic Dhows or more modern cruise boats and enjoy our delicious gourmet cuisine. Call Dubai cruises 04 389 4773. US$70 per person.

brunch: a combination of breakfast and lunch
souk: market
double-decker: bus with two levels
resort: place where a lot of people go for holidays

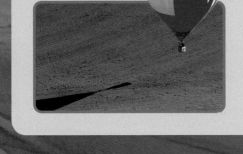

January
16 Monday

7.00

Plans day 1

8.00

9.00

a.m. – brunch at Mall
or ballooning?

10.00

11.00

12.00

13.00

p.m. – desert safari?

14.00

15.00

16.00

17.00

evening – shopping?
Mall

18.00

19.00

January
Tuesday **17**

7.00

Plans day 2

8.00

9.00

a.m. – skiing?

10.00

11.00

12.00

midday – bus tour

13.00

14.00

15.00

p.m. – shopping
for Gold?

16.00

17.00

18.00

evening –
dinner cruise?

19.00

8 Work in pairs. You are work colleagues going to Dubai. You have 48 hours to do some sightseeing and you have a budget of US$450 per person. You have already made a plan but now you want to change it. Agree on the activities that you will do a) together and b) individually.

9 One of you falls ill just before the trip to Dubai! Find another partner and plan a new itinerary.

Writing: A budget increase

10 Write an email to your manager saying what you are planning to do and how much it is going to cost (make sure it is within budget). Ask for extra money so you can do another activity that you would really like to do. Give reasons.

Interaction

3

A Base form with *to* or *-ing* form
B Food and entertaining
C Quantifiers
D Communication strategies Saying 'no'
E Interaction The visit (board game)

Be my guest

Base form with *to* or *-ing* form

Reading: Taking your food seriously

1 What rules of etiquette do people follow when they are eating in your country? Consider the following things.

- using a napkin
- waiting to be seated
- sitting on the floor
- serving yourself first
- putting your elbows on the table
- talking loudly
- leaving a little food on your plate
- eating with your fingers

2))) **1.11** Listen to someone describing a meal they had. What was the situation and what happened? What would you think if this happened to you?

3))) **1.12** Listen to the boss's version of the story. Why didn't the woman get the job?

4 Discuss these questions.

1 Why does the boss take job candidates to a seafood restaurant?

2 Do you think it's a good way for bosses to find out who to hire?

3 In what ways can sharing a meal help people get along?

5 Read some tips for international dining. Match each tip to one of the countries in the box. Then check your answers in File 29, page 135.

Turkey   Japan   Saudi Arabia   Germany

Dining etiquettes of the world

Cross-cultural understanding is important for today's global businessperson. A lack of cross-cultural awareness* can result in misunderstandings, which may offend others and have a negative impact on your business. One area of importance is the different dining etiquettes* of the world.

A _____ Do not begin eating until the host signals to do so. *It is impolite to rest your elbows on the table. You should eat everything on your plate.* Indicate you have finished by laying the knife and fork parallel across the right hand side of the plate.

B _____ *An honoured guest starts eating first* and sits at the centre of the table furthest from the door. *Learn to use chopsticks* – never point them, never pierce food with them and place them on the chopstick rest when breaking for a drink or a chat. *It is polite to try a bit of everything. People usually prefer to talk quietly.*

C _____ Meals are a social affair and *people enjoy having loud conversations.* The head of the family or honoured guest is served first but it is good etiquette* to insist on the most senior person being served first. If you go to a restaurant, the person who made the invitation must pay.

D _____ Traditionally, meals are eaten on the floor. Sitting with your legs crossed is normal behaviour*. Never sit with your feet stretched out. Guests are served specialities such as head, eyes, etc. Eat with your right hand only. *Do not be afraid of making a mess.* When you have finished, leave a little food on your plate. If you don't, it will be filled immediately. *Asking for more food is a compliment.*

awareness: knowledge or understanding of a subject or situation
etiquette: formal rules for polite behaviour
behaviour: things that a person does

6 Read the dining tips again and rewrite them so that they are true for your country.

Asking for more food is not very polite.

7 What other things are good manners when you are dining out in your country? For example, punctuality.

Grammar: base form with *to* or *-ing* form

8 Look at the information in the table. Complete the example sentences from the article.

the base form with *to* or *-ing* form

1 We use the base form without *to* after modal verbs.
You **should** _____ everything on your plate.

2 Some verbs are followed by the base form with *to*.
Learn _____ chopsticks.

3 Some verbs are followed by the *-ing* form.
People **enjoy** _____ loud conversations.

4 A few verbs can be followed by the base form with *to* OR the *-ing* form.
Do not **begin eating** until the host signals to do so.
(or **begin to eat**)
An honoured guest **starts** _____ .
(or **starts to eat**)
People usually **prefer** _____ quietly.
(or **prefer talking**)

5 Use the *-ing* form when the verb is the subject of the sentence.
Sitting with your legs crossed is normal behaviour.
_____ for more food is a compliment.

6 Use the *-ing* form after a preposition.
Indicate you have finished **by** _____ the knife and fork parallel.
Do not be afraid **of** _____ a mess.

7 Use the base form with *to* after *It is* + adjective.
It is impolite _____ your elbows on the table.
It is polite _____ a bit of everything.

>> For more information on the base form and the *-ing* form, see page 173.

9 Look at the information about dining etiquette in China. Complete the sentences using the correct form of the verbs in brackets. There may be more than one possibility.

Speaking: Copy your host

10 Work in groups of three. You work as cross-cultural consultants and are giving advice on dining etiquette to a group of international MBA students. Student A: Turn to File 1, page 132 for information about Russia. Student B: Turn to File 30, page 139 for information about Argentina. Student C: Turn to File 39, page 140 for information about India. Choose four of the most important tips to memorize and tell your partners.

11 What are the main differences when dining in someone's house in these countries? Make notes about the main points.

When in China

1 Take off your shoes before _____ (enter) someone's house.

2 Chinese people prefer _____ (entertain) at home.

3 If you don't want _____ (eat) delicacies like fish eyes, you should _____ (not serve) them to others.

4 It's important _____ (revolve) the serving tray to other people around the table.

5 _____ (eat) the last piece of food from the serving tray is considered _____ (be) impolite.

6 You can _____ (show) your appreciation of the meal by _____ (knock) on the table.

7 Insist on _____ (pay) for the meal, although your host will _____ (refuse) your offer.

8 Next time you meet your host, it is polite _____ (offer) a meal of a similar quality.

TALKING POINT
- Describe the last time you had a formal lunch or dinner at someone's house.
- When was the last time you had a meal with people from work? Who was it with, where and why? What did you eat? Who paid the bill?

Listening: What the locals eat

1 Do you like trying new dishes when you travel? What is the most unusual dish you have ever eaten?

2))) **1.13** An Australian couple, Richie and Barbara, are on holiday in the Philippines. Listen to their conversation and complete the travel blog.

Balut are common in the Philippines, Cambodia and Vietnam. They are a popular ¹_____ typically sold by ²_____ _____ . A balut is a fertilized ³_____ or chicken ⁴_____ that is ⁵_____ and eaten in the shell. It is usually eaten with a ⁶_____ _____ _____, although some people prefer chilli and vinegar with their balut.

3))) Listen again and <u>underline</u> the expressions you hear.

1 We must try the balut. / We could try the balut. / We should try the balut.

2 It's very tasty. / It's very sweet. / It's very salty.

3 I can't stand raw egg. / I can't eat raw egg. / I can't eat boiled egg.

4 What is it? / What's in it? / What's it like?

5 It's quite chewy. / It's very chewy. / It's kind of chewy.

6 It's a sort of boiled egg. / It's like a normal boiled egg. / It tastes like boiled egg.

4))) **1.14** Back home in Australia, Richie takes a business client to dinner in Sydney. Look at the waitress's pad, listen to the conversation and write their order.

5))) Listen again and complete the expressions.

1 What would you _____?

2 OK, that _____ good.

3 I think I'll have _____ _____.

4 For the main course, you _____ _____ the grilled emu.

5 It's a _____ of big, funny-looking bird.

6 It's _____ _____ an ostrich.

7 What does it taste _____?

8 No, it's _____ beef, only it's healthier.

9 What does it come _____?

10 _____ _____, hello.

6))) **1.15** Richie invites Enrique to a barbecue at his home. Listen to their conversation and put the items in the order that they are discussed.

1 Food that Enrique doesn't like to eat.

2 An anecdote about food in the Philippines.

3 A dish Enrique wants to try.

4 The food served at a typical barbecue.

7))) Listen again. Tick (✓) the expressions you hear and correct the other expressions.

1 Thank you for inviting me.

2 It's more prawns than steak these days.

3 Can I help you with anything?

4 Help yourself to the buffet.

5 Is there anything you don't eat?

6 Is there any fruit in the salads?

7 This tastes good. What's in it?

8 I wouldn't eat that with your salad, Enrique.

The Blue Emu
Bondi Beach

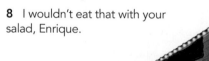

Entrée
2 _____ _____

Side order
2 _____

Main course
1 _____ _____
1 _____ _____

Word focus: Food and entertaining

8 Put these words into three groups.

> knife and fork   boiled   salty   grilled   salt and pepper   roast   delicious
> sweet   oil and vinegar   fried   spicy   chewy   baked   rich   tasty
> steamed   smoked   chopsticks   serviette   stewed   oily   tender   plate
> spoon   tough   menu   glass

A how food is cooked

B taste and texture

C things on a table

9 Match the correct combinations.

1	grilled / tender / tough / raw	**a**	ice cream
2	fresh / frozen / white / tuna	**b**	stew
3	rare / medium / well-done / fillet	**c**	water
4	green / prawn / fruit / egg	**d**	steak
5	chicken / beef / lentil / tripe	**e**	vegetables
6	steamed / stir fried / boiled / roasted	**f**	salad
7	bottled / tap / still / sparkling	**g**	meat
8	low-fat / chocolate / homemade / strawberry	**h**	fish

10 Think of two other combinations for each of the items (a–h) in exercise 9.

11 Discuss these questions.

1 What is your favourite meat dish, fish dish, snack, ice cream, fruit and vegetable?

2 What food and dishes do you never eat?

3 What starter, main course and dessert would you usually order in a restaurant?

4 What do you usually drink with your meals?

Speaking: I'd recommend …

12 Work in pairs. Prepare to act out a conversation. Student A: You are the host. Student B: You are the guest. Read the information below and roleplay the situation. Then change roles.

Student A:

Student B is an important business client and you are taking him/her to lunch.

● Decide which restaurant you are taking him/her to.

● What is special about the restaurant? e.g. the food, the price, the location, the service, the atmosphere? Mention this to your guest.

● What is on the menu? Write down three or four typical starters, main courses and desserts from your country/region.

● Show your guest the menu and be prepared to describe and recommend dishes.

Student B:

You are a very important client of Student A, and he/she is taking you to lunch.

● Respond to information Student A gives you about the restaurant and ask questions about it.

● You have never seen any of the dishes on the menu before. Ask lots of questions about the food, e.g. *How's it cooked?*

● Tell Student A about either a) your numerous food allergies or b) your special diet.

● Ask if you can have a side order that isn't on the menu.

TALKING POINT
● How often do you entertain guests at home? In a restaurant?
● Which factors are the most important for you when choosing a restaurant?

Reading: Food quiz

1 In three minutes, write down everything you have eaten and drunk in the last 24 hours. Compare your lists. What is healthy about your diets? And what is unhealthy?

2 Are you making healthy food choices? Do the food quiz with a partner. Then turn to File 4 on page 132 to check your answers.

3 Which information surprised you most in the quiz?

What is Healthy Eating?

We all know we should eat lots of fruit and vegetables, but nutritionists say consumers often don't have enough information about the fat, sugar and salt levels in food to make healthy choices.

So, what do you know about healthy eating?

1 Which best describes your attitude to breakfast?
- **a** I usually take the time to have a good breakfast.
- **b** I skip it. I'm not hungry in the mornings.
- **c** I just need some coffee to wake me up.
- **d** I don't have enough time for breakfast most days.

2 Which of the following facts about sugar are true?
- **a** There are two types of sugar – those found naturally in fruit and milk (unprocessed) and artificial or processed sugars that are added to food.
- **b** There are about nine teaspoons of sugar in a can of fizzy drink, such as cola.
- **c** Sugar contains fewer calories than other carbohydrates and provides essential nutrients.
- **d** The body needs a little added sugar – it's essential to a healthy diet.

3 You are having a busy day at work. Which of the following is true for you?
- **a** I sometimes forget to have lunch.
- **b** I often grab a sandwich and have a quick lunch break.
- **c** I'm always multi-tasking, so eating and working is easy!
- **d** I usually make time for a good meal.

4 Eating too much saturated fat is believed to increase 'bad' cholesterol, which is a risk factor for heart disease. How many grams of saturated fat are there in a medium cheese pizza?

a 6–8   **b** 10–12   **c** 15–22

5 Which of these foods are also high in saturated fat?
- **a** butter and margarine
- **b** milk and yoghurt
- **c** meat and meat products
- **d** biscuits, crisps and cakes
- **e** nuts
- **f** fish
- **g** cheese
- **h** olive oil

6 How would you describe your salt consumption?
- **a** I never add salt in cooking or at the table.
- **b** I add a bit of salt to food I'm cooking.
- **c** I add lots of salt to my food, even before I taste it.

7 Salt is essential for our health, but experts say too much salt can lead to high blood pressure and heart problems. How much salt should an adult eat per day?
- **a** 3g (half a teaspoon)
- **b** 6g (a teaspoon)
- **c** 12g (two teaspoons)

Grammar: Quantifiers

4 Look at the information in the table. Choose the correct alternative to complete the rules.

Quantifiers

1 We use **much** with *countable / uncountable* nouns and we use **many** with *countable / uncountable* plural nouns, in negative sentences and in questions.

2 We use **a lot of** and **lots of** with countable and uncountable nouns to talk about *large / small* quantities. We use **a lot** when there is no noun.

3 We use **a little** with *uncountable / countable* nouns and **a few** with *uncountable / countable* nouns. **A little** and **a few** mean a small quantity.

4 We use **(very) little** and **(very) few** to suggest that there is not as much, or many, of something as we would like.

5 We use **too**, **too many** and **too much** when we say there is *more / less* of something than we need or want. We use **(not) enough** when we say there is *more / less* than we need or want.

>> For more information on quantifiers, see page 171.

5 Choose the correct option to complete these sentences.
1 There isn't *much / many* sugar in my diet.
2 How *many / much* grams of saturated fat are there in this?
3 I eat *a lot of / much* fruit and vegetables.
4 More than 20g of fat per 100g is *lots / a lot / a lot of*.
5 I often add *a few / a little* sugar to yoghurt.
6 He went for a walk to burn *a little / a few* calories.
7 *Very little / Very few* people know where saturated fat comes from in their diet.
8 There is *very few / very little* information on food labels.
9 Most people eat *too many / too much* salt.
10 I think there are *too much / too many* additives in food.
11 Fizzy drinks are *too / not enough* sugary for me.
12 Consumers don't have *too much / enough* nutritional information.

6 Make six questions using words and phrases from three or four columns in the table. Then work with another student. Take turns to ask and answer your questions.

How much chocolate do you eat?

How	much	nutritional information	do you eat?
Do you eat	many	chocolate	do you drink?
Do you drink	a lot of	cakes and biscuits	varied enough?
Is your diet	a lot	water	in your diet?
Is there	too much	fruit juice	on food labels?
	too many	takeaway and ready meals	
	enough	variety	
	very little	fruit and vegetables	

Speaking: It's all too much

7 Work in pairs. What would you say in each of these situations?

1 Your new assistant has reserved a meeting room and ordered lunch for you and two colleagues. She has booked the boardroom which seats 30 people, ordered 30 sandwiches and two small bottles of water. Tell her what the problems are and what you want her to do.

2 You're having a meal in a restaurant with a friend. The soup is cold, the bottled water is warm, the portions are small, the food is expensive and there's a 20% service charge. What do you say to each other? What do you say to the waiter?

3 Your teenage brother/son loves pizza and pasta and never eats any fruit or vegetables. He also plays video games for hours but never does any exercise.

TALKING POINT • How has the diet in your country/region changed? What do people eat and drink more or less of?
• How can you get children and teenagers to eat fewer unhealthy snacks?

Speaking: Hosts and guests

1 When is it polite to argue with people? Think of some situations where it is polite to say 'no' and disagree with other people.

2 Look at the man and the woman in the photos. Each one is having a conversation with another person. Read their half of the conversation. Which person is a host and which is a guest? What are they arguing about?

Conversation 1

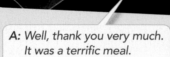

A: Is that the check? Let me get that.

A: No, no. Why don't we split it?

A: Are you sure?

A: Well, that's very kind of you.

A: Well, thank you very much. It was a terrific meal.

Conversation 2

A: Have some more paella.

A: Some more shrimps then?

A: You don't need to lose weight!

A: Just a few more?

A: Good, and a little more paella?

3 What would you say to the host and guest in exercise 2 if you were talking to them? Use these phrases to create the two complete conversations.

1 I do!

2 It's our pleasure.

3 No really, I'm full. I'm trying to diet.

4 I'm glad you enjoyed it. Don't forget your doggy bag.

5 No really. I'll have to pass on that, but thank you.

6 No, no I insist. You're our guest.

7 No, no. It was terrific, but I couldn't manage any more.

8 Oh no. This is on me.

9 Well … maybe just a few then.

10 Yes, the company's paying.

4 🔊 1.16 Listen to the two complete conversations and check your answers.

5 What qualities does a perfect host have? What qualities does a perfect guest have?

6 Look at some things that English speakers often do when they turn down invitations. Then label the different parts of the refusal using items 1–6 from the table.

Saying 'no'
1 Give an excuse
2 Apologize
3 Hesitate
4 Suggest an alternative
5 Say something positive
6 Say thank you

3

Oh … It sounds great. I'm so sorry, but I have to study. Thanks for thinking of me. Perhaps we can meet up another time?

Listening: An invitation

7 When was the last time you said 'no' to an invitation? What was the event and why did you turn it down?

8 ◀) **1.17** Listen to one half of a telephone conversation. What's the event and why can't Gabriella go?

9 Look at what Gabriella said. What do you think Sandy said?

Hello. … Sandy! Great to hear from you. How are you? … Not too bad. How's Peter? … Oh, nothing exciting. I've got some exams coming up so I'm studying all weekend. … Oh … I don't think I can. Sunday, you say? … It sounds great, but I have two exams the next day – Marketing and Accounting. … I'm really sorry, but I have to study. … Thanks for thinking of me. Look, when my exams are over, perhaps you and Peter can come over to my place for a meal? … OK, choose a restaurant you want to go to and it'll be my treat. … No, no, I insist. It'll be your birthday present. … OK, I will. And have a lovely birthday on Sunday. … Bye.

10 ◀) Now listen to the complete conversation. Were your answers similar?

11 ◀) Try to remember the missing words from the conversation. Then listen again and check your answers.

1 Listen, what ¹_____ _____ _____ this Sunday?

2 Can you ²_____ _____ _____ ? It's my birthday and I'm ³_____ a party.

3 Oh, what a ⁴_____ !

4 It's OK, I ⁵_____ .

5 ⁶_____ be nice. Or ⁷_____ _____ all go out to a restaurant together.

6 Oh no. We'll pay for ⁸_____ .

7 No, you ⁹_____ _____ _____ do that. Let's talk about it later.

12 Look back at what Gabriella says in exercise 9 and <u>underline</u> the different ways she uses to say 'no'.

13 Look at the audio script on page 146. Are there any things people might say differently in your culture?

Speaking: Turning someone down

14 Work in pairs. Think of different ways to say 'no' in these situations. Try to think of good excuses.

1 Have you ever tried sheep's brains/insects/fish eyes? Do try some. They're a delicacy.

2 We're going jogging at six o'clock tomorrow morning. Would you like to join us?

3 *Terminator 10* is playing at the Roxy Cinema. Do you want to come and see it?

4 I'm going to the library to study. Would you like to come?

5 We need to clean out the garage. Would you like to help?

15 Work in pairs. What could hosts and guests say in these situations?

1 A classmate invites you to a late-night party this Friday. You have to work on Saturday.

2 Your English teacher invites all the class to see a Shakespeare play. It will last about three and a half hours.

3 Your Polish host offers you tripe soup in a restaurant.

4 Your cousin, who lives in Canada, invites you to visit him this winter. He says he'll pay for the flight. The ticket is expensive and it's very cold in Toronto in winter.

5 Your new boss invites all the people in your department for a meal after work on Tuesday.

6 Your supplier offers you two free flights to Rome but it is company policy not to accept expensive gifts.

16 Work in pairs. Act out situations 1–3. Student A: Turn down the offer or invitation. Student B: Insist a little. Then change roles and act out situations 4–6.

Reminder

Grammar reference page 171

There are many ways of turning down an invitation politely. You can apologize, give an excuse or suggest an alternative.

Oh, I'm so sorry but we're going to be on holiday then.
No, really. It was delicious but I'm on a diet.

We use *many, a few, few* and *too many* with countable nouns.
How many visitors are coming?
There are a few questions I want to ask.

We use *much, a little, little* and *too much* with uncountable nouns.
I don't have much information about their visit.
We have a little time to visit the factory before lunch.

Speaking: Gift-giving

1 When was the last time you gave or received a gift? What was it and who was it to or from?

2 Which of these gifts would you prefer to accept from a business contact? Why?

- a key ring
- local handicrafts (e.g. a wooden box)
- a book
- the company calendar
- a bouquet of flowers
- a potted plant
- a packet of tea/coffee
- quality chocolates
- a pen with the company logo
- tickets for a cultural event

3 What kinds of gifts are popular in your company and country? What taboos are there?

1
You greet a group of international visitors at the airport. Act out the situation.

8
In the corridor, you meet the Marketing Manager. Introduce him/her to the visitors.

9
One of the visitors asks where the nearest restroom is. Give her the wrong directions. Miss a turn.

10
You attend some presentations. Offer the best seat to the visiting director. When he turns it down, insist. Act out the situation.

✲ FINISH

18
At the airport, you say goodbye to the visitors and exchange small gifts. What do you give? Offer the gifts and when they refuse, insist.

17
At the end of their visit, you take the guests to the airport. You give them gifts of pen knives. Go back two spaces.

Board game: Entertaining

4 Work in pairs. Discuss these questions.

1 Do you ever have important visitors to your company or department? Who are they? How often do they visit and why?

2 When was the last time you were a visitor? Where did you go and why?

3 What kinds of things can sometimes go wrong with visits?

5 Play this game in pairs. An important group of international visitors come to your company/organization.

Rules

1 Toss a coin to move. Heads, move one square, tails move two.

2 Follow the instructions on each square. Answer the question or act out the conversations.

3 If you land on a square someone landed on before, move on to the next new square.

4 The first person to finish is the winner.

2
While having a coffee, you chat to your guests. Your guest asks you about the food in your country.

3
You're presenting the programme for the visit. Some of the visitors ask if they can change the order of some of the items on the programme. Act out the situation.

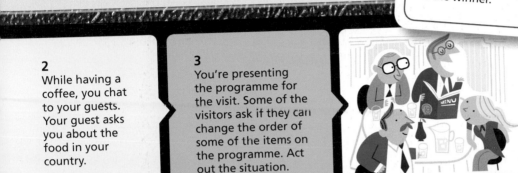

4
After the morning meeting you take the visitors to lunch. You give them a brief summary of the kind of food on the menu and recommend one of the dishes.

7
You offer the visitors a tour of the company. Act out the situation.

6
One of the visitors comes up to you and tells you that one of the members of the group has his 50th birthday that week. You discuss what gift would be appropriate and how to celebrate the event.

5
You suggest eating out this evening but one of the guests says 'no' and gives an excuse. What does he/she say? *The thing is …*

11
Arrange a time and a place to meet your visitors before dinner this evening. One of the guests can't come to the pre-dinner venue. Act out the situation.

12
In the restaurant that evening, a visitor who does not eat meat asks you to recommend some regional dishes. What do you suggest?

13
Complete these questions to ask your guests.
_____ bottles of water would you like?
Would you like _____ bread with your meal?
_____ side dishes with that?

16
Your visitors invite you to go sightseeing the next day but you have a lot of work. What do you say?

15
After the main course, you recommend a typical dessert from your country. One of the guests doesn't want it. What does he say?

14
The waiter takes your order. What do you order for everyone as a starter and for the main course? (There is one vegetarian and one diabetic.)

Writing: A thank-you note

6 You have recently returned from an overseas visit to another company. Write an email thanking your hosts for organizing your visit and for the gifts you received. Say something nice about the food in their country.

Review 1–3

1 Match the verb tenses to example sentences.

1 The present simple
2 The present continuous
3 The *will* future
4 The *going to* future
5 The present continuous for future
6 The past simple
7 The past continuous
8 The present perfect

a I've always wanted to have a personal trainer.
b We were sitting on the beach in Mallorca this time last week.
c Why are you wearing a tie today?
d Do you usually walk to work?
e I'll finish this work tomorrow.
f She's starting her new job on Monday.
g They bought their car on eBay.
h I'm going to make a healthy salad for dinner.

2 Read this article and put the verbs in brackets in the correct past or present tense.

Commuting by water

Commuters in many parts of the world travel to work by water. Services like the Star Ferries of Hong Kong and Sydney Ferries in Australia ¹_____ (offer) an easy way to commute. These ferry services in recent years ²_____ (become) symbolic of their cities. A huge double-decker ferry in New York ³_____ (carry) up to 5,000 people in a single rush-hour trip, and the number of services ⁴_____ (increase) to meet growing demand.

In London, in recent years, many people ⁵_____ (decide) to commute on the river. Mark Hardwick regularly ⁶_____ (use) the London River Services: 'For years I ⁷_____ (take) the underground to work but I ⁸_____ (always be) fascinated by the River Thames. Commuting by water ⁹_____ (make) me feel more relaxed. It's a bit expensive, but there ¹⁰_____ (not be) a more pleasant way to get to work.'

3 Match each phrase 1–8 to a suitable response a–h.

1 Why don't we stop for lunch now?
2 How about taking the high-speed train to Brussels?
3 Is that the bill? I'll get this.
4 Her designs are the best. What do you think?
5 Is there anything you don't eat?
6 Would you like some baklava?
7 Pizza is a healthy choice, isn't it?
8 Do you want to come to lunch on Sunday?

a That's very kind of you, but it's my treat.
b Thank you. It looks great but I couldn't eat another thing.
c Yes, good idea. I'm starving.
d Well, I'm not sure. Doesn't it contain a lot of fat?
e Let's check the price of flights first.
f Yes, actually, I'm allergic to peanuts.
g It's my mother's birthday. Perhaps we can make it another time.
h That's true. But the price is important, too.

4 Read this article. Put the verbs in brackets in the correct form (base form with or without *to* or the *-ing* form). Sometimes more than one answer is possible.

Breakfast meetings are common in US corporations, and now the 'power breakfast' is becoming more popular in Europe and Asia as well. A lot of women executives especially prefer ¹_____ (have) breakfast meetings. Helena Downey, a marketing director from London, says that she doesn't like ²_____ (take) a lot of time out of her working day for business lunches. She often chooses ³_____ (meet) clients before she gets to the office: 'By ⁴_____ (get up) an hour earlier, I can often ⁵_____ (leave) the office earlier.

It's easy ⁶_____ (get) a table for breakfast in a good hotel. And I've found people who might ⁷_____ (say) 'no' to lunch because they have a busy schedule, are happy ⁸_____ (meet) for breakfast.' Cost is another consideration: 'Lunch for two can ⁹_____ (be) over £100, but breakfast will ¹⁰_____ (cost) less than £30.' There are other advantages to the working breakfast: 'It's quicker, more informal and dining etiquette isn't such an issue.'

5 Read this description of a seasonal food and complete the missing words. The first letter is given.

> If you ever go to Catalunya in north east Spain in late winter or early spring, you ¹ s _ _ _ _ _ try the calçots. These are a ² k _ _ _ of long onion that ³ t _ _ _ _ quite sweet. Calçots are typically eaten outdoors at a popular lunch called a calçotada. The onions are ⁴ c _ _ _ _ _ on the barbecue and ⁵ s _ _ _ _ _ with a special sauce called romesco, which is ⁶ m _ _ _ with olive oil, nuts, tomatoes and a ⁷ s _ _ _ of chilli pepper called a ñora. You eat the white part of the onion. Use your hands to peel off the outer leaves and then dip it into the sauce. You'll need a big ⁸ n _ _ _ _ _ to protect your clothes and don't be afraid of making a ⁹ m _ _ _. After the calçots, for the main ¹⁰ c _ _ _ _ _ people usually eat lots of ¹¹ g _ _ _ _ _ _ meat, such as lamb, and often finish the meal with a traditional ¹² d _ _ _ _ _ _ , such as crema catalana.

6 Underline the word or expression that is different.

1 Which of these is NOT a cooking method?

roast / boil / stew / tender

2 Which of these is NOT associated with taste and texture?

salty / baked / tough / chewy

3 Which of these is NOT put on a dining table?

spicy / chopsticks / spoon / knife

4 Which of these is NOT used to describe fish?

white / frozen / homemade / fresh

5 Which of these is NOT used to describe water?

tap / bottled / sparkling / low-fat

6 Which of these is NOT used to describe steak?

well-done / still / medium / rare

7 Complete these staff complaints about the company canteen. Choose the correct quantifiers.

1 There aren't *enough / too much / little* healthy options.

2 It closes *early too / too early / early enough* in the afternoon.

3 I prefer not to eat meat but there are *little / a few / few* vegetarian dishes.

4 It costs *too much / too / much* to eat there every day.

5 There isn't *many / much / too* space between tables.

6 The queues are long at lunchtime so there's very *little / much / few* time to eat.

7 The canteen isn't *too big / enough big / big enough*.

8 There are *a little / much / a lot of* starters but there aren't *many / much / few* desserts.

8 Underline the future forms that can complete the sentences. Sometimes more than one option is possible.

1 I haven't made any plans for the weekend, but _____ to the cinema.

a I'll probably go   b I'm going   c I go

2 Sandra's got her ticket booked for Bali. She _____ on the 25th.

a leaves   b is leaving   c probably leave

3 _____ into the office tomorrow?

a Do you come   b Are you coming   c Are you going to come

4 We _____ a lot next month. It's too expensive.

a aren't going to eat out   b don't eat out   c won't eat out

5 I think _____ some more coffee. Want one?

a I'm making   b I'll make   c I'm going to make

6 Tomorrow evening he _____ his favourite series. He never misses it.

a is going to watch   b is watching   c watches

9 Match the words in each column to form compound nouns.

1 double / single /queen-size   a TV

2 cable /satellite / flat screen   b suite

3 honeymoon / executive / luxury   c trip

4 round / desert / business   d facilities

5 fast food / traditional / seafood   e restaurant

6 airport / hotel / modern   f bed

10 Put each word in the boxes into the correct group according to its stress pattern.

Unit 1 | appointment   commute   knowledge   management   suggestion   stressful   schedule

Unit 2 | arrangements   delay   exchange   hotel   departures   sightseeing

Unit 3 | business   chocolate   delicious   dessert   etiquette   healthy   restaurant

Oo	oO	Ooo	oOo
survey	career	passenger	assistant

4

A *can, could* and *be able to*
B Personal characteristics
C Comparatives and superlatives
D Communication strategies Building on ideas
E Interaction Training solutions

Learning curve

can, could and be able to

Reading: Mental abilities

1 How often do you do puzzles? What type of puzzles do you like?

2 Look at this puzzle. You have to make words that contain the letter N. How many words can you find in three minutes?

3 Did you enjoy the puzzle? Why?/Why not? Do you think puzzles like this are good exercise for your brain?

4 Read the article about brain power. Find six ways to improve your mental abilities.

5 What do you think is the best advice in the article?

6 Find words in the article that mean the following.

1 increase or improve something (paragraph 3)

2 make someone do something they don't want to do (paragraphs 3 and 4)

3 something that tests skills and abilities in an interesting way (paragraph 4)

4 make someone use all their abilities or intelligence (paragraph 5)

5 how well a person or thing does a particular activity (paragraph 5)

Easy ways to improve your brain power

I can remember the name of my first teacher but I can't remember what I did yesterday. I was able to learn things a lot faster when I was a child. Are you able to remember things easily? Could you learn things quicker when you were younger?

What can we do to improve our memories? Google 'improve brain power' and you'll find all sorts of tips on the subject. Most of them involve physical exercise, balanced nutrition and complex mental exercises. It would be cool* to incorporate all these tips, but it is hard work.

Fortunately, for the lazy people like me there are easier things to boost the way the brain functions. By changing the side of your mouse pad you force yourself to use your non-dominant hand. This will stimulate the neural connections between the right and left hemispheres in your brain. Ideally, you want to do as many activities as possible with your non-dominant hand.

Force yourself to remember things. You can stimulate the brain just like your muscles and the more you exercise it, the stronger it will get. For example, last year I couldn't remember my mobile phone number. Every morning for a month I forced myself to write down the number from memory. Now I am able to memorize phone numbers very easily. Remembering names, memorizing phone numbers and not writing shopping lists is a great challenge for the brain.

By playing games that involve some thinking you will be able to keep your brain in shape. Activities as simple as sudoku or crosswords stretch the thinking process and soon have an impact on your brain's performance. Regularity is the key here, so try to make these games or exercises part of your routine.

*cool: great, very good

Grammar: *can*, *could* and *be able to*

7 Read the information in the table. Find all the examples of *can*, *could* and *be able to* in the article.

---

can, could and be able to

1 When we talk about abilities people have now, we generally use *can*.
I **can** remember the name of my first teacher.

2 *Be able to* and *can* sometimes have the same meaning.
You **can/will be able to** integrate this into your life fairly easily.

3 When we talk about abilities people will have in the future, we use *will be able to*.
You **will be able to** keep your brain in shape.

4 We use *could* and *was able to* to describe abilities people had in the past.
I **could/was able to** learn things a lot faster when I was younger.
I **couldn't** remember my mobile phone number.

>> For more information on *can*, *could* and *be able to*, see page 167.

! We don't use **could** when we talk about one specific situation or occasion in the past that involved a challenge or difficulty.
Instead we might say '*It was a hard test but she **managed to** pass it.*'

---

8 Choose the correct form to complete the sentences. Sometimes more than one answer is possible.

1 The world's changing so fast. We all need to *be able to / could / can* learn new things.

2 You *can't / won't be able to / couldn't* keep your brain in shape if you don't exercise it.

3 *Can / Could / Is able to* a regular brain training programme help you?

4 Many retired people do a crossword every day, so they *can / could / are able to* keep their brains active.

5 If you practise regularly, you *will be able to / can / could* get better at certain types of puzzles.

6 *Being able to / Can / Could* remember faces and names is very important when you work in a job like mine.

7 Even people who *weren't able to / can't / couldn't* do Maths when they were at school found that this game helps them to improve.

8 *Will you be able to / Could you / Can you* remember new words when you finish this lesson?

Speaking: I'd like to be able to sing

9 Read the instructions and write your answers inside the shapes below.

1 Something that you could do well when you were younger but can't do now.

2 Something that you can do better now than you could ten years ago.

3 Something that you can never remember.

4 Something that you think you'll never be able to do.

5 Something that you would love to be able to do.

10 Look at your partner's answers and ask questions about what he/she has written. Do you have any abilities in common?

TALKING POINT
- What do you have a good/bad memory for? For example: actors' names, faces, birthdays, shopping, passwords, prices.
- Are you right-handed or left-handed? What activities could you try with the opposite hand?

Listening: Life skills

1 What skills do you need in your job? Complete three of the sentences. Then compare with a partner. Could you do his/her job? Why?/Why not?

1 You need to be able to …

2 You should be capable of …

3 You have to be …

4 It's important to be good at …

5 You want to know how to …

> **!** *Job* is generally a noun:
> *What's your* **job**? *I'm a software engineer. Have you finished all those* **jobs**?
> *Work* can be a verb or a noun.
> *She* **works** *for a software company. We start* **work** *at 8 a.m.*
> Notice that *work* is an uncountable noun, so it cannot be plural.
> *Have you finished all that* **work**? NOT ~~Have you finished all those works.~~

2 🔊 **1.18** Listen to a recruitment specialist talking to a group of job seekers. Make a note of the skills that they say employers look for.

3 🔊 Listen again and complete these notes with one to three words.

1 Employers would like all staff to have certain skills, called _____ skills.

2 They want people who are able to express _____ _____ well, and who are good _____ .

3 You need to be able to work with all _____ _____ _____ .

4 Being organized and maintaining a _____ _____ shows you can work efficiently.

5 You'll need to research _____ _____ _____ and find _____ .

6 Looking at routine problems and using _____ _____ _____ is part of most jobs.

7 Show you are prepared to improve professionally by _____ _____ _____ .

Word focus: Personal characteristics

4 Match the adjectives to describe skills and personal characteristics to the definitions.

If you are		you are able to …
1	analytical	**a** convince other people to do things
2	self-sufficient	**b** plan things carefully and keep things tidy
3	organized	**c** have the necessary knowledge to use computers
4	sensible	**d** do things for yourself without the help of others
5	computer literate	**e** examine things very carefully and logically
6	efficient	**f** do basic mathematics
7	persuasive	**g** be practical and have good judgment
8	numerate	**h** work quickly and effectively

5 Tick (✓) the words below that employers would consider to be negative characteristics. Use a good dictionary to help you with the meaning of the words.

> responsible hard-working unreliable resourceful
> self-confident messy flexible conscientious
> motivated bossy unpunctual friendly

6 Match these job skills with the correct verb or phrase below.

- team worker/player
- common sense
- logical thinker
- good attention to detail
- a sense of humour
- problem-solving
- work on your own initiative
- think on your feet
- writing
- an outgoing personality
- meet deadlines
- customer care
- work well under pressure
- decision-making

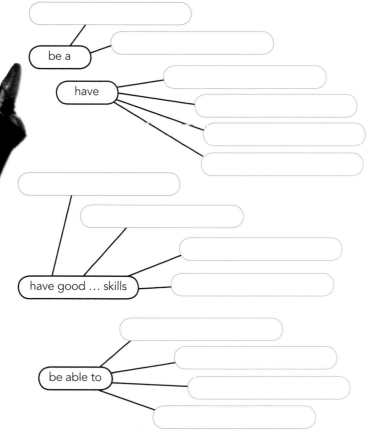

be a

have

have good ... skills

be able to

7 Choose three skills from exercise 6 which you think a person needs for these jobs.

civil servant

flight attendant

journalist

sales rep

lawyer

dancer

chef

surgeon

software engineer

Speaking: Tricky questions

8 Read the story about James Cash Penney. What do you think of his interview technique?

J.C. Penney, the founder of the US chain of stores, was known for interviewing people over a 6 a.m. breakfast. If the person put salt and pepper on their food before tasting it, the interview was over. In Mr. Penney's estimation, this was a person who made decisions before they had all the information.

9 Have you ever attended a job interview where they have asked you questions about your personality? What did they ask you?

10 Many interviewers ask difficult questions to find out about the candidate's personality. Work in pairs. Interview each other using these questions.

1 Can you describe yourself in three words?
2 What are your best skills?
3 What is your biggest weakness?
4 How would your previous boss describe you?
5 What aspects of your day-to-day work do you dislike?
6 Do you prefer to work by yourself or with others?
7 What's the biggest career mistake you've made so far?

11 Which questions in exercise 10 were the most difficult to answer?

TALKING POINT
- Qualifications, personality and work experience are all important factors in finding a job. Which do you think is the most important? Why?
- Do you think your age can affect your ability to do certain jobs? Give examples.

Listening: Getting an education

1 What are the people in the photos learning to do? Which things are best learnt by hands-on practice and which by formal study? What is the best age to learn the activities in the photos?

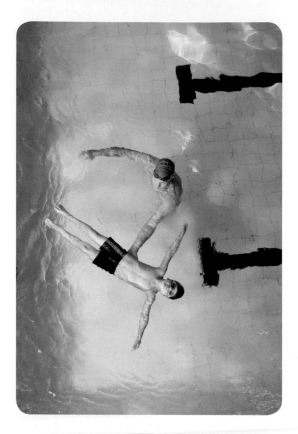

2 ◁)) **1.19** Listen to Mark talking about his own education and his son Nathan's education. Are these statements true (T) or false (F)?

1 Mark was successful at school and passed all his exams.

2 Mark needed few qualifications for his job.

3 Mark was not very self-motivated when he started studying again.

4 Mark wanted a law degree that was flexible.

5 The Open University course is less expensive than a traditional course.

6 Nathan's law degree is assessed by exams.

7 Nathan is less confident about his course than his father.

8 Nathan can study his course more slowly than his father.

3 ◁)) Listen again. What are the similarities and differences between the two courses?

Grammar: Comparatives and superlatives

4 Complete these sentences from Mark's story using a comparative or superlative form of the words below. Listen again and check your answers.

> bad   flexible   stressful   easy   slowly   good   cheap

1 Studying online is much _____ than attending full-time classes.

2 It's also a bit _____ than a traditional course.

3 Nathan got a place at one of _____ universities in the country.

4 Nathan says _____ part for him is all the exams.

5 My course is _____ because it's mostly continuous assessment.

6 Studying for a degree when you are young is _____ than at my age.

7 Fortunately, I can take it _____ .

5 Read the information in the table on the comparative and superlative forms and complete the examples.

Comparative and superlative adjectives

1 We use **-er** to form the comparative and **-est** to form the superlative with short adjectives.

Online courses can take _____ to finish _____ traditional courses. (long)

My university course was _____ _____ course I have ever taken. (long)

2 Adjectives ending in **-y** are formed by changing **-y** to **i** in the comparative and superlative forms.

Studying when you are young is _____ _____ at my age. (easy)

That was _____ _____ test I've ever done. (easy)

3 We use **more** to form the comparative and **most** to form the superlative with long adjectives.

Studying part-time is much _____ _____ _____ attending full-time classes. (flexible)

Modular courses are the _____ _____ way to study in my opinion. (flexible)

The opposite of *more* is *less*. The opposite of *most* is *least*.

>> For more information on comparative and superlative adjectives, see page 172.

Comparative and superlative adverbs

1 We use **-er** to form the comparative and **-est** to form the superlative of adverbs which have the same form as the adjective.

He learns new concepts _____ _____ me. (fast)

She works _____ _____ in the group. (hard)

2 We use **more** to form the comparative and **most** to form the superlative of adverbs ending in -ly.

I'm progressing _____ _____ than I expected. (slowly)

3 There are a few irregular adjectives and adverbs that change their form completely.

adjective	adverb	comparative	superlative
good	well	_____	_____
bad	badly	_____	_____

>> For more information on comparative and superlative adverbs, see page 172.

6 Choose the correct option to complete the comparative and superlative forms in this article.

Is e-learning right for you?

E-learning is now an essential part of higher education and many universities are finding that online enrolment is growing faster **1** *that / than* student enrolment. Many academics agree that the quality of online instruction is the same as or even **2** *better / best* than face-to-face teaching.

Advantages

- Participants are learning more **3** *active / actively* by taking responsibility for their studies.
- For shy students, the online environment is **4** *least / less* intimidating.
- Adult learners trying to balance work, family and study generally value the freedom and flexibility that e-learning offers.
- There is often a **5** *more / the most* supportive and collaborative environment than in the traditional classroom thanks to email contact with tutors and student forums.
- Study can be much **6** *more / most* affordable.

Disadvantages

- The e-learner has to be **7** *most / more* organized, disciplined and determined about studying than in a traditional classroom.
- Making friends is **8** *more difficult / more easily* than in a face-to-face, social environment. Younger students are often **9** *the least / less* satisfied with online learning than older students for this reason. Although many people enjoy chatting online to classmates.
- The e-learner is more dependent on technology for their learning. Some of them find using computers **10** *more slowly / harder* than others.

Speaking: What do you think?

7 The writer in exercise 6 makes the following statements. Do you agree? Why?/Why not?

1 Many academics agree that the quality of online instruction is the same as or even better than face-to-face teaching.

2 Most adults value the freedom of e-learning.

3 E-learning is a more supportive and collaborative environment than the traditional classroom.

8 Discuss these questions.

1 Would you like to learn English online? Why?/Why not? In what ways would it be better/worse than a classroom course?

2 What other subject would you like to learn online?

Writing: Asking about a new course

9 You see a website advertising an English course by e-learning. There are two types of course available: a three-year course and a six-month intensive. Write an email to the website stating your situation and asking for more information to find out which course is suitable for you.

TALKING POINT
- What new skill would you like to learn?
- What method of learning do you prefer for your chosen skill/subject?

Reading: Improvisation skills

1 Improvisation is doing things without preparing first. Are you a planner or an improviser? Do this quiz with a partner. Then turn to File 5 on page 132 and find out.

---

1 You're cooking a meal with a friend. Which one of these things are you most likely to say?

a 'Could we follow the recipe exactly?'
b 'Why don't we make things up as we go along?'
c 'What we could do is change a couple of ingredients.'

2 There's no shower cap in the hotel you're staying in and your husband/wife doesn't want to get their hair wet. What do you say?

a 'Don't have a shower then.'
b 'What if we use a plastic bag just for the top of your head?'
c 'Let's call room service and find out if they have one.'

3 You've driven half way to the campsite when you realize you've forgotten to pack the camping chairs. What do you say?

a 'Oh, no. We'll have to go back home and get them.'
b 'Oh, it doesn't matter. I'll work something out*.'
c 'Let's wait and see – maybe there's a camping shop on the way.'

4 Which is closest to your philosophy of life?

a 'It's always best to plan, plan, plan.'
b 'I like to adapt: life is full of surprises.'
c 'I try to be organized but you've got to be flexible sometimes.'

work something out: think of a solution to a problem

---

2 Discuss these questions.

1 What kinds of people often improvise?

2 People often have to improvise because of unexpected events. Do you have to improvise much in your job? How?

3 Is improvisation a natural skill or is it something people can learn? Why? Read the article and find out if the writer agrees with you.

The skill of improvisation

Organizations need their employees to look ahead and plan for the future. They also need them to improvise when the unexpected happens and adapt to new situations. Improvisation isn't just a natural talent. It's something people can learn, and more and more organizations are employing improvisation experts to help them train their staff. So who are these experts? Surprisingly, the new company trainers are comedians.

Improvised comedy is one of the most risky forms of comedy but also one of the most fun. There are no scripts, so nobody knows their words in advance, and there are no rehearsals*, so nobody practises first. The audience provides the ideas and the comedians make things up* on the spot. Many comedians are now teaching company executives and employees the skills they had to learn.

A key skill they teach is how to say 'Yes …, and …'. Many people like to stick to* their own ideas and they resist new ones. So when they hear another person's suggestion, they automatically want to raise objections. The first thing you have to learn when you're improvising is to think 'That's a good idea'. So you can't say, 'Yes, but…'. You have to say 'Sounds great to me' instead.

'Yes …, and …' is a powerful technique with two parts. The first part is the 'yes' which means 'I'll go along with* that'. The second part is the 'and' which means you have to build on the idea. So instead of resisting the idea you add to it. It's a great way to develop creativity. Organizations have found it's a powerful way to build teams and encourage employees to take risks in the workplace, too.

rehearsal: a time when actors prepare for a public performance
make up: invent things
stick to: stay fixed or attached to
go along with: agree to someone's ideas

4 Discuss these questions.

1 Do you know anyone who often resists new ideas? Think of examples.

2 Do you know anyone who's good at improvising and coming up with new ideas? Think of examples.

3 Do you think training in the 'Yes …, and …' technique sounds useful? Why?/Why not?

5 Find four expressions in the article in exercise 3 that you could say if you like an idea. Then find one expression you can say if you don't.

6 Work in pairs. Experiment with the 'Yes …, and …' technique. Use the phrases in the box to make suggestions about these ideas.

> Learning to ride a motorbike
> Taking classes in Latin
> Buying everyone in the office a mobile phone
> Driving across Australia on your next summer holiday

Building on ideas	
What if we _____?	*Yes, I'll go along with that and …*
Could we _____?	*Great idea! And we could …*
Let's _____?	*Sounds good to me. And …*
Why don't we _____?	*Fantastic! And what we could do is …*

1 First have a 'Yes, but …' conversation where you don't build on one another's ideas. Try to resist your partner's ideas and raise objections.

2 Then have a 'Yes …, and …' conversation. Use the responses in the box and add to your partner's ideas.

7 Compare the conversations you had with 'Yes, but …' and 'Yes …, and …'.

1 Which conversation generated the most ideas?

2 Which one was easier? Why?

3 What other expressions did you use to resist ideas?

4 Some people say 'Yes …, and …' is a good way of thinking because it opens your mind. Do you agree? Why?/Why not?

Speaking: Improvising and organizing

8 Work in pairs or groups. Read about the situation and brainstorm some ideas. When you disagree with each other's ideas, you can use 'Yes, but …' But also try to use the 'Yes …, and …' technique to build on ideas.

> The head of marketing in your organization is visiting your offices in four weeks' time.
>
> During her visit you want to:
> - introduce her to all the team
> - give a presentation about your department's work
> - arrange a special fun event which will show off your team's creative talents, e.g. a talent show, concert, or sports day
>
> The members of the team each have special skills and talents. Look at File 10, page 134 and choose one of the roles.
>
> The head of marketing is visiting company offices around the world. There is a prize for the most creative team!

9 When you have finished, compare your ideas with your group, or the rest of the class.

1 Who thought of the most original and creative event?

2 Who had the best organizational skills?

3 Who was able to make the most of all the team's personal skills?

10 Congratulations! Your team won! Turn to File 43, page 141 and look at the information.

Communication strategies

Reminder

Grammar reference
pages 167 and 172

When we talk about skills and abilities we use *can/could* but *be able to* as the base form.
I'd like to be able to give good presentations.
I can't/won't be able to do a course on Saturdays.

We use comparatives and superlatives to compare ideas.
This course will be more interesting than that one.
It's the best course for me.

Some people say, *'Yes …, and …'* because it helps people to build on ideas.
We can use these expressions when responding to people's ideas.
Yes, I'll go along with that, and …
Great idea! And what you could do is …
Sounds good to me.

Listening: Staff training needs

1 Think of two or three training courses you've attended. What were they about? What was good about them?

2 ◁)) 1.20 Look at the photos of three employees from a&k. Listen to them talking to the Training Manager, Oskar. What are their training needs?

3 Look at the brochure for the training company Total Training Solutions. Which course(s) do you think Karen, Ricardo and Nadia could do? Why?

a&k is a Swedish company based in Stockholm that manufactures electronic cards and high-tech security systems for banks, financial institutions and other leading companies worldwide.

1 Karen Barnes,
Research Assistant, 26

2 Ricardo Sanchez,
Computer Technician, 30

3 Nadia Hudak,
Product Manager, 46

TOTAL TRAINING SOLUTIONS

TTS has developed a series of one-day or two-day courses using theoretical knowledge* and modern psychology. Training is in groups or one-on-one.

Assertiveness

Learn to communicate your preferences while taking into consideration other people's needs. Delegates practise how to express their own needs in an honest, direct and positive way and build their self-confidence.

Presentations Across Cultures

Our cross-cultural course on presentation skills assists managers, academics and salespeople to improve their awareness of intercultural differences. The course provides analysis of presentation styles and looks at how people deliver and understand presentations internationally. Learn how to adapt your presentation in areas such as: content, using your voice, body language and maximizing impact.

Advocacy and Mediation

In these advocacy training sessions, you learn the art of effective persuasion. We teach you techniques that lead to positive results quickly and easily. This two-day seminar provides a systematic approach for anyone who has to persuade others: directors, managers, salespeople and consultants.

Ex-pat Relocation

How can we reduce the impact of culture shock for people who are going to be relocated*? Our training provides an introduction to the country and gives you an understanding of the culture's values, customs and etiquette in work and social life. We give tips on working with international colleagues and how to deal with cultural differences. Courses are given by cross-cultural

specialists with knowledge of working in the target country. Additional language classes can also be provided.

Playing Golf with NLP

Reduce negative self-talk and create positive game plans. Using fast, effective NLP (Neuro-linguistic Programming) techniques, you will learn to stay in control and improve your performance when playing golf even in the most challenging games.

Call us to discuss your specific requirements*. Courses run from Monday to Saturday. One-day courses, €349 + VAT; two-day courses, €549+ VAT per person.

knowledge: information, skills and understanding gained through learning and experience
relocate: move to a different place
requirements: something that someone needs

4))) **1.21** Listen to Karen talking to the Training Manager, Oskar. Which course(s) would she like to do and why? What do they agree to do?

5 Look at Oskar's email to Karen. What has happened?

Subject: a&k Meeting and Training Course

Dear Karen

Congratulations on your recent promotion! I hear you have been asked to attend the annual a&k meeting in Copenhagen next month and present our latest electronic card technology. Let me know if you need any help with this.

I am also writing to confirm that the company has agreed to pay for one of your training courses, although you will attend two. Please let me know if you have any questions.

Best wishes

Oskar

Training Manager
a&k

---

6 Work in pairs. Student A: Look at your information below. Student B: Turn to File 6, page 132. Roleplay the situation.

Student A:

You are Karen. You think a&k should pay for both of your courses now that you have been promoted. Persuade your training manager that your point of view is right.

Make some notes before you begin. Make sure you mention the benefits to the company of doing both courses.

7 Would you be interested in doing any of these courses? Why?/Why not?

Speaking: Persuading the boss

8 Work in pairs. Student A: Look at the information below. Student B: Look at the information in File 11, page 134. Act out the situation. Then change roles.

Student A:

You are an employee at a&k. Choose the most suitable course(s) for you from the TTS brochure and negotiate with your training manager. The company will pay for one course but maybe you can persuade them to let you do some more. Consider these points before you begin.

1 Your motivation

2 Benefits of the training to you and the company

3 Cost, e.g. How many courses can you do? Do you have to pay for part of the cost yourself? (You are prepared to pay for up to 20% of the costs but it depends on the course. Do not tell this to your manager.)

4 Length and time, e.g. Will you be able to attend in company time? It is difficult for you to make up lost time in the office/factory because you do shift work and have family commitments.

5 Your attendance – You sometimes work in the evening and at weekends so this will affect your attendance.

5

A Present perfect and past simple
B used to
C Conversation topics
D **Communication strategies** Socializing
E **Interaction** Choosing a candidate

Getting on

Present perfect and past simple

Reading: Talented people

1 Look at the photos of these people.
Who are they and what do you know about them?

2 Read the three profiles quickly and match
them to the photos.

3 These texts were written in 2009.
What changes to the lives of these people do you
know about since that year?

PROFILE A

Born in Mallorca, this sportsman has taken the tennis
world by storm in recent years. In 2001 he turned
professional at the age of 15. His coach is his uncle.
Like Björn Borg, he has won four consecutive singles
titles in the French Open. In 2008 the Spanish champion
won four titles including the French Open, the US Open,
Wimbledon and a gold medal in the Olympic Games.
He won the Australian Open for the first time in 2009.
He is the first male tennis player to hold Grand Slam*
singles titles on three different surfaces at the same
time. He has been especially successful on clay*
courts, which is why he is known as the King of Clay.

Grand Slam: important sports event in a particular sport
clay: a type of red earth

Profile B

Born in 1969, she is one of the
most talented performers on
cinema screens today. She has
played diverse roles such as
Elizabeth I in *Elizabeth*, the elf
queen in *The Lord of the Rings*
trilogy and Bob Dylan in the film
I'm Not There. She has starred
alongside famous actors such as
Dame Judi Dench, Brad Pitt and
George Clooney. She has won
several acting awards*. In 2006
she won an Academy Award
for Best Supporting Actress in
Martin Scorsese's *The Aviator*.
But she has not received an
Oscar for Best Actress yet. Her
husband is playwright Andrew
Upton and they have been
artistic directors of the Sydney
Theatre Company since 2008.

award: prize or money given to reward
someone for something they have done

PROFILE C

This writer was born in Kyoto in
1949. Both his parents taught
Japanese literature. Since
childhood, Western culture has
influenced him, particularly music
and literature. He ran a jazz club
in Tokyo before he became an
author at the age of 30. His best
known novels include *Norwegian
Wood*, *The Wind-up Bird
Chronicle*, and the international
bestseller, *Kafka on the Shore*,
for which he received the Franz
Kafka Prize in 2006. In addition
to writing books, he enjoys
running. He is a skilful translator
of English works and has
translated his own novels into
English. There are translations of
his work in 34 languages.

4 Read the profiles again and answer these questions.
There is sometimes more than one possible answer.

1 Who has won an award?

2 Who won four titles in the same year?

3 Who likes doing sport?

4 Who has had two jobs?

5 Who started working in their profession in his/her
thirties?

6 Who has relatives who work in a similar field?

5 Which of these talented personalities would you most like to
meet? Why? What would you like to talk about with him/her?

6 Find five words in profile A related to sports; five words in profile
B related to films and five words in profile C related to books.

Grammar: Present perfect and past simple

7 When do we use the past simple and present perfect tenses? Look at the table, choose the correct options and complete the examples.

Present perfect and past simple

1 We use the *present perfect/past simple* to talk about finished actions and events in the past. We can give a definite time when the events happened.

Haruki Murakami _____ (become) an author at the age of 30.

2 We use the *present perfect/past simple* to talk about life experiences in an indefinite time in the past.

Cate Blanchett _____ (not/receive) an Oscar for Best Actress yet.

3 We use the *present perfect/past simple* to talk about an action or situation that started in the past and which is still continuing now.

They _____ (be) artistic directors of the Sydney Theatre Company since 2008.

4 We use the *present perfect/past simple* to talk about present results of past actions and to announce news.

Rafael Nadal _____ (just/win) the match.

>> For more information on the present perfect and the past simple, see pages 161 and 163.

8 How many more examples of the present perfect can you find in the texts? Why did the writer use the present perfect and not the past?

> **!** We use *for* with time periods and we use *since* to refer to the start of an event or situation.
> *They have been artistic directors **since** 2008.*
> *He's been a writer **for** over thirty years.*
> When we speak about 'unfinished time', we often use the adverbs **already** and **yet**. **Already** is used to say something has happened sooner than expected.
> *He has **already** won four consecutive singles titles.*
> **Not yet** is used when something you expected to happen hasn't happened.
> *She has**n't** received an Oscar **yet**.*

9 Do we use *for* or *since* with these time expressions?

> many years   2007   May   ages   he was 15   two minutes
> 15 years   a long time   months   last Monday

10 Look at these sentences. What is the difference in meaning?

1 **a** She has already starred with Dame Judi Dench.

   b She hasn't starred with Dame Judi Dench yet.

2 **a** He hasn't won the Australian Open yet.

   b He has already won the Australian Open.

11 Which sentence in exercise 10 is true for the people in the texts? Using *yet* and *already*, make more sentences about the people in the texts.

12 Work in pairs. Look at some more information about one of the three people. Student A: Turn to File 2, page 132. Student B: Turn to File 13, page 134. Write questions in the present perfect or past simple to complete your information. Ask your partner the questions.

Speaking: 'A' list

13 Who are the most talented people in your country? Make an 'A' list and add a new category of your own. Write one or two sentences about each of them. Compare with your partner.

> **1** Best sports personality:
>
> _____
>
> **2** Best actor/actress:
>
> _____
>
> **3** Best author:
>
> _____
>
> **4** Best musician/singer:
>
> _____
>
> **5** Category(ies) of your choice:
>
> _____

14 Compare your 'A' lists with another pair and explain your choices. If all the people are from the same country, vote for the most talented.

TALKING POINT
- Who do you think is the most talented personality of your generation? Why?
- Why is it too late to start in some professions at the age of 30?

Reading: Career change

1 How did you become interested in your job or field of work?

2 What are some of the similarities and differences between the lives of a photojournalist and an investment banker? Compare your ideas and then read the article.

Bleasdale swapped his banking job for a camera

Banker-turned-photojournalist

As an investment banker, Marcus Bleasdale used to earn £500,000 a year. By 30 he was the owner of two houses and a Porsche, and he spent weekends skiing in the Alps. Bleasdale is now a photojournalist. He owns a flat but no car, and at 40 earns £60,000 a year. At short notice he is sent to report on conflicts around the world. 'I just like life being real,' he says.

Bleasdale studied Economics and Finance at university and in 1996 was working for ABN Amro in Amsterdam.

'I used to get up at 5.30 every morning and be in bed by 10.30. Everyone thinks it's glamorous, but it's not that glamorous. I didn't want to be sitting in front of computer screens when I was 40.'

Then, he found something that completely changed his life. 'A girlfriend wanted a camera for her birthday,' he explains. He picked it up one day, started taking pictures of nature and did some evening courses.

The move in 1998 was dramatic.

'I remember reading about the Balkans. I got into work the next day and someone said, "Have you seen the newspaper headlines?" I said, "Yes, horrific isn't it?" He said, "What do you think that's going to do to the price of the dollar?" I knew I didn't want to be a banker any more.' Within 24 hours he was on a plane to the Balkans.

Why did he go? 'I just felt I needed to be there. I loved the freedom, the energy.' On his return to London, he enrolled* on a photojournalism course and then won an award for best young photojournalist.

Since then Bleasdale has worked for *Time*, *Newsweek*, and *National Geographic*.

He now lives modestly in Norway with his wife. His savings have long gone, spent on subsidizing his new career, and also on an orphanage* in eastern Congo. 'It's not easy to come back and fit back into normal life,' he says. But it is the camaraderie* of banking that he misses most. 'The life of a journalist is quite lonely.' Does he feel he has changed?

'I think I appreciate life a lot more. I think I'm more sensitive. I'm a nicer guy.'

enrol: officially arrange to do a course
orphanage: a large house where children who are orphans live
camaraderie: feeling of friendship, especially when working together

3 Read the article again. Find evidence to support the following statements.

1 Marcus was a successful investment banker.

2 He was unhappy as a banker.

3 He is very flexible in his approach to life and work.

4 He is very talented.

5 He contributes to charity.

6 He has changed as a person.

4 In what ways is Marcus Bleasdale's life better than before? In what ways is it worse?

Grammar: *used to*

5 Look at the information in the table and choose the correct options.

> **used to**
>
> **1** We use *used to* when we talk about *present/past* habits, which we no longer do, or to describe states, which are not true now.
> *Marcus Bleasdale* **used to** *earn £500,000 a year.*
> *He* **didn't use to** *enjoy his work but he loves it now.*
> **Did** *he* **use to** *work in a bank? Yes, he did./No, he didn't.*
>
> **2** We can also use the *past simple/present perfect* to describe past habits.
> *He* **drove** *fast cars. (He* **used to drive** *fast cars.)*
>
> **3** We use the *present simple/used to* with an adverb of frequency when we talk about present habits.
> *Marcus* **is** *usually* **away** *from home six months of the year.*

>> For more information on *used to*, see page 164.

6 Complete the information about Marcus Bleasdale's life using *used to* and the verbs in the box.

> sit   love   help   say   not appreciate   eat out   live   wear

1 As a boy, Marcus _____ his family pay the bills.

2 His father _____ , 'You should make sure you earn enough money.'

3 When Marcus worked as a banker, he _____ in expensive restaurants twice a week.

4 In the bank he _____ in front of computers.

5 Marcus _____ smart suits. Nowadays he usually wears trousers and a shirt that he can wash easily at night.

6 He _____ life as much as he does now.

7 Marcus _____ cities but he hates them now.

8 He _____ in Amsterdam but now he lives in Norway.

Speaking: Guess what I used to do

7 Work in pairs. Student A: You used to be rich. Look at the information below. Student B: You used to be poor. Turn to File 16, page 135.

Student A:

1 You used to be a rich businessperson but you lost all your money. Complete these sentences about your former life. Then answer your partner's questions.

- I used to drive _____ . (form of transport)
- I used to own _____ . (type of business/company)
- I used to work _____ . (working hours)
- I used to have _____ . (possessions)
- I used to spend my holidays in _____ . (places)
- I didn't use to … (type of problems)

2 Ask Student B questions to guess what he/she used to do.

Did you use to work in an office?

8 Write down three significant changes in your life. Talk about them with your partner and ask each other questions. What do you both have in common?

> **TALKING POINT**
> - Which job would you like to do for one month/one year? Why?
> - Who do you know who has reinvented himself/herself? How did they do it?

Listening: Making small talk

1 Small talk is light informal conversation. How many small talk topics can you find?

televisionsportspoliticsfashionartnovelsfamilyarchitecturethe
economicclimatemusicpetstheweatherreligionfoodandrestaurantstravel
experiencesholidayplansthenewssalariesyourhometownhealthweekend
activitiesfilmsandcinemayourjobhobbiescelebritygossipfestivals

2 Which items in exercise 1 are your favourite small talk topics? Which topics are not suitable in a lot of local situations? Why?

3 Look at the blog entry. What does this woman say are her favourite small talk topics? What is her theory, and how does she get her customers talking?

I'm the queen of small talk because I'm in sales. My favourite safe topics are: weather, travel, what are you reading? movies, kids, pets. One of my never-miss topics is pursuing my theory that everyone knows of one amazingly beautiful and special place where they live. There exist beautiful places even in areas that you wouldn't expect beauty. But if you investigate a bit, they will share and it's so cool to go to those places and see neat things that only the locals know about, like waterfalls, fields of flowers, architecture, historical monuments, etc. People love talking about where they live and how it's cool – and I LOVE learning from my customers, so I ask a lot of questions – it's like an imaginary vacation.

> **!** *News* is an uncountable noun. We can say: *I heard some **news*** or *It's an interesting piece of **news***, but not *I read a **news** about him.*

4 On what occasions do you usually make small talk and what about? Think of four situations, e.g. *When I arrive at work on a Monday morning, I ask my colleagues about their weekend.*

5))) **1.22** Listen to six people starting a conversation. Which six of these topics are they talking about?

> the weather   the physical environment   the news   the town   television
> weekend activities   celebrity gossip   work

6))) Listen again and complete what they say.

1 Are you _____ _____ _____ the match on Saturday?

2 _____ you _____ the rain we're having this week?

3 Have you _____ _____ _____ _____ the physics experiment in Switzerland?

4 _____ _____ _____ the big boss is coming from France next week.

5 What do _____ _____ _____ that new shopping centre?

6 _____ you _____ the beautiful spring flowers outside the office?

7 How could you respond to each person in exercise 6?

8 Choose one of the expressions in exercise 6 and use it to start some small talk with your partner.

> A: I hear that there is a flower festival in town at the moment.
>
> B: Yes, I read about it in the local newspaper. I think I'll go. Do you like flowers?

9))) **1.23** Listen to the start of two phone calls. Which call doesn't begin with small talk? Why do you think that is? In what kind of situations is small talk inappropriate?

10))) Listen again. How does Marco move from small talk to work talk?

Word focus: Conversation topics

11 Look at these groups of words. What is the small talk topic for each one?
Which word does not belong to each group? Why?

Topic:

1 _____ storm, flood, boiling, exhibition, changeable, _____ _____

2 _____ the sales, flu, casual wear, designer label, suit, _____ _____

3 _____ plot, the ending, main course, leading actor, thriller, _____ _____

4 _____ mayor, local council, author, taxes, elections, _____ _____

5 _____ flight delays, tie, campsite, lost luggage, first class, _____ _____

6 _____ aunt, nephew, library, anniversary, in-laws, _____ _____

12 Put the words in the box with the correct category in exercise 11.
Think of three more words to add to each group.

> T-shirt   soundtrack   niece   flip-flops   politician   director
> check-in   vote   traffic jam   freezing   daughter   shower

13 Choose a topic from exercise 1 and write four words that relate
to it and one that does not. Test another person in the class.

Rules

1 Use a coin to move forward. Heads move one space. Tails move two.

2 Talk for a minute about the subject without repeating a word or hesitating. Then, your partner will ask you two questions.

3 If you can't talk for a minute, move back to your previous position.

4 If you land on 'partner's choice', your partner chooses the subject you talk about.

Speaking: Keep talking

14 Work in pairs. Read the rules. Then play the game.

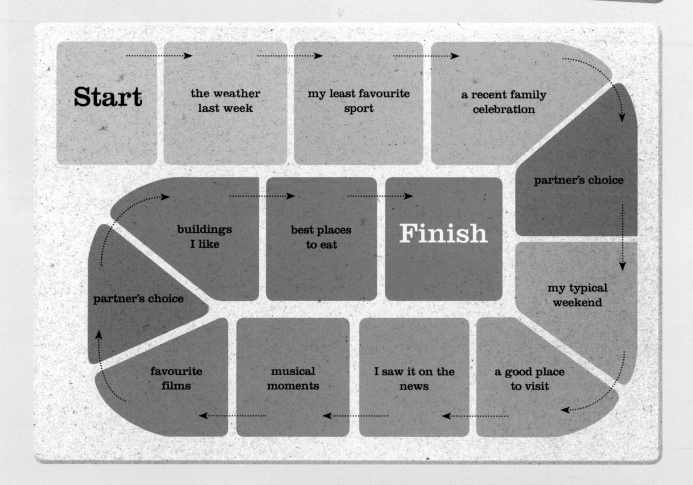

| TALKING POINT | How important is small talk in your job? |

Listening: Meeting and greeting

1 Look at the information about greeting people in Honduras. How is it similar or different from greeting people in your country? Discuss these points.

- Greeting family and close friends
- Meeting acquaintances
- Differences when greeting men and women
- Introductions with business contacts
- Meeting people for the first time

> Hugs and kisses are common in Honduran culture. Women usually greet each other with a little hug and a kissing gesture on the cheek, even when meeting for the first time.
>
> Men who are relatives or close friends may greet women that way, too. Among each other, men will usually shake hands, sometimes accompanied by a hug and a pat on the back if they are friends or family. The same gestures are exchanged again when parting.

2 🔊 1.24 Listen to six greetings. How would you respond to each one? Choose the correct option a), b) or c).

1. a I'm going to get a drink. Want one?
   b She's fine. Thanks for asking.
   c Not bad. And yourself?

2. a Yes, it's been a long time since the last conference.
   b I've been looking forward to meeting you, too.
   c You haven't changed a bit either!

3. a Hi, I'm Helena Coltrane. Nice to meet you, Sandra.
   b Great to see you again, too, Sandra. How have you been?
   c So, where are you working now?

4. a No, it's old. I've had it for ages.
   b Oh, not much. What are you up to these days?
   c No, I haven't watched the news today.

5. a Of course.
   b Can I have your name, please?
   c Yes, that's right. Do I know you?

6. a Not at all. Please do.
   b Yes, I'll join you later.
   c I don't mind.

3 Which people in exercise 2 have met before? Which conversations were the least formal?

> ❗ *How do you do?* is not often used nowadays. It's more common to say *Nice to meet you.* or *Pleased to meet you.* when meeting people for the first time.
>
> There are also many informal expressions for meeting and greeting such as: *Long time, no see! How are things with you?*

4 Complete the gaps with informal greetings from the conversations. Do you know any others?

How are you doing?

Hey, what's ¹ _____?

Long time, no see!

Hi! How's ² _____ _____?

Hey, what's new?

5 Look at the other responses in exercise 2 again. In what situations are they appropriate responses?

> *I'm going to get a drink. Want one?*

= When you want to explain why you're leaving someone you're talking to.

D

Reading: Compliments

6 Look at this travel blog. Do North American customs sound similar to your country? Why?/Why not?

Things are going well for me in Chicago. I've found people are very friendly. They don't wait to be introduced here, and they start conversations with strangers very easily.

Something unusual I've noticed is that Americans pay a lot of compliments – even to people they don't know. I don't think we do that much in the UK. Yesterday I was waiting in the queue at the supermarket when the customer next to me said, 'I love your coat'. I didn't know how to reply at first. I wanted to say 'Oh, it's old – nothing special', but that seemed unfriendly. So I said 'Thanks, I like your coat, too', and then we started chatting. In the next three minutes, this complete stranger told me her whole life story. It's an interesting way to start a conversation, but I don't know if I'll ever be good at it.

7 How would you respond to these compliments? Choose a, b or c.

1 That was a great presentation!
  a I know. I'm fabulous, aren't I?
  b Do you think so? I was really nervous at the start.
  c Thanks a lot. I think it went well.

2 Cool shirt!
  a Thank you. I like yours, too.
  b I'm not so sure about it myself. It's a bit loud.
  c Do you mean that? Or are you just saying it?

3 Your apartment is really beautiful.
  a Yes, we'd like to renovate the kitchen though.
  b Yes, but it's a noisy neighbourhood.
  c I don't deserve it.

4 I love your dress.
  a Thanks! It's a bit tight on me now. I've put on weight.
  b Thanks! It was a birthday present from my husband.
  c Yeah, it's all right. Nothing special.

5 You did a nice job on the product launch.
  a It really wasn't me. I had a lot of help from Ivan.
  b Thanks. I'm sure Ivan will appreciate hearing that, too.
  c It was a bit of luck really.

8 Read some strategies for responding to compliments. Then look at the responses in exercise 7. Decide which strategy the speaker was using and write it in the table. The first two are done for you.

Responding to compliments

It's sometimes difficult to respond to compliments. On the one hand, we want to be modest. But, on the other hand, we don't want to be disagreeable. Here are some typical strategies.

Strategy	Examples
Accepting the compliment	
Responding with a compliment	
Questioning the compliment	1b
Sharing the praise with someone else	
Downgrading the praise, so it seems less important	
Giving an explanation	
Joking	1a

9 Make up some compliments. Think of some words to complete the spaces in the table. Then compare your compliments to another student's. In what situations could you use them?

Paying compliments

1 Your _____ is _____ .
2 That _____ was really _____ .
3 I _____ your _____ .
4 That was a really _____ party.
5 This is a _____ _____ .

Speaking: Social chit-chat

10 Work in pairs. You meet your colleague who you know well in the corridor or lift. Think of a compliment you can pay him/her and start a one-minute conversation. Change partners and start another conversation.

11 Work in pairs. Imagine you don't know each other and you meet for the first time at a party at work. Greet each other, include a compliment if appropriate, and talk for two minutes.

Communication strategies

53

Reminder

Grammar reference
pages 161 and 163

We use the past simple to talk about finished actions and events in the past.
When I started I had very little money.

We use the present perfect to talk about life experiences at an indefinite time in the past.
Zahir Rahman has received many social enterprise awards.

We use the present perfect to talk about events that started in the past and which still continue today.
His company has sold solar panels for several years.

There are many ways of responding to compliments. For instance, we can share the praise, we can give an explanation or we can respond with a compliment.
A: You're doing a great job with the youth orchestra.
B: Thank you. I'm lucky I have a very supportive partner.

Listening: Social enterprise

1))) **1.25** What is a social enterprise? Listen to the first part of an interview with Zahir Rahman and complete the definition with one to three words in each gap.

A social enterprise is an organization that provides
1_____ like any other business and uses the same 2_____. A social enterprise focuses on 3_____ and needs. Unlike commercial businesses, the 4_____ generated are put back into the business rather than going into the 5_____ of owners or shareholders.

2))) Listen again and write down three examples of social enterprises.

3))) **1.26** Listen to the second part of the interview and correct this biographical information about Zahir Rahman.

1 Zahir Rahman has run his social enterprise for twelve years.

2 He has more than 118,000 customers today.

3 He thinks that a social entrepreneur is an inventor.

4 He qualified in engineering.

5 He went to live in the US twelve years ago.

6 He has just started a clean water company.

4 Would you like to work for a social enterprise? Which social needs would you focus on? Why? Look at the following suggestions.

> health   education   housing   transport   children
> the elderly   the unemployed

5 Read this advertisement. Who's offering the Social Enterprise Award and what does the prize include?

Social Enterprise Award

We're giving away £500,000

The *Daily Times* newspaper and the Northern Hibernia Bank offer annual awards worth £500,000 to social entrepreneurs and enterprises that have innovative ideas to achieve social change.

People can apply in one or more of these categories:

- Making profits for social purposes
- Transforming people's health
- Bringing communities together
- Passion for the environment

What we're offering:

- £300,000 for the overall winner
- £200,000 to be divided between the other three finalists

The four winners will also each receive a free consultation from one of the UK's leading social entrepreneurs as well as publicity in the *Daily Times*. Nominations for this year are now open.

Speaking: Four finalists

6 Work in pairs. Student A: Look at this information about David Horn and Carla D'Silva and ask Student B questions to complete the other two profiles. Then answer Student B's questions about Sally Warren and Jamie Barnes. Student B: Turn to File 15, page 135.

Name: David Horn
Company: Top Note Orchestra (TNO)
Started: ¹ _____ years ago

Main achievements:

- TNO aims to develop aspiring talent, especially young people who can't afford music lessons.
- TNO has trained ² _____ young musicians from poor city areas.
- The orchestra has given concerts ³ _____ . The musicians play with an energy and passion that audiences love.
- TNO uses the money from concerts to ⁴ _____ and set up new projects.
- TNO gives music workshops to people with learning difficulties.

Name: Carla D'Silva
Company: D'Silva Arts Centre
Started: ⁵ _____ years ago

Main achievements:

- Carla, who graduated from art school in ⁶_____ , has won several awards for her art.
- She opened ⁷_____ with her prize money and government grants.
- D'Silva Arts Centre has helped ⁸ _____ people change their lives through art therapy.
- The Centre organizes public exhibitions and raises money through sales of art to continue the project.
- The Centre runs street art courses for children having problems at school.

Name: Sally Warren
Company: City Leisure Unlimited (CLU)
Started: eight years ago

Main achievements:

- CLU started as a local council sports centre. After cuts in the service, employees bought the centre and have reduced costs by 10%.
- CLU operates a flexible pricing policy, with reduced prices for customers on a low income.
- CLU now has three centres and has created 350 jobs in the local community.
- CLU provides financial support for talented young sports people. Sally Warren, who used to be an Olympic runner, remembers how hard it was getting money to continue training.

Name: Jamie Barnes
Company: Barnes Apprentice Restaurants
Started: six years ago

Main achievements:

- Jamie runs three high-quality restaurants in fashionable parts of London.
- He has written eight cookbooks and some of the money from sales goes into his apprentice restaurant chain.
- The restaurants create opportunities for people who have been unemployed for a long time.
- Professional staff in the restaurants work with and train new apprentices for six months.
- 80% of the apprentices who graduate have found permanent jobs.

7 Work in pairs. Student A: Read the information below. Student B: Turn to File 37, page 140.

The finalists for the award are staying in the same hotel. There is a party at the hotel for them to socialize the evening before the award ceremony. Decide if you are Sally Warren or Jamie Barnes. Make small talk with one of the other candidates. Compliment him/her on something he/she is wearing and ask him/her questions.

8 Decide which is the strongest candidate with your partner. Then explain your choice to the rest of the class.

9))) 1.27 Listen to each of the finalists telling the judges about their plans for the future and make notes.

10 Work in groups. Discuss these ideas and come to a final decision.

1 Choose the winner. Is it the same person as your strongest candidate in exercise 8?

2 How much of the remaining £200,000 will you give to each of the other three finalists? Give reasons for your decisions.

3 What conditions should there be for spending the money?

Writing: Choosing the winner

11 You are one of the judges for the Social Enterprise Award. Write a short article for the *Daily Times*. Provide some background information about the award and announce this year's winners. Give your reasons for choosing the overall winner and the three finalists and explain how the £500,000 prize money is divided.

6

A can, have to, must, need to and should
B Obligation in the past
C Writing emails 1
D Communication strategies Giving advice
E Interaction Helping new people

Rule of thumb

can, have to, must, need to and should

Reading: Happy Computers

1 What makes your company, organization or school a good place to work or study? Make a list.

2 Quickly read the article about a company called Happy Computers. Find three things that make it a great place to work. Were any of these on your list?

3 Read the article again and find the information that supports these statements.

1 Staff can choose their own working hours.

2 People can work fewer days and achieve more.

3 The company's business has expanded in new directions.

4 Staff can contribute to the company's planning processes.

5 There is open communication within the company.

6 There are a lot of people interested in working for Happy.

Happy Computers show the way ahead

Happy Computers, last year rated* as one of the UK's top 10 companies, shows that there are many ways to achieve a contented and productive workplace.

The London-based firm aims to keep its staff happy. They don't have to give a reason for wanting a flexible timetable. 'There are no specific rules,' says Sabina Barbato, who is in charge of human resources. 'The simple reason that you need to have flexi-time is good enough for us to give it to you.'

For instance, when one staff member asked to take Mondays off* to recover from a weekend of clubbing*, the company agreed. 'It worked very well because he was much more productive on the other four days,' she says.

Happy believes that learning should be fun. Originally focused on IT training, the 50-employee company now offers management and personal development courses as well. Its chief executive Henry Stewart passionately believes that staff should have the freedom to do things their way.

He lets staff participate in business and financial decisions and allows them to vote on most major decisions. They can also have a say in* pay rises and bonuses, which are all team-based and set* by staff. A spreadsheet posted on the company intranet shows the salaries of all Happy employees.

'Nothing is secret. We're very open about things like finances and people's salaries,' says Ms Barbato. 'The reason behind that is if you ask for a pay rise then you have to be able to justify it in front of everybody.'

The company's reputation as a good employer has brought it many awards. And Happy doesn't need to pay for recruitment agencies or job advertisements. It currently has about 2,000 people signed up to receive information when a position at the company becomes available.

At Happy, having no rules such as 'You must park only in allocated spaces.' or 'You should work from 9 to 5', means that employees are much freer in their approach to the working day. No 'shoulds' or 'musts' obviously produce a very contented workforce.

rated: considered
take (time) off: have a holiday from work
clubbing: going to clubs and discos
have a say in: participate in decisions about
set: established

Grammar: *can*, *have to*, *must*, *need to* and *should*

4 Complete the first column of the table with the correct form of *can*, *have to*, *must*, *need to* and *should*. Then complete the examples.

can, have to, must, need to and should		
1 _____	possible or permitted	*They _____ in pay rises and bonuses.*
must **2** _____	necessary, important, an order, a rule, a law	*Visitors **must** sign in at reception.* *You _____ to justify it in front of everybody.*
3 _____		*The simple reason that _____ flexi-time is good enough for us.*
4 _____	a good idea or the right thing to do	*Happy believes that learning _____.* *Staff _____ to do things their way.*
shouldn't	a bad idea or wrong to do	*Staff **shouldn't** worry about making mistakes.*
mustn't **can't**	not permitted	*You **mustn't** make overseas phone calls.* *You **can't** wear jeans to work.*
5 _____ **6** _____	not necessary	*They _____ a reason for wanting a flexible timetable.* *Happy _____ for recruitment agencies.*

We also use **let** and **allow** when you have permission to do something.

*He **lets** staff participate in business and financial decisions and **allows** them **to** vote on most major decisions.*

>> For more information on *can*, *have to*, *must*, *need to* and *should*, see pages 167 and 168.

5 Complete these sentences with *mustn't* or *don't have to*.

1 We _____ park our cars in the Director's space. She doesn't like it.

2 Please help yourself to tea and coffee. You _____ ask.

3 We _____ go into the production area. It's for authorized staff only.

4 Food in the canteen is quite cheap. We _____ pay much for lunch.

5 I _____ attend the meeting tomorrow. It's not very important for me.

6 We _____ smoke anywhere in the building. It's against the law.

7 I _____ forget to call Sandy. It's her birthday today.

8 We have plenty of time. We _____ rush.

> **!** *Have to* and *need to* are more common in conversation than *must*. In American English the contraction *mustn't* is never used. See the grammar notes on page 167 for more information.

Speaking: Unwritten rules

6 What is an 'unwritten rule'? Suggest words and phrases to complete some unwritten rules.

1 You shouldn't stare at …

2 Don't sit next to another passenger on a bus if …

3 If you want to get noticed at work, you have to …

4 You should never overtake …

5 Close your umbrella when …

6 You don't have to be rich …

7 Match these endings to the correct rules in exercise 6. Are these unwritten rules true for your country or culture?

a there's a free seat somewhere else.

b to show generosity to others.

c you go inside.

d volunteer for important assignments.

e a police car.

f other people in public places.

8 Work in pairs. What are the unwritten rules in these situations? Write them down.

1 in a lift   3 when using a mobile

2 in the cinema   4 in friendship

9 Read your rules to the class.

Who had the most rules?

Whose rules were the most interesting?

Whose rules were the funniest?

TALKING POINT Could you run your organization like Happy Computers? Why?/Why not?

Listening: A memorable boss

1 Do you remember your best boss? What made him/her a good boss?

2))) 1.28 Listen to five people talking about a present or past manager. Pause after each speaker and discuss these questions with a partner.

1 Does the speaker think their manager is/was good or bad? Why?/Why not?

2 Would you like to work for this particular boss? Why?/Why not?

3))) Listen again. Who says the following? Match the speaker to the information.

Speaker 1   a   His/Her boss allows some staff to work less than others.

Speaker 2   b   His/Her boss recognized and credited the staff's good work.

Speaker 3   c   His/Her boss didn't like to mix with staff.

Speaker 4   d   His/Her boss preferred to communicate by email.

Speaker 5   e   His/Her boss doesn't overwork the staff.

Grammar: Obligation in the past

4 Put the correct past forms of *have to*, *need to* and *be allowed to* in the table.

Obligation in the past

There is no past form of the modal verb of obligation *must*.
Instead we use the past forms of *have to* and *need to*.

Present	Past	Example
1 have to	had to	*I had to do most of it.*
2 need to		
3 don't have to		
4 don't need to		
5 isn't/aren't allowed to		

6 We use ¹_____ and _____ when something was necessary in the past.

We use ²_____ and _____ when something was not necessary in the past.

We use ³_____ when something was not permitted in the past.

>> For more information on obligation in the past, see page 168.

5 Look at the audio script for exercise 3 on page 149 and find examples to complete the table.

6 Imagine these were some of the rules in your last job. Rewrite the rules using the past forms.

1 I have to start work at 9 a.m. and finish at 6 p.m. every day.

2 We must wear a uniform and an ID badge for work.

3 We aren't allowed to surf the internet for fun.

4 I need to leave my mobile phone on during meetings.

5 We aren't allowed to smoke anywhere in the building.

6 Sometimes everyone has to do some overtime.

Speaking: Those were the days

7))) **1.29** Listen to two colleagues talking about a TV show and answer the questions.

1 What's the show called?   **2** What's it about?   **3** Where's it set?   **4** When's it set?   **5** What does one colleague like about it?

8))) **Listen again. What do they say about working lives at this time?**

1 In those days people were allowed to
_____ .

2 Men had to wear _____ to the office.

3 Women were basically second-class citizens and had to _____ then.

4 They usually had to work as _____ or _____ or stay at home with the kids.

5 A secretary had to _____ and give the boss his hat and coat when he left the office.

9 How have the lives of your family changed over the years? Make five or six sentences and then ask your partner questions about his/her sentences.

1 When I was a child	I	had to …
2 When I was at school/university	we	didn't have to …
3 When I left home	they	was/were allowed to …
4 When my parents were young	people	wasn't/weren't allowed to …
5 In my first/previous job		
6 Twenty years ago		

10 In what ways do you think working lives were different in the past? Were there more or fewer rules and regulations? Think about some of the following.

- the age people started work and retired
- dress code
- attitudes to people in authority
- health and safety regulations
- equal opportunities legislation

TALKING POINT What are some of the most memorable rules for places you have visited, worked in or studied at in the past?

Reading: Informality in writing

1 Look at the examples of punctuation. Identify a comma, full stop, semicolon, colon, an exclamation mark, a letter in lower case and a capital letter.

2 What does C u l8r mean? Where do you usually see it written?

3 Look at this message and punctuate it. Then read the first paragraph of the article and check your answers.

i sadly will be late for our meeting the underground is running with long delays

C u l8r informality

Last week I received a text message from a young colleague that read: 'I, sadly, will be late for our meeting; the Underground is running with long delays.'

He's a 26-year-old man. So if he sends punctuated text messages, does this signify the end of an era? Could it be that the lower-case, c-u-l8r age of business language is over?

The next day I read an email from the UK head of internal communications at Google. It did not begin 'Hi'. Instead it started: 'Dear Ms Kellaway'. It was an invitation to speak at an event and finished: 'I look forward to hearing from you'. The message was signed off 'Yours sincerely'. If Google employees have given up the language of the internet and are now composing emails in this manner, something must be changing.

To find out more, I have just carried out some research and discovered some surprising results. I examined the latest 100 unsolicited* emails in my inbox and graded them for style, punctuation and formality. I then compared the results with those of a similar test I did in 2000.

The results prove that the pendulum has swung away* from informality towards correct usage. In 2000, more than a quarter of emails were entirely written in lower case. In my recent research only one email didn't use a capital letter.

In my earlier audit there was a rich variety in email sign-offs, but almost all were ugly. One of the most common was 'rgds', a horrible little abbreviation. But in the recent group there was only one 'rgds', and instead 'Yours sincerely' and even 'Yours faithfully' have come back.

There has been a corresponding return of surnames. Nearly 40 per cent of the recent emails addressed me as 'Ms Kellaway', 'Mrs Kellaway' or 'Lucy Kellaway', and before the name came 'Dear'. This is firmly back in fashion, while 'Hi' and 'Hey' are on the way out*.

This is no surprise. Just as recession encourages people to put on ties, it also makes them look more kindly on capital letters and semicolons. When people are losing their jobs, correct dress and correct usage of words seem like a good insurance policy.

unsolicited: unwanted
the pendulum has swung away: tendency of ideas to change regularly to the opposite
on the way out: soon to be replaced by something else

4 Read the rest of the article and discuss these questions in pairs.

1 Does the writer prefer more informal or formal emails from people she doesn't know? What about you?

2 What research did the writer carry out?

3 What does she think is happening to business writing nowadays? Do you agree? Why?/Why not?

Writing: Emails 1

5 Work in pairs and answer these questions.

1 When do we usually write 'I look forward to hearing from you'?

2 What is the difference between *Ms Kellaway* and *Mrs Kellaway*?

3 What is *rgds* an abbreviation of?

4 How do you usually sign off emails in your company or organization?

5 When do we usually use *Yours sincerely* and *Yours faithfully*?

6 Which of these are correct forms of address to someone you don't know?

Hey Lucy, Dear Ms Kellaway, Hi Lucy, Dear Lucy Kellaway, Dear Mrs Kellaway

6 Work in pairs. Look at this email that John Moore has written to Lucy Kellaway. Discuss what you would need to change to write it in a more formal style. Consider the following points.

- form of address
- signing off
- organization of paragraphs
- use of formal/informal words and expressions
- punctuation and spelling
- use of abbreviations
- the impact your email will have on the reader

dear lucy
how's it going? we want you to speak at an event that we're organizing it's about how business writing is changing and it's going to be on thurs. 21 feb. write soon.
rgds
john

7 Work in pairs again. Rewrite the message in exercise 6 in a more formal style. One person writes; the other checks spelling and grammar.

8 Look at another message for Lucy Kellaway. What advice does the man ask for? What advice would you give him?

Dear Ms Kellaway
I am writing to your blog as I would very much like your advice on a personal issue. Three years ago I resigned as a manager and since then I have thoroughly enjoyed more meaningful leisure activities such as gardening, fishing, writing and so on. However, lately, I have been concerned that my utopian existence is no longer sustainable, so I went to see a recruitment agency. When I explained the past three years to one of their staff, he looked completely shocked. I fear any future employer will react similarly. How should I present my current circumstances and curriculum vitae to best effect at the next interview?
Yours sincerely
MB
Unemployed, male, 41

9 Rewrite the message in exercise 8 in a more informal style and make it shorter.

Speaking: Formal and informal styles

10 Discuss these questions in pairs or groups.

1 Who do you usually write emails and letters to? How informal or formal are they? How informal or formal are those you receive?

2 Is there a common writing style in your organization? How formal/informal is it?

3 If you don't have a common writing style, what do you think it should be?

4 How important is formality in your place of work or study? Consider the way you dress, speak, address people and generally behave.

TALKING POINT
- How well-written are the SMS or text messages that you send?
- What abbreviated words or expressions do you know in English?, e.g. 4u, asap, TBD, BTW, LOL.

Listening: What should I do?

1 Look at these sentences. Which ones are true for you? Discuss your answers in groups.

1 I only give people advice when they specifically ask for my opinion.

2 I think giving advice shows you care about someone.

3 I'm a terrible backseat driver. When someone else is driving I always make comments.

4 It's very annoying when everyone tells you how to bring up your children.

> **!** Advice is an uncountable noun; you ask for, give, or get *some* advice. Alternatively, you can say *a bit of/a piece of* advice.

2 1.30 Listen to two conversations in which people give some advice. What are they talking about in each conversation? There are two items you don't need.

a career advice

b taking time off work

c holiday plans

d a job interview

3 What do you think is the relationship between the speakers? What advice is given?

4 Listen to the two conversations again and complete these dialogues.

Conversation 1

Kelly: Robert, I have a question. I want to ask Kristof for a few days off next month but I think he'll say no. It's one of our busy periods. I wonder what I should say to him.

Robert: 1_____ _____ _____ just tell him why you need to have the time off.

Kelly: OK, I'll try that.

Robert: And 2_____ _____ _____ _____ make sure your work is up to date before you go away.

Kelly: Yes, that's a good idea. And I'll tell Kristof I'll do that.

Robert: And 3_____ _____ _____ do is leave information with me, you know, so I can cover for you. Tell Kris I'll take care of things, no problem.

Kelly: Really? That's excellent. Thanks Robert. I'll do the same for you some day.

Conversation 2

Kelly: You know that job interview I went for last week.

Jake: Yeah, did you get the job?

Kelly: Well, I dunno. I haven't heard from them yet. But I thought the interview went really well. Do you think I should phone them?

Jake: No, 4_____ _____ _____ yet. It'd 5_____ _____ to send them a thank-you note first.

Kelly: A thank-you note? You must be joking!

Jake: No seriously, that's pretty standard in the States. An email will do. Then you follow up with a phone call.

Kelly: Oh no. I don't think that would work. We don't do that here.

Jake: Oh, OK. I think 6_____ _____ phone them then.

Kelly: Yeah, perhaps. I'll give it another couple of days.

5 Which of these phrases for giving advice were used in the first conversation? Which were used in the second?

Giving advice
You might want to …
You should …
No, don't do that …
It'd be better to …
What you could do is …
Maybe you could …

6 Look at the phrases in the box in exercise 5 and decide which are more forceful.

Speaking: If you want my advice

7 Who would you probably go to for advice about the following? Why?

- buying a new car or another major purchase
- investing or saving money
- feeling stressed or overworked
- your job and career options
- where to go for a holiday
- a good place to eat out in your town
- what to wear on a special occasion
- ideas for decorating your home

8 What advice do you think these people might give you? Would they say it forcefully or not? Use phrases from the box in exercise 5 to say what they might say.

9))) 1.31 Listen to six people receiving advice. What's the advice about? Which responses sound positive and which negative? Do you think the person will follow the advice?

10 Work in pairs or small groups and take it in turns to be the person asking for and giving advice in these situations. Remember to respond to the advice you receive.

1 You are a junior manager. You're thinking of introducing some changes in your department and you ask your senior manager(s) for some advice. You want to improve dress standards by getting everyone to wear business suits and ties to work every day. You also want to improve the level of English of your employees and would like all formal meetings to be in English from now on.

2 You recently got married and you've found that your partner is incredibly messy around the home. You want to hire a cleaner but your partner doesn't. You are having constant arguments about housework and cleaning. Confide in a close friend or family member and see if they can give you any useful advice.

3 Your company wants to make some staff redundant and there is a generous package of six months' salary. You want to leave to travel around the world for a year. The economy is experiencing a downturn and it isn't a good time to leave a secure job either but you want to take the risk. You've asked a lot of people for advice. Now ask your colleague(s) at work what they think you should do.

4 Your teenage son is doing badly at school this year and seems to be going through a rebellious stage. Ask your mother and/or father (his grandparents) for some advice. They have more experience of bringing up children than you do.

5 You have been given the responsibility for organizing a surprise birthday party and buying a present for your boss's 60th birthday. You aren't sure what to get or what sort of event it should be. Ask your colleague(s) for some advice.

Reminder

Grammar reference
pages 167 and 168

We can use several modal verbs to talk about rules and obligation.

We have to sign in every morning.

You don't have to pay for tea and coffee. It's all free.

We're not allowed to smoke in the building.

We give other people advice in more or less forceful ways depending on the type of relationship we have with them.

You should arrive early for your first day at work.

You might want to introduce yourself to the other staf

What you could do is work with someone with more experience.

Listening: First-day nerves

1 Why do people often feel nervous about starting a new job? Read the newspaper article and compare your answers.

FIGHT THOSE FIRST-DAY NERVES

Recent research shows that starting a new job is one of the situations we most fear – worries about the unknown, strange surroundings and unfamiliar faces can be frightening even for the most confident recruits.

In a survey of 500 job-seekers, independent recruitment agency Pertemps discovered that almost three-quarters of them (72%) suffered from acute first-day nerves. When asked to classify the level of their fears on a first day, around half of the sufferers (46%) said it was more stressful than moving house.

2 Discuss these questions.

1 Can you remember any situations when you have (or someone you know has) had first-day nerves?

2 What do you remember about your first week in your company or present job?

3 What were some of the rules and procedures you had to learn?

4 How did your company and colleagues help you in the first few weeks?

5 What do new staff need to know when they start work in your company/ department?

6 Is there an induction or orientation programme for new staff? What does it include?

3))) **1.32** Listen to two people describing their first day at work. Who enjoyed their first day more, Julia or Saul?

4 Match these words and expressions from exercise 3 to the meanings.

1 show (someone) around
2 it's up to me/you, etc.
3 get to know
4 get things wrong
5 take in
6 be in trouble
7 team up

a it's someone's responsibility or decision
b do things incorrectly
c understand and remember new information
d become familiar with a person or place
e have done something which someone will not be happy about
f join with someone in order to work on something
g go around a place with someone when they first arrive there, to show them what is interesting and useful

5))) Listen to Julia and Saul again and answer the questions.

	Julia	Saul	both
1 Who started work without an induction programme?			
2 Who admits he/she made mistakes?			
3 Who wasn't able to concentrate?			
4 Who started conversations with people?			
5 Who was more confident?			
6 Who got help and advice from his/her boss?			

6 Did Julia and Saul's companies do enough to help them in their new jobs? What else could they do to help new staff?

Speaking: What should we do?

7 Work in pairs. Student A: This is your first day at work. Student B: You are the manager. Prepare a short dialogue and roleplay the conversation.

Student A:

This is your first day at work. You didn't sleep well last night because you were nervous.

Today you haven't taken in much information and you've got things wrong several times. Your boss asks to speak to you. You think you're in trouble.

Student B:

You can see your new member of staff is nervous. Ask him/her how he/she feels after the first day at work.

Find out why he/she doesn't take in instructions and gets things wrong. Give him/her some advice.

Tell Student A that you're going to team him/her up with an experienced member of staff tomorrow and advise him/her what to do.

8 Work in pairs. Student B: You are a new member of staff. Ask Student A for advice on how to make a good impression in your first week at work. Student A: Give advice to Student B.

9 You are going to design an induction programme for new staff or students. Look at the agenda for your project meeting and decide what points you want to discuss.

Agenda

Aim: Design an induction programme

1 Reasons for programme
2 Personal experiences
3 Feedback on existing programme
4 Brainstorm new programme
5 Content of induction booklet
6 Time needed
7 AOB

10 Work in pairs. Student A and Student B consider the questions below and prepare for the meeting.

Student A:

- Will new staff need to have a security pass?
- Should we show a new person around? What should we show him/her?
- Who will need to go through the job description and the appraisal system?
- What should a new team member know about professional development and training?
- Should the line manager give some guidelines on how he/she would like a new employee to communicate with him or her, e.g. email or face-to-face?
- More suggestions?

Student B:

- What organizational policies does a new person need to know, e.g. parking, smoking, internet and email, data protection?
- Should the team socialize with the new staff? What sort of formal and informal social events?
- What technology training is required, e.g. how to log on to the computer system and use certain software packages?
- Do new employees get a staff handbook? What information is included, e.g. health and safety?
- More suggestions?

11 Work in groups. Decide who is going to lead the discussion and hold the meeting.

12 Summarize and present your ideas for the induction programme to the class. Imagine you have only five PowerPoint slides to summarize your ideas.

Review 4–6

1 Complete the sentences with the correct form of *can* or *be able to*.

1 Nowadays most people ___*c*___ understand some English.

    a aren't able **b** couldn't **c** can

2 I spent a long time doing the sudoku but I ___*a*___ complete it.

    a couldn't **b** were able to **c** was able

3 Being ___*a*___ type is a very useful skill when using computers.

    a able to **b** can **c** able

4 She would like _____ speak more fluently but she isn't very confident.

    a be able **b** be able to **c** to be able to

5 Our computers crashed so we _____ to finish the work.

    a couldn't **b** weren't able **c** can't

6 He _____ speak some German years ago but he _____ remember any of it now.

    a could / can't **b** can't / couldn't **c** wasn't able to / be able to

7 How will you _____ get a good job if you don't study harder?

    a can **b** be able to **c** are able to

8 Have you _____ to think of some new ideas for the project?

    a able to **b** could **c** been able

2 Read the definitions and complete these words related to learning.

1 Process of teaching and learning
e _ _ _ _ _ _ _ _

2 Series of lessons in a particular subject
c _ _ _ _ _

3 Course or qualification that is given by a university or college d _ _ _ _ _

4 Available through the internet o _ _ _ _ _ _

5 Go to a meeting or class a _ _ _ _ _

6 Ability to do something well, especially because you have trained for it s _ _ _ _

7 Someone who teaches the particular skills for a job t _ _ _ _ _ _

8 Job or profession that you do for a long period of your life c _ _ _ _ _

9 Someone who learns using the internet and not face-to-face e- _ _ _ _ _ _ _

10 Another word for requirements n _ _ _ _

3 A new employee is talking about the company where she used to work. Complete the dialogue. Choose the correct options.

A: You [1] *use / used / didn't use* to work for McDormand's, didn't you?

B: That's right.

A: So, what was it like compared to here?

B: Well, I liked the people but I wanted something [2] *much / least / more* challenging. And the pay is [3] *good / better / the best* here.

A: Really? Did you [4] *use / used / accustomed* to have a company car?

B: Yes, and we had free medical insurance and the canteen was a bit [5] *cheap / the cheapest / cheaper*.

A: I'm sure the food was better and the portions were [6] *biggest / bigger / more big*!

B: Actually, it was much [7] *worse / bad / worst* at McDormand's.

A: And were the working hours [8] *the longest / longer / more long*?

B: No, they were more or less [9] *same / the same / same as*.

A: And what do you think of Sam?

B: Oh, Sam's great. He's a lot friendlier [10] *as / that / than* some of the people I used to work with. He's [11] *much more / the most / much* hard-working, too.

A: Yes, but he isn't [12] *less / as / more* easy-going as he used to be. Before, he used to [13] *let / make / allow* us wear jeans on Fridays, but that has all changed now.

B: Do you mean [14] *for / since / during* the former director retired?

A: Yeah, new management, eh? They think they [15] *must / should / have* to change everything. Sorry, what did you say your name was?

B: Actually, I'm Alicia, the new Managing Director.

4 Complete these sentences. Put the verbs in brackets in the correct tense: either past simple or present perfect simple.

1 She _____ (play) tennis since she _____ (be) four years old.

2 He _____ (retire) from athletics in 2006 after a serious sports injury.

3 _____ (you/learn) to play the piano when you _____ (be) a child?

4 The women's hockey team _____ (just/win) a gold medal!

5 _____ (you/see) her latest film yet?

6 She's only 25 and she _____ (already/publish) two novels!

7 He _____ (live) in Sydney for a long time, but he _____ (not/be born) there.

8 Since she _____ (start) her acting career, she _____ (star) in over 30 films.

5 Match each phrase 1–8 related to making small talk to a suitable response a–h.

1 I haven't seen you for ages!

2 What did you think of the new TV series last night?

3 How's the new job going?

4 I love your shoes!

5 You're pretty good at presentations, aren't you?

6 Do you mind if I join you?

7 What are you up to these days?

8 Great to see you again!

a Oh, not much. How about you?

b Yes, it's been a long time, hasn't it?

c Thanks. I've just done a course.

d Good to see you, too! How are the kids?

e Not at all. Please do.

f Fine, thanks. It's really interesting.

g Thanks. I bought them in the sales.

h Great, wasn't it?

6 Tick (✔) the correct sentences. Sometimes more than one option is possible.

1 a We have to send the order by 5 p.m. today.

  b We need to send the order by 5 p.m. today.

  c We must to send the order by 5 p.m. today.

2 a You need find a new job before you leave this one.

  b You must find a new job before you leave this one.

  c You should find a new job before you leave this one.

3 a I had to make a lot of decisions in my last job.

  b I must make a lot of decisions in my last job.

  c I should make a lot of decisions in my last job.

4 a Did you have to study much on the training course last week?

  b Should you study much on the training course last week?

  c Did you need to study much on the training course last week?

5 a They shouldn't reduce the training budget.

  b They mustn't reduce the training budget.

  c They were able reduce the training budget.

6 a You don't have to stay until late if you don't want to.

  b You can't stay until late if you don't want to.

  c You don't need to stay until late if you don't want to.

7 Put each word in the box into the correct group according to the topic of conversation.

> movie Grand Slam boiling novel author
> leading actor director changeable screen
> politician flood bestseller vote role
> government champion storm sportsman
> literature freezing translate medal
> local council match mayor

Cinema	Sport	Books	Weather	Politics

8 Put the words in these sentences in the correct order for giving advice.

1 their let Don't trainers choose staff .

2 should degree I you online think do an .

3 to new might You skill a want about learning think .

4 choose be their better let courses to It'd everyone .

5 let you've you Maybe passed when me could know .

6 could us to courses allow What work-time is do you do to in .

9 Underline the word that has different word stress.

1 Oo

   bossy friendly relaxed quiet

2 oO

   advice punctual recruit employ

3 Ooo

   numerate organized sensible efficient

4 oOoo

   reliable easy-going intelligent responsible

5 oOo

   persuasive assertive efficient logical

6 Ooo

   practical hard-working confident literate

Tell us a story

Past continuous

Some of the most famous people in the world started their working lives in the most humdrum jobs. In his early twenties, Brad Pitt dropped out of a degree in advertising and journalism, and drove to Hollywood to pursue his childhood dream of becoming an actor. As for many aspiring actors, the early days were tough and Pitt did various part-time jobs while he was taking acting lessons. He worked as a limo chauffeur, a fridge removal man, and he even dressed up in a chicken costume to attract customers when he was working for the Mexican fast food chain El Pollo Loco.

Actor Johnny Depp dropped out of school at 15. As a teenager he played guitar with a rock band called The Kids. After that, he worked as a phone salesman, a position he once called his 'first acting job' because he used different voices when he was bored. 'You're calling people who don't want you to call them,' he recalls. 'You put on your best fake voice and try and sell them ballpoint pens with their name printed on them.' Depp was still selling pens when his friend Nicolas Cage suggested that he try acting. At 22, he got his first role in *A Nightmare on Elm Street*.

At the age of 12, the founder of Dell computers, Michael Dell was washing dishes in a Chinese restaurant for $2.30 an hour. Dell had several more jobs like that and by the age of 16 he was selling newspaper subscriptions. He recalls, 'I'd call people on the phone and try to convince them to buy the newspaper. I discovered that people who were moving into new houses or apartments were buying more newspapers than other people, so I tried to find those people and that worked very well.' By the time Dell enrolled at the University of Texas, he was already a successful businessman.

Reading: First jobs

1 Which jobs do you think these people did before they were rich and famous?

> Brad Pitt   Johnny Depp   Michael Dell

> removal man   dish washer   driver   telemarketer
> musician   promotions representative

2 Read the texts quickly and check your predictions.

3 Read the texts again and find this information.

1 Who went to university?   _____ and _____
2 Who got some good advice about work?   _____
3 Who trained to be an actor?   _____
4 Who worked in telesales?   _____ and _____

4 Find the words and expressions in the texts which have a similar meaning to these expressions.

1 boring and having no variety (text 1)
2 left a course before it finished (texts 1 and 2)
3 try to achieve something he's always wanted (text 1)
4 it was difficult at first (text 1)
5 not real (text 2)
6 remembers an event from the past (texts 2 and 3)

Grammar: Past continuous

5 Find seven examples of the past continuous in the texts.

6 Match the uses of the past continuous in the table to the examples in exercise 5.

Past continuous

1 We use the past continuous to describe past actions or situations which were in progress at a particular time in the past.

2 We often use the past continuous together with the past simple. The past continuous gives the background details or describes longer events.

3 We can also use the past continuous to show two or more actions were in progress at the same time.

While he *was studying* at university, he *was* also *running* a successful business.

When, *while* and *as* often introduce the action or situation in progress which is interrupted by another action or event. The shorter action can be introduced by *when* but not *while*.

>> For more information on the past continuous, see page 165.

7 Complete these celebrity anecdotes with the past simple or past continuous form of the verbs. The first one has been done for you.

1 At the age of 19 Jennifer Lopez ___was working___ (work) in a legal office in New York during the day and _____ (dance) in nightclubs in Manhattan in the evenings. She was also _____ (take) dancing lessons in her free time.

2 Cameron Diaz _____ (work) as a model when she _____ (get) a part in *The Mask*, a film that _____ (transform) the 21-year-old into an instant star.

3 In 1990 J K Rowling _____ (sit) on a train in London when the idea for Harry Potter _____ (occur) to her. She recalls, 'Really, the best thing about working in an office was that I _____ (can) type up my stories on my computer when no one _____ (look).'

Speaking: Recalling the past

8 Work in pairs or groups. Ask and answer the questions.

1 What were you doing at this time:
a yesterday?
b last week?
2 What were you doing when you were:
a 12 years old?
b 15 years old?
3 Were you working when you were:
a 18? (How much were you earning?)
b 22?

9 What were your parents doing when they were these ages? And what about your grandparents? Did any of them have unusual jobs?

TALKING POINT
• How old were you when you got your first job? What was the best/worst thing about it?
• What's the most unusual job you've ever done?

Reading: Humour in hard times

1 Look at the photos. What kind of business does Anya Hindmarch have? Do you think this type of company does well or badly in times of an economic recession?

2 Read the article about handbag designer, Anya Hindmarch and put these events in chronological order.

a When the writer visited Anya's office, the male employees were growing beards.

b During the recession Anya gave a humorous presentation to motivate her staff.

c The web team had the idea of a beard-growing competition while they were having dinner with Anya.

d By the age of 19, Anya Hindmarch had set up her own business, although she hadn't been to business school.

e One evening she invited members of staff to her home for dinner.

f Her handbag stores became successful.

A Fun-and-Games Strategy
Part One

When I walked into the handbag designer Anya Hindmarch's head office in London last month, I was surprised to see all of the men were growing long beards. 'It was a beard-growing contest, with prizes for growth and creativity,' says Ms Hindmarch. 'It was the web team's idea,' she explains. 'We had them for supper at home and my husband James hadn't shaved* that morning. We were joking around* when we came up with the plan.'

Last year sales at the handbag store were up four per cent at a time when most luxury businesses were experiencing hard times. Perhaps Ms Hindmarch's shop was successful because she had set up her company by the age of 19, or perhaps because she hadn't gone to business school, or perhaps because she had made her name with stylish evening bags and fun bags with personalized images.

Ms Hindmarch says her strategy is about humour and cost-cutting. She first began her fun-and-games strategy a year ago when she made an internal presentation to staff. Instead of talking through the sales figures from her 53 stores around the world, she used slides* of war-time propaganda posters of the 'Keep Calm and Carry On*' kind. 'It made them laugh,' she says. She explains the idea was about working hard and building a sense of community in hard times.

shave: cut hair very close to the skin, especially from the face
joke around: say things that are funny
slide: a single page of a presentation created with software like PowerPoint
carry on: continue doing something

3 Discuss these questions in pairs.

1 What do you remember about Anya's fun-and-games strategy?

2 Would you like to work for someone like Anya? Why?/Why not?

Grammar: Past tenses

4 Read and complete the table with these tenses: past simple, past perfect or past continuous. Then find two other examples of the past perfect in part one of the article.

Past tenses

We form the past perfect using _____ + _____ of the main verb.

1 We use the _____ to talk about things that happened in the past.

She first began her fun-and-games strategy a year ago when she made an internal presentation.

2 We use the _____ to talk about things that were in progress at a particular time in the past.

We were joking around when we came up with the plan.

3 When we want to show that one action or event happened before another in the past, we use the _____ to talk about the earlier one.

They came for dinner and my husband hadn't shaved that morning.

4 We can use the _____ to talk about life experience before a point of time in the past.

She had set up her company by the age of 19.

See pages 164 and 165 for more information on past tenses.

5 Look at these things that are mentioned in part two of the article. What do you think happened next?

> ice cream   manicure   little girl
> makeover   £50 note

6 Read part two of the article quickly and find out if you were right.

7 Complete part two of the article by putting the verbs in the past simple, past continuous or past perfect. Sometimes more than one option is possible.

A Fun-and-Games Strategy
Part Two

After her presentation, Ms Hindmarch handed out £50 notes that she 1 _____ (photocopy) to every employee saying: 'If you can think of a way to save £500, I'll give you a real note.' The aim 2 _____ (be) to think about saving, so that people were rethinking business travel and 3 _____ (not/order) expensive office equipment. By the end of the year, the company 4 _____ (save) £25,000.

To motivate her employees, she 5 _____ (offer) them a weekly manicure* so that they 6 _____ (not/have to) leave the office to get one. This way they 7 _____ (spend) more time at work. The handbag designer then 8 _____ (extend) her ideas to her customers and started joint ventures with other brands: an ice cream brand* 9 _____ (serve) icecream in-store for a week; and a cosmetic brand 10 _____ (give) customers makeovers*.

As a result, more people came into the stores. 'Our customers felt we 11 _____ (treat*) them like friends,' she says. 'One mother came in to buy her daughter an icecream and the daughter announced the next time she 12 _____ (want) both an icecream and a handbag.'

manicure: a treatment for hands and nails
brand: a name given to a product so that it can be easily recognized
give someone a makeover: make someone more attractive by giving them new clothes, a new hair style, etc.
treat: behave towards someone in a particular way

Speaking: Success stories

8 Work in pairs. You are going to tell each other a success story. Student A: Turn to File 7, page 133. Student B: Turn to File 20, page 136.

9 What similarities and differences were there in the two stories?

Writing: A story

10 Your local newspaper is holding a writing competition: A success story. Write about a successful person, or a company or organization that you know. Include different past tenses and these expressions in the story: *when, while, by the age of …, then, after (that)* and *as a result.*

> **TALKING POINT** • Think of two people who have been successful. Why were they so successful?
> • Who are some of the most successful businesspeople in your country?

Word focus: Humour

1 Which are your favourite TV comedy shows and cartoons?
How often do you read funny stories and jokes?
When was the last time you laughed out loud? Why?

2 Do this quiz in pairs and find out what kind of a sense of humour you have.

Quiz: the funny side of life

1 A colleague sends you an email with a funny joke. What do you do?

  a Delete it and tell him/her not to send you any again.
  b Laugh but delete it later.
  c Forward it to a few friends.
  d Forward it to all your workmates, family and friends.

2 Some friends are planning to play a practical joke* on a friend who is getting married. What do you do?

  a You hate practical jokes so you warn your friend.
  b You laugh nervously but you don't get involved.
  c You join in the fun – if it isn't too cruel.
  d You play a practical joke. It was your idea.

3 You see your manager has food on his beard/moustache. What do you do?

  a Point out the problem diplomatically.
  b Smile to yourself but say nothing.
  c Ask, jokingly, if he enjoyed his lunch.
  d Say nothing but tell all the staff about it behind his back.

4 You've just finished lunch with an important client and they tell you an amusing* story after lunch. What do you do?

  a Smile politely and ask for the bill.
  b Ask him/her to tell another story.
  c Tell a humorous anecdote yourself.
  d Laugh out loud and tell your own funny story.

5 At a party, someone is telling a joke in English that you don't understand. What do you do?

  a Say, 'Sorry, I didn't understand.'
  b Laugh, although you didn't understand everything.
  c Smile but ask a friend to explain the joke later.
  d Say, 'Hey, listen to this. I've got a funnier joke!'

6 Your boss asks you to give a presentation for next week. What do you do?

  a Say you have a doctor's appointment at the same time.
  b Say you're not very good at giving presentations.
  c Agree and think of a funny anecdote to include in your talk.
  d Agree and think of a couple of jokes to start the talk.

practical joke: a trick you do to make people laugh
amusing: humorous

3 Now turn to File 21, page 137 to check your answers to the quiz. Do you agree with the answers? Why?/Why not?

> ⚠ Don't use *fun* and *funny* in the same way.
> Use *fun* to talk about situations or activities that you enjoy.
> *The picnic was (good/great) fun. NOT ~~funny~~.*
> *Funny* is used to describe someone or something that makes you laugh.
> *The joke was really funny. NOT ~~fun~~.*

4 Work in pairs. <u>Underline</u> the word that is the odd one out. Then compare and justify your answers with a partner.

1 comedian joke story anecdote
2 fun funny humorous amusing
3 story joke history anecdote
4 irony clown comedy satire
5 laugh frown grin smile
6 laugh at a joke tell a joke forget a joke say a joke
7 hilarious serious amusing funny
8 lots of fun no fun good fun great fun

Listening: Humour across the globe

5 Read an article about a researcher who wanted to find the world's funniest joke. What research questions did he want to answer? What do you think the answers to the questions were?

THE FUNNIEST JOKE IN THE WORLD

from LaughLab,
University of Hertfordshire, UK

Few people have had so much fun at work as Richard Wiseman. Richard is a psychology professor who spent a year doing research into jokes and humour. More than 40,000 people from all over the world sent their favourite jokes to the LaughLab website and 1.5 million rated how funny they were.

The project aimed to answer some serious questions about the psychology of humour:

1 *Do people from different countries laugh at the same jokes?*
2 *When is the best time of day to tell a joke?*
3 *When is the best time of the month to tell a joke?*
4 *Which animal do people find the funniest?*

So what's the world's funniest joke? The funniest joke is interesting because it works across many different countries and different kinds of people find it funny: men and women, young and old. This joke had universal appeal.

6 🔊 **2.1** Listen to one of the researchers talking about their findings. What were the answers to the four questions?

7 🔊 **2.2** Listen to the world's funniest joke about two hunters. Discuss these questions.

1 What does the telephone operator say?
2 What happens at the end?
3 How funny did you find it?

8 Look at the audio script on page 150. What tense is used? Try to remember the joke and practise telling it in pairs.

> When we are telling stories informally, we often use present tenses.

Speaking: Find someone who

9 Ask and answer these questions in groups.

Find someone who …

1 enjoys the same TV comedy show as you. (Which one?)
2 used to like the same cartoons as you. (Which ones?)
3 has laughed out loud recently. (Why?)
4 has sent/received a funny email recently. (What?)
5 liked playing practical jokes as a child. (What?)
6 thinks that there's no best time to tell a joke. (Why?)
7 likes the same comedy films as you. (What?)
8 thinks that a sense of humour is the most important thing in a relationship. (Why?)
9 thinks humour is important at work. (Why?)
10 is good at telling jokes. (Can they tell you one?)

10 When you have finished, report back to your teacher.

> **TALKING POINT**
> • Why are jokes often 'lost in translation'?
> • What kind of humour is popular in your company or organization and culture?

Listening: A night bike ride

1 Discuss: 'Everyone loves a good story.' Is it true? Can you remember a good story that a friend or relative told you? Why do you remember the story so well?

2 2.3 Listen to Ben telling the first part of a story to a friend, Georgia. What do you think happened next?

3 2.4 Listen to the second part of Ben's night ride story. Were you right? What two words were confused at the end of the story?

4 Listen again to part one. How does Ben start his story? How does Georgia respond? Which expressions do you hear?

1 **a** A funny thing happened to me when … **b** Did I tell you about the time …?
2 **a** No. What happened? **b** No, you didn't.
3 **a** Did you? **b** Really?
4 **a** So, what happened next? **b** And then what happened?

5 Listen again to part two. How does Georgia respond? Which expressions do you hear? How does she introduce her own story?

1 **a** You mean, you'd just started! **b** You mean, you've just started!
2 **a** I don't believe it! **b** You're kidding!
3 **a** That's interesting. **b** Oh no!
4 **a** Oh, I see! **b** I understand now.
5 **a** That was fun. **b** That's so funny.
6 **a** Actually, that reminds me of the time … **b** A similar thing happened to me when …

6 Which tenses did Ben use when telling his story? When did he change tense? Why? Look at the audio scripts on page 151 and check your answers.

7 Complete the notes on storytelling with the phrases below.

a So, what happened next?
b They were too fast for you.
c That reminds me of the time (when) …
d Did I tell you about the time when …?
e That's so funny!
f Really?

Storytelling	
Starting	
A: 1________ **B:** *No. What happened?* *I'd like to tell you about the time when …* *I'll never forget the time …*	
Showing interest	
Responding:	2________ *You're kidding!* *I don't believe it!* 3________
Asking questions:	4________ *What did you do?*
Repeating or paraphrasing:	*A: As they were going down the hill, I was falling behind.* *B:* 5________
Linking a story to someone else's	
6________ *A similar thing happened to me when ….*	

Word focus: Linkers

8 Read this story. Think of a good title.

_____

I'll never forget the time my parents left me in the car.
¹ _____ I was about six years old and we'd just
driven all the way from Bristol to Birmingham to visit
some distant Italian cousins of ours. I had fallen asleep
on the way ² _____ my parents decided to leave me
asleep in the car ³ _____ they didn't want to wake
me up. ⁴_____ I woke up, I didn't know where I was
or where my parents were, ⁵ _____ I got out of the car and started to look for them. In fact they had
parked right outside our friends' house ⁶ _____ I didn't know that. ⁷ _____ , I asked some people
in the street if they knew any Italian people living in the area. ⁸ _____ they found the house where my
family was staying, but it was one of the scariest moments of my life. ⁹ _____ , I was OK, ¹⁰ _____
I was really annoyed with my parents for leaving me in the car!

9 Complete the story in exercise 8 using these linkers.
Do you know a similar story?

1 At the time   Then   At the moment
2 but   so   after that
3 so   although   because
4 While   When   Then
5 luckily   then   so
6 so   but   and
7 Although   Anyway   In fact
8 In the end   At the time   At the moment
9 Suddenly   Unfortunately   Luckily
10 although   finally   anyway

> ! We use _eventually_ to say that something happens
> after a long time.
> **Eventually** he told us what had happened.
> We use _in the end_ to say what the result or outcome was.
> _She found them_ **in the end**.
> We use _finally_ to introduce the last point you want to make
> in a series or a list.
> **Finally**, I'd like to end with a story.

10 Read these short stories and complete them using
these linkers.

> and   because   while   although   when
> after that   in the end

1 I thought I'd lost my bag with my keys, purse and
everything but _____ a taxi driver found it.

2 She'd been in hospital for a long time because she'd
broken her leg _____ skiing in Canada.

3 We went to the police station on holiday _____
someone had found my husband's wallet.

4 They decided to leave their well-paid jobs in the city
_____ bought a farm in the country.

5 He was young, good-looking and successful, _____ he
had a terrible haircut!

6 We were so happy _____ we adopted Ainoa because
we'd waited such a long time.

7 They met in Venice. _____ , she never saw him again.

11 Choose one or two of the stories in exercise 10 to tell to
your partner. What else happened? Add some more details.

Speaking: One-minute stories

12 Work in pairs. Student A: Turn to File 3, page 132. Student B: Turn to File 22, page 137.

13 When you have finished, change partners and retell two of the stories: your favourite one and one
of the stories your partner told you.

Reminder

Grammar reference
pages 163, 164 and 165

We use the past continuous to describe actions or situations in progress in the past.

*We **were doing** well when suddenly we lost all our customers.*

We use the past perfect to talk about actions or events that happened before something else in the past.

*It **was** my first job. I **had never worked** in an office before.*

We use linkers to connect the different parts in a story.

*It was a weird experience, **although** I learnt a lot.*

We can use different expressions to start a story or respond to someone's story.

***I'd like to tell you about** my proudest moment.*

***That reminds me of the time** I was working in advertising.*

Listening: Elevator pitch

1 Work in pairs. What is the best office space you have worked in? What did you like about it?

2 Look at this website. What kind of business is Instant Desks?

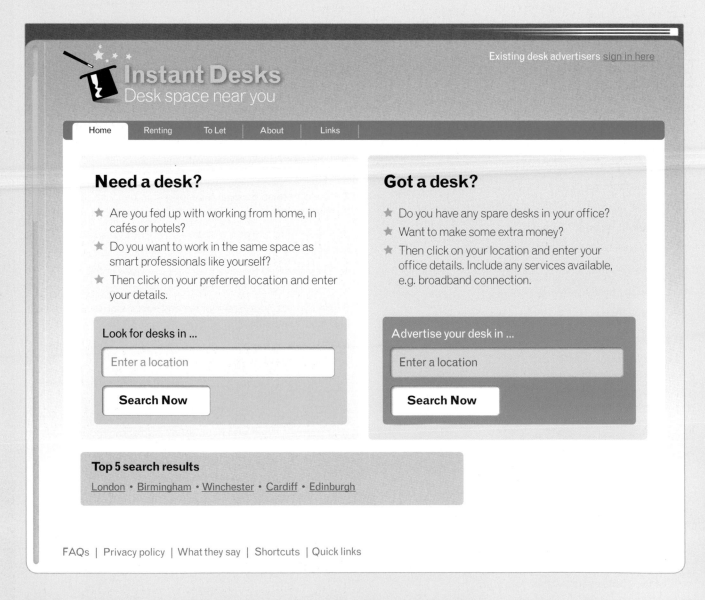

Instant Desks
Desk space near you

Existing desk advertisers <u>sign in here</u>

| Home | Renting | To Let | About | Links |

Need a desk?

★ Are you fed up with working from home, in cafés or hotels?

★ Do you want to work in the same space as smart professionals like yourself?

★ Then click on your preferred location and enter your details.

Look for desks in ...

Enter a location

Search Now

Got a desk?

★ Do you have any spare desks in your office?

★ Want to make some extra money?

★ Then click on your location and enter your office details. Include any services available, e.g. broadband connection.

Advertise your desk in ...

Enter a location

Search Now

Top 5 search results

<u>London</u> • <u>Birmingham</u> • <u>Winchester</u> • <u>Cardiff</u> • <u>Edinburgh</u>

FAQs | Privacy policy | What they say | Shortcuts | Quick links

3))) **2.5** Listen to entrepreneur Sam Harris giving a presentation about his new business venture to a group of potential investors. What is he doing in this part of the talk?

4)) You are an investor interested in Instant Desks. Listen to the start of the presentation again and make notes on these questions.

1 What does Sam Harris do?

2 How many online businesses does he mention?

3 Is his new business making any money?

5)) 2.6 Listen to part two of the presentation and answer these questions.

1 What exactly is Instant Desks?

2 Who are 'deskers'?

3 How does it work for advertisers?

4 How does the website make money?

6 Would you invest in the website? Why?/Why not?

7 Tick (✓) the presentation techniques that Sam uses to make his talk more interesting. Which techniques do speakers often use in your culture? Anything else? What?

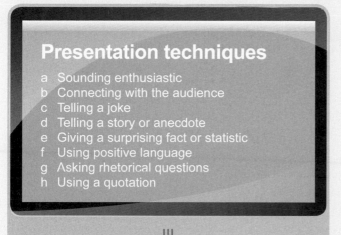

Presentation techniques

a Sounding enthusiastic
b Connecting with the audience
c Telling a joke
d Telling a story or anecdote
e Giving a surprising fact or statistic
f Using positive language
g Asking rhetorical questions
h Using a quotation

8 Look at these sentences. Which of them make a better impact in a presentation? Check your answers in the audio script on page 151.

1 a Here are a few facts about me.

  b Let me tell you a bit about myself.

2 a I'm an e-commerce entrepreneur, which is my real passion.

  b I'm an e-commerce entrepreneur.

3 a It's my new company and it's making a bit of money.

  b It's our new business venture and it's already profitable.

4 a Now I'm going to describe my company's services.

  b So, how does Instant Desks work?

5 a You're probably thinking, 'How much does it cost?'

  b This is what it costs.

6 a The great thing about Instant Desks is it's absolutely free.

  b Instant Desks is free.

9 Match the correct sentences in exercise 8 to some of the presentation techniques that Sam uses in exercise 7.

Speaking: A proud moment

10 Prepare a short presentation about yourself for some work colleagues who you are meeting for the first time. Use some of the correct expressions from exercise 8. Practise it in pairs.

11 Prepare an elevator pitch about the benefits of your company's products or services. Try to do it in two minutes and choose one of these audiences. Practise it in pairs.

1 a group of potential advertisers

2 a group of potential customers

3 a group of potential investors

4 a group of work colleagues

5 a group of students aged 16–18

6 your teacher's mum

12 Present your elevator pitch to the whole class. While you listen to your classmates, think of one or two questions to ask them.

13 What do you remember about your classmates' presentations? Which presentation techniques did they use? How could you improve your presentation next time?

14 Prepare a short anecdote for your presentation on one of these topics. It doesn't have to be funny but, if you want to, you can use humour. Practise it in pairs

1 My proudest achievement(s) at work

2 A proud moment in my life

3 My real passion(s)

4 My biggest challenge

5 Our closest competitors

6 My weirdest business experience so far

15 When you have finished, retell your anecdote to the rest of the class. Who told the most unusual/surprising/funniest anecdote?

Interaction

77

8

A	Zero and first conditionals
B	Products
C	Second conditional
D	**Communication strategies** Problem solving
E	**Interaction** Planning a green office

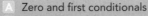

Green chic

Zero and first conditionals

Listening: Eco-revolution 1

1 Read about how three major companies are going 'green'. Do you know any organizations that have taken similar initiatives? Think of two other green initiatives.

> **British Telecom fuelled by renewable energies**

> **Cisco's videoconferencing plan saves carbon emissions**

> **Japanese Giant Sanyo recycles 99.8% waste**

2 Match these verbs and nouns. Then make sentences using these verb and noun combinations.

1	reduce	a	paper and envelopes
2	replace	b	a recycling scheme
3	reuse	c	light bulbs with low-energy ones
4	drive	d	energy costs
5	launch	e	fuel-efficient cars

3 🔊 2.7 Listen to part one of a radio programme about green business. Tick (✓) the initiatives that are mentioned in exercise 2. What other ideas do you hear?

4 🔊 Listen to part one of the programme again and correct this advice to companies about going green. There are nine errors.

1 If you exchange your old light bulbs with low-energy ones, it can increase your electricity bills.

2 Switch to less fuel-efficient cars if you have a fleet of company buses.

3 If you drive a recycling scheme, it probably won't save you time, but it will help to replace your employees.

4 Unless you have a lot of time and energy, it makes sense to start with these big initiatives.

Grammar: Zero and first conditionals

5 Read the information in the table and complete the sentences.

> **Zero conditional**
>
> *If + present simple, present simple.*
> It is possible to change the order of the clauses.
> **1** *If he _____ (leave) the office, he _____ (switch off) the light.*
> **2** *_____ (switch off) the light **if** you _____ (leave) the office.*
> We can use **unless**, **when** or **whenever** instead of *if* in the main clause.
> **3** ***When/Whenever** she _____ (leave) a room, she _____ (switch off) the lights.*
> **4** ***Unless** you _____ (have) a lot of time and money, it _____ (make) sense to start with simple initiatives.*
> We use the zero conditional to talk about situations and events that are generally true.

6 Complete these company guidelines to staff about going green. Put the verbs in the correct form using the zero conditional.

> be save clean turn not print use pay help

> ### Eco Guidelines
>
> **1** You save trees when you _____ recycled paper.
> **2** You reduce the use of paper if you _____ emails and documents.
> **3** Every time you _____ down the thermostat, you cut down on electricity consumption and carbon emissions.
> **4** When you car share with colleagues, you _____ yourself money and _____ to protect the environment.
> **5** If there _____ plants in your office, they _____ the air and provide more oxygen.
> **6** If you _____ attention to the small things, it is easy to have a greener, more pleasant office.

7 Read the information in the table and complete the sentences.

First conditional

If + present tense, *will* + base form (or an imperative). It is possible to change the order of the clauses.

1 We use the first conditional to talk about real possibilities now and in the future.
If we _____ (use) recycled paper, it _____ (be) more eco-friendly.

2 We use *unless* to mean 'if not'.
*Air quality _____ (get) worse **unless** we _____ (reduce) carbon emissions.*

3 We can use other modal verbs such as *may, might, must, have to, can, should* instead of *will* in the first conditional.
*You _____ (save) money **if** you _____ (turn) the heating down a bit.*

>> For more information on the zero and first conditionals, see page 169.

8 Complete these sentences using the first conditional.

1 If I _____ (have) time later, I _____ (take) these newspapers to the recycling bin.

2 He _____ (help) you if you _____ (not understand) anything in the guidelines.

3 If we _____ (not turn down) the heating, our bill _____ (be) enormous this month.

4 Our client _____ (go) to another supplier if we _____ (not implement) a green energy policy.

5 They _____ (not be) very happy if they _____ (not get) that new contract.

6 People _____ (not buy) more of our products unless we _____ (reduce) the prices.

Listening: Eco-revolution 2

9))) 2.8 Listen to part two of the radio programme and complete the journalist's notes.

One major corporation that is introducing more innovative green projects is ¹_____ .
The company have installed ²_____ solar panels on the rooftops of their headquarters.
These panels can provide ³_____% of the company's electricity at peak times. The investment will pay for itself in ⁴_____ _____ and then they'll have cheap electricity for many years.
The company makes donations to charity if staff ⁵_____ _____ _____, _____ or _____ to work. It also provides a ⁶_____ service for staff. And if they must use their cars, they get cash incentives to ⁷_____ _____ _____ _____ .
PB Copy is a small ⁸_____ _____ company in Canada. They use an ⁹_____ _____ to power their equipment. Customers can help by ¹⁰_____ _____ _____ while they're waiting for their copies.

10 Look at the audio script on page 152 and find three more examples of conditional sentences.

Speaking: Bright ideas

11 Work in groups. Look at the ideas in exercise 6 again.

a Brainstorm more ideas for reducing an organization's impact on the environment.

b Rank your ideas in order of importance.

c Prepare a five-point proposal to present to another group.

d Give reasons why your ideas will be effective.

TALKING POINT Has your place of work/study gone green? How? Why?

79

Word focus: Products

1 Our 'carbon footprint' is the amount of carbon dioxide emissions we generate in our daily activities. Which two items represent the majority of most people's carbon dioxide emissions?

1 Holidays
2 Transport
3 Shopping
4 Leisure activities
5 Home energy
6 Food and drink

2 Match these words and phrases to the definitions.

> recycling packaging appliance pollute organic
> eco-friendly disposable reusable

1 word to describe something that can be used again
2 relating to methods of growing food without using artificial chemicals
3 intended to be used once, then thrown away
4 process of treating used objects and materials so that they can be used again
5 container or material that a product is sold in
6 not bad for the environment
7 make the air, water, earth dangerously dirty
8 piece of (electrical) equipment used in the home

3 Match the pictures a–h to the words. How many other appliances and types of packaging can you think of?

> glass bottle cardboard box fridge-freezer washing machine
> carton can cooker fan

4 <u>Underline</u> the item in each group that does NOT combine with the adjective.

1 energy-efficient   appliance / air conditioning unit / plastic / dishwasher
2 eco-friendly   pollution / cleaning products / detergent / washing-up liquid
3 fuel-efficient   hybrid car / bicycle / vehicle / train
4 reusable   canvas shopping bag / container / glass bottle / electricity
5 refillable   ink cartridge / water bottle / marker pens / paper
6 biodegradable   carton / packaging / battery / plastic
7 disposable   camera / computer / pen / plastic cups
8 recycled   glass / water / light bulbs / paper

5 Choose the correct options to complete these adverts. Which products would you buy?

These natural cotton grocery bags carry much more weight than plastic ones and they are ¹ *reusable / disposable*, so they won't pollute the environment! Five-bag set $39.99 + free shipping.

Creating art from ² *fuel-efficient / recycled* products has become a growing trend in South Africa resulting in unique and imaginative folk art. Papier maché bowls $12.99 each.

Discover the many shapes and sizes of ³ *energy-efficient / biodegradable* lighting. GE Energy Smart bulbs give you the high-quality lighting you expect. Save energy – up to 75% less energy! Last up to ten times longer!

Simple Green produces ⁴ *eco-friendly / refillable* cleaning products that are non-toxic and ⁵ *biodegradable / disposable*. Our all-purpose cleaner tackles the toughest cleaning jobs.

Speaking: Your carbon footprints

6 Work in pairs. Ask and answer the questions in this quiz to find out how green your lifestyle is. Turn to File 24, page 137. Look at the analysis. Do you agree with it?

How Green is Your Lifestyle?

1 You need to buy some food for dinner. What would you probably do?

a Walk to the local market with your reusable shopping bag, and buy some organic food.

b Drive your gas guzzler* to the supermarket, buy more than you need and put it all into disposable plastic bags.

c Make a meal from whatever you find in the cupboards.

d Phone for a pizza, eat half of it and throw the rest in the bin along with the box.

2 How do you usually deal with waste* at home?

a I don't give it much thought. Everything goes in the same bin.

b I carefully separate out paper, plastic, metal, glass and organic waste for recycling.

c As well as recycling my waste, I often buy recycled goods.

d In the past I used to separate my rubbish and recycle packaging, but I've stopped doing it.

3 You see an advert on TV for a new eco-friendly car. What do you probably think?

a If it's a reasonable price I might buy that when I need a new car.

b That's just marketing. It probably pollutes as much as standard cars.

c Not another green message. I'm so bored with these ads.

d It would be better if we all used public transport and bicycles.

4 Which description best reflects your electricity consumption at home?

a I go round switching off the lights – sometimes when people are still in the room.

b We leave all the lights on and have TVs switched on in different rooms.

c I have low-energy light bulbs and energy-efficient appliances. I don't use the dishwasher or the washing machine unless there is a full load.

d I used to be more energy-conscious but I don't think the things I can do will help the environment.

5 When you think about air travel and pollution what do you do?

a Feel guilty about flying and always pay the carbon offset charge* to the airlines.

b Don't feel guilty – it's up to the government and businesses to deal with carbon emissions.

c Feel guilty about flying but don't pay the carbon offset charge to the airlines.

d Know you have made a conscious effort to stop travelling by plane so often.

gas guzzler: car that consumes a lot of fuel

waste: unwanted materials or substances

carbon offset charge: money donated to environmental projects to compensate for the CO_2 emissions

TALKING POINT In what ways were our parents and grandparents' generations greener than this generation?

Reading: Electric cars

1 How do you normally travel to work? Which of these forms of transport is the most/least eco-friendly? (1 = the most friendly). Why do you think that is?

> bus skateboard electric scooter train underground car hybrid car bicycle motorbike

2 What do you think are the advantages and disadvantages of driving an electric car? Look at the article about the smart ed and check your ideas.

The smart ed (Electric Drive)

With high fuel prices and carbon emissions*, now is a good time to think about alternative transport to the petrol engine. The people at Smart have designed an all-electric car.

The smart ed is powered only by electricity – charging* it takes about eight hours. The car has a top speed of 60 mph/97 kmph and a range of up to 70 miles/113 km, although this is reduced as your speed increases.

Smart say a trip from London to Brighton (54 m/87 km) will cost you around £1 (€1.26) in the UK. I suspect that the car would get to Brighton, but it wouldn't get back without recharging, and only if you didn't drive over 40 mph/64 kmph.

Smart ed emits no harmful* emissions, although generating the electricity to drive the car will. But the car emits no carbon dioxide, or carbon monoxide, or even noise as you accelerate.

The two-seater smart ed has plenty of room in the front but a very small boot. It's brilliant if you're just driving to work. Great if you have only one passenger. If you were just a couple, you could probably fit a week's shopping in it.

Another problem is charging the car. They recommend you charge the car whenever it is not in use. If you live in a house with a garage that has a supply of electricity, you'll be fine. I do not have a garage, but I live in a house where I can park the car directly outside – so I can put an extension cable out of the window to the car. This is not something I would do overnight or if I were out one evening.

If you had a garage, worked somewhere where you could charge it safely and only wanted to use it for commuting, this would be an ideal second car. But if you are thinking of changing your existing family car for a smart ed, you will probably have to wait a few more years.

emissions: gases like carbon dioxide that are sent into the air
charging: take in and store electricity
harmful: causing damage or pollution

3 How many words do you know that are related to cars? Find words in the text which mean the following.

1 liquid used to supply power to vehicles (two words)
2 part of a car that produces power to make it move
3 rate at which something moves or travels
4 start to go faster
5 for two people
6 space in the back of the car used for luggage
7 building where you keep a car
8 regularly travelling a long distance to work

4 Discuss these questions.

1 Do people have garages in your area? If not, where do they usually park?

2 Have you ever driven or been in a two-seater, or an electric car? What was it like?

3 Would you drive a smart ed? Why?/Why not? How easy would it be to charge?

Grammar: Second conditional

5 Look at the information in the table. Complete it and choose the correct options.

> ### Second conditional
>
> **1** We form second conditional sentences using *If* + _____ , + _____ + base form.
> We can change the order of the clauses.
> *This* **would be** *an ideal second car* _____ *you* **wanted** *to use it for commuting.*
>
> **2** We use the second conditional to talk about 'unreal', imaginary or unlikely possibilities.
> *If you* **had** *a garage, this* **would be** *an ideal second car.*
>
> **3** We can also substitute the modal, *would* for *might* or _____ .
> *If you were just a couple, you* **could** *probably fit a week's shopping in it.*
>
> **4** Sometimes we can use either the zero, first or second conditional. It depends how likely it is.
> *If you* **have** *a garage, this* **is/will be** *an ideal second car. (likely / unlikely)*
> *If you* **had** *a garage, this* **would be** *an ideal second car. (likely / unlikely)*
>
> >> For more information on the second conditional, see page 170.

6 A politician is standing for election as mayor. He is being interviewed by some journalists. They are interviewing some local people, too. Complete some of the things they say, forming second or first conditionals.

1 When I'm elected, I _____ (introduce) a bike-sharing system in our town like they have in Paris or Barcelona. I've already included a proposal in the election programme.

2 If I _____ (be) a politician, I would probably reduce the number of cars per household.

3 As soon as I _____ (be) in power, I _____ (pass) a law to reduce the speed limit.

4 Politicians aren't doing enough about carbon emissions. I _____ (encourage) people to use public transport more regularly if I were the mayor.

5 We _____ (not/fine) companies for business travel when I _____ (be) mayor, but we'll run a campaign to reduce air miles.

6 I _____ (probably/ban) big cars like 4x4s if I were in a position of power.

7 I'm a local shop owner. If I were mayor, I _____ (not/charge) drivers for going into the town centre because it _____ (be) bad for my business.

8 We _____ (definitely/put up) car prices for big cars and we _____ (offer) money to citizens if they _____ (stop) driving their old cars.

7 Compare your answers with a partner, then report back to the class. Consider these questions.

a Who said what? The politician or a local person?

b Did they use a first or second conditional? Did they think it was a likely or an unlikely possibility?

> ⚠ We use *journey* to talk about travelling a long distance or travelling regularly.
> *She has a long* **journey** *to work.*
> *Trips* are short journeys or journeys you don't make regularly.
> *He's not in the office today. He's gone to Brighton on a business* **trip***.*
> Sometimes we can use either word.
> *You could use a bicycle for shorter* **trips/journeys***.*

Speaking: Eco-friendly travel

8 Work in groups. You are going to do a class survey. If you wanted to be responsible travellers, what would you do? Look at the ideas and prepare ten questions.

> **1** share a car?
> **2** cycle everywhere?
> **3** how/reduce your air miles?
> **4** stop going abroad?
> **5** ban 4x4s?
> **6** how/encourage people/ use public transport?
> **7** put up petrol prices?
> **8** how/reduce number of car journeys?
> **9** what kind of tax/impose on cars?
> **10** how/reduce the speed limit?

9 Ask and answer the questions. Then report back to your teacher. Which were the most popular ideas?

TALKING POINT
- Would you share a car to commute to work? Why?/Why not?
- What do you think are the pros and cons of a bike-sharing system in a big city like Barcelona or Paris?

Word focus: Talking about problems

1 Think of a problem you are facing at the moment. It can be any problem you like, e.g. you own something that is lost or broken, you have a work problem or a 'people-problem'. Don't tell anyone what your problem is yet.

2 Read an article and see if it contains any ideas that could help you solve your problem.

Problem-solving techniques

Step 1: Identifying the problem
Before you start to tackle any problem, make sure you have a clear understanding of what's wrong. Gather information and, if you discover that you're facing many problems, prioritize them so you can deal with the most urgent ones first.

Step 2: Brainstorming solutions
Try to think of new ways to look at the problem and come up with as many different solutions as you can. Ask other people to suggest solutions, too. Don't worry if some of your options don't look attractive at this stage. You can always reject them later.

Step 3: Making decisions
Examine each option and think about what the consequences will be if you implement it. Remember, no solution is perfect, and you can always revise your plans later. It may take several attempts before you find a solution that works so don't be afraid to take risks.

3 Read the article again and answer these questions.

1 What should you do if you have identified more than one problem?

2 What can you do to help generate more possible solutions?

3 What can you do if your first solution doesn't work?

4 Look at these definitions and put the verbs in the correct space.

> work out   come up with   deal with

1 to do something to make sure the problem no longer exists. _____

2 to find a solution to a problem or make a decision after thinking carefully. _____

3 to think of an idea, answer, etc. _____

5 Underline verbs in the article that are used with a) problem(s), b) solution(s), c) option(s) and plan(s).

6 Tell another student about the problem you thought of in exercise 1. Discuss the best way to tackle it. Which ideas in the article can you use? Think of another idea to add to the article.

Listening: Working together

7 2.9 Listen to a conversation and answer these questions.

1 What relationship do the speakers have?

2 What problem do they discuss?

3 What possible solutions do they discuss?

4 What decision is made?

5 Can you see any possible problems with the solution?

8 Listen again and complete the expressions in the table.

Problem solving
Step 1: Identifying the problem
A: 'Can I have [1] _____ _____ ?'
B: 'Sure, what's [2] _____ ?'
We've got a [3] _____ problem with the photocopiers.
It's a bit of a [4] _____ .
Step 2: Brainstorming solutions
So, [5] _____ if we do a little experiment?
Then we'll know [6] _____ it's a problem with the copiers or the recycled [7] _____ .
Step 3: Making decisions
'I like that idea.'
'It's a [8] _____ .'
'That's right and we can [9] _____ what _____ .'
'We haven't [10] _____ it out yet, but I think I [11] _____ what to do now.'
'That was [12] _____ . Thanks!'

9 Here are some phrases from another problem-solving discussion. In which stage of the discussion do you think you will hear them? What do you think the discussion is about?

a So we have a plan of action now.

b It's a real headache.

c If we buy one second-hand, it'll be cheaper.

d I'm glad you thought of that.

e Not if we borrowed against the house.

10 2.10 Listen and find out if you are right. Then answer the questions in exercise 7 for this conversation.

Speaking: We can work it out

11 Work in small groups. Discuss these scenarios and come up with a plan of action.

1 One person describes the problem.

2 Think of as many solutions as possible and then discuss each option and its consequences.

3 Make a decision and sum up each discussion at the end.

Office temperature

The room temperature is causing many arguments in your office. Some employees say it's too hot, some too cold. Your heating and air conditioning bills are very high. As office managers, how are you going to keep everyone happy and also keep your bills down?

Old IT equipment

You have a lot of old computers and IT equipment which you need to dispose of. There is a lot of data on the hard disks, so security is an issue. On the other hand, the equipment still works well so it could be useful to other people. What can you do with it?

Recycling

Your organization has a six-storey office block with a recycling collection point in the basement. Every individual employee has to bring all their waste there and sort it into one of twelve categories. Employees are complaining that the collection point is too far from their desks and they don't know which bins to put things in.

Writing: Presenting solutions

12 Write some PowerPoint slides presenting a solution to a problem to your colleagues. You can write about one of the problems in exercise 11 or choose your own problem. Include the information below.

1 A description of the problem

2 Some different options and their consequences

3 The decision you've made and why you think it's the best solution

Reminder

Grammar reference pages 169 and 170

We use conditional sentences to talk about the real, likely or unlikely consequences of an action or event.

If we improve the ventilation, staff will feel better and be happier at work.

If the roads were safer, I would cycle to work.

When we're discussing problems and possible solutions we can use several expressions:

We've got a little problem …

So what/how about if we do a little experiment?

Speaking: A new look

1 What are the advantages and disadvantages of open-plan offices compared with walled offices in your experience? Use these words to help you compare the two.

> privacy   communication   individual space
> noise and interruptions   walls   access to fresh air
> ability to control heating and lighting
> access to natural light

2 Complete these sentences using one of these words.

> soundproof   screen   renovate   perimeter   refurbish
> partition   cubicle

1   When you _____ or _____ a building or an office you repair and decorate it so that it is in good condition again.

2   A _____ room or wall, etc. is one that noise cannot pass out of or into.

3   The _____ is the border of an enclosed area, such as an office or car park.

4   A _____ is a thin wall that separates one part of a room from another. If this wall can be moved around it is called a _____ .

5   A _____ is a small part of a room separated from the rest of the room for individual use.

3 Look at the two photos. Which of the three descriptions match the photos?

A Meguro Office

Japanese design team Nendo created this office space in Tokyo by using giant U-shaped partitions. It redesigns the traditional office space structures of cubicles and conference rooms. You have to step over the lowest point in the partition to get from one section of the office to another. Spaces that need some privacy are separated by soundproof plastic curtains.

B Olanto Call Centre

Olanto's refurbished office space in San Francisco has reduced electricity consumption by 40% and water consumption by 30% and has created a healthier and more productive work environment for employees. The office is mainly open plan, with high screens providing privacy for administrative and management staff. A moveable wall system allows training rooms to be divided into smaller meeting rooms.

C Devalon Headquarters

Devalon successfully converted this old factory into modern, open-plan offices. Many original features, such as the brick arches, have been conserved. A glass wall at one end of the building and skylights in the roof make use of natural light and create a bright environment for all employees. The split-level design makes excellent use of space and offers a meeting area for teams away from their desks.

4 Which of these offices would you most/least like to work in and why?

5 Work in pairs. Look at this office that needs to be renovated. Discuss what you would do to refurbish it. Which ideas would be the most expensive?

Listening: Sustainable offices

6 🔊 **2.11** Listen to an architect giving a presentation to a group of company managers about green office design. In what order does she mention these points?

a   materials used to build and furnish the office

b   travelling to the building

c   conservation of water

d   quality of light and air

e   saving energy

7 🔊 Listen to her presentation again and complete these notes from the meeting.

Ways to reduce the negative environmental impact of an office and improve conditions for the occupants:

- The building should be easy to get to on foot, by bike and by [1] _____ _____.
- The good use and saving of water is a priority.
- Carbon emissions are controlled by using [2] _____ equipment.
- The office is built using [3] _____ _____ and organic and low chemical-emitting paints and products.
- Access to [4] _____ _____ and improved ventilation makes people feel better and increases productivity.

The extra costs of building a green office should be paid back through savings in [5] _____ _____. For example, the software maker Adobe Systems spent $ [6] _____ million on a green office project at its San Jose headquarters and earned that back in savings in less than 10 months.

Speaking: A greener place to work

8 Work in groups of three. You are the project team responsible for refurbishing the office where you work to make it greener. Student A: Turn to File 8, page 133. Student B: Turn to File 19, page 136. Student C: Turn to File 26, page 138.

9 Discuss your proposals and the possible consequences of each, and decide which ideas you want to implement first and which you will leave for a second stage. Decide who is going to lead the meeting.

Points to consider

1   transport and building location
2   water usage
3   reducing CO_2 emissions
4   materials selection
5   indoor environmental quality

10 In your groups, prepare five PowerPoint slides to explain your proposal.

Interaction

9

A Passive forms
B Active or passive
C Telephoning
D Communication Strategies Making requests
E Interaction Remote manager

IT generation

Passive forms

Reading: The cellphone novel

1 Would you like to read a novel on your mobile phone? Why?/Why not?

2 Read these sentences about phone books in Japan and predict the missing information. Then read the article quickly and check your answers.

1 Last year _____ of Japan's top ten novels were originally mobile novels.

2 The top _____ novels were all written by new authors.

3 Nearly _____ US dollars a year is spent on electronic books in the country.

4 It's estimated that there are _____ mobile phones in Japan.

5 It costs between _____ and _____ to buy a mobile novel.

6 _____ films were shown at Japan's first mobile phone film festival.

3 Read the article again and answer the questions.

1 How did one author find time to write her cellphone novel?

2 When and where are people typically reading Keitai novels?

3 Why did one woman change her opinion about Keitai novels?

4 What three elements do most mobile phones now have?

5 What can you do with the latest models of mobile phone?

6 Which two innovations have made it easier to read comics on the mobile?

Japan ♥ phone books

The cellphone novel, or Keitai novel, is now a big part of Japanese popular culture. Half of last year's top ten bestselling novels originated from the (very) small screen and the top three books were all written by first-time cellphone authors. One bestselling novel was tapped out* on a mobile phone while the young author commuted to work, then uploaded to her blog.

The mass media*, which uses the phrase 'oya yubi seddai', the thumb generation* to describe Japan's cellphone users, is now asking: are real novels dead? It was recently estimated that the market for e-books was nearly 20 billion yen ($200m), and it is growing by more than 200 per cent a year. The books are being read in cafés, during work breaks and during Japan's famously long commutes to work.

'I thought the idea of a Keitai novel was a bit dumb because the screens are so small,' said Eriko Saito, 25. 'But you quickly get into them because the stories are so irresistible.'

The mobile phone is Japan's most popular accessory – there are now 100 million of them in circulation. Standard features* include internet browsers, games and digital cameras, while newer models are used to watch television, go through train-ticket barriers and pay bills. Bigger screens and faster downloads have made manga comics* increasingly possible. Thousands of Japanese books are now being accessed for about 210 to 450 yen ($2.10 to $4.50) each – cheaper than a paperback book.

'Is the cellphone the library of the future?' asked one magazine. Perhaps it might become the new cinema, too. Japan's first Pocket Film Festival has recently been launched in Yokohama, screening 400 movies made on camera-equipped cellphones.

tapped out: written
mass media: television, radio and newspapers
thumb generation: people, who as adolescents communicated by text messaging on mobiles
standard features: typical parts
manga comics: Japanese comic books.

Grammar: Passive forms

4 Complete the sentences from the article in the table below. Then complete the rules.

Passive forms

1 To form passives, we use the appropriate tense of the verb _____ and the _____ form of the main verb.

When we want to say who did an action, we use the preposition _____ .

2 We use passives when we are more interested in what happens to someone or something than who does it.

Newer models _____ _____ to watch television.

(We are more interested in the new models than who uses them.)

Japan's first Pocket Film Festival _____ recently _____ _____ in Yokohama.

(We are more interested in the Film Festival than who launched it.)

3 We often use passives when we don't know who did the action.

Thousands of Japanese books _____ now _____ _____ for about 210 to 450 yen.

(We don't know who is accessing them.)

The top three books _____ all _____ by first-time cellphone authors.

(We don't know who wrote them.)

>> For more information on the passive form, see page 170.

Speaking: Mobile facts and figures

5 Work in pairs. Student A: Read the facts and figures about mobile phones below. Student B: Turn to File 35, page 140 for your version of the facts and figures. Ask your partner questions to complete the missing information in your text.

Student A:

1 The first call on a mobile phone was made by Dr Martin Cooper of Motorola, in _____ (when?). He called his rival at AT&T's Bell Labs in New York.

2 In December 1992 the first SMS text message was sent on Vodafone's network.

3 Around _____ text messages (how many?) are sent worldwide each day.

4 Chatting on your mobile phone is forbidden in 'quiet' train carriages in the UK.

5 The train's windows are covered with _____ (what?) that blocks phone signals.

6 The world's most expensive mobile phone number is 666 6666. It was sold for 10m riyals ($2.75m) at a charity auction in Qatar.

7 The ring tone was first launched _____ (where?) in 1998.

8 The first full internet service on mobile phones was introduced in 1999 and was called i-Mode.

9 As early mobile phones were too large to carry they were installed in _____ (where?).

10 A standard charger for mobile phones was agreed in February 2009 by the GSM Association.

TALKING POINT
• What other inventions have changed the world? In what way?
• Which invention do you think has been the most useful? Why?

Reading: Online social networking

1 What's the most important web technology that you use each day? Discuss some of these ideas in pairs.

> email   social networking   blogs   customer forums   chatrooms
> downloading music files   consulting the company intranet
> photo sharing   listening to podcasts   online gaming

2 What are the advantages and disadvantages of using the internet at work? Does anybody not use the internet at work? Read the article and compare your answers.

Social networking sites – opportunity or threat?

Social networking sites are the next big change for the internet. What are they exactly? They are online ways of social networking (YouTube, Myspace, Facebook, LinkedIn, etc.) which have been made as interactive as possible.

Not surprisingly this new technology is being adopted by many companies. Employees are encouraged to access employee blogs, customer forums, multimedia content and self-created encyclopaedias (wikis).

A recent survey of these social networking sites shows that more than 39% of people are typically accessing such a site for more than an hour a day. This is especially true for 16 to 25-year-olds. These Web technologies can be accessed at work. Now during the working day not only personal emails are being sent. These days photos, music files and videos can also be shared between colleagues and friends.

As with all new technologies, there are issues for companies. First of all, privacy is threatened*. Professional information can be stolen on the web. There is a danger that photographs and private information could be used without permission. There is also the issue of financial cost: increased use of the company's computer system for private networking means that employee productivity has been decreased.

This is not just a problem for a few techies*. Use of social networking technologies at work needs to be controlled.

threaten: likely to be harmed or destroyed
techies: (informal) people working in or very interested in IT

Grammar: Active or passive

3 How many examples of the passive can you find in the text? Which tenses are used?

4 Read the information in the table and choose the correct options.

Active or passive

1 We tend to use the passive form more often when *writing / speaking*. But sometimes both active and passive forms are possible.

*This new technology **is being adopted** by many companies. (active / passive)*

*Many companies **are adopting** this new technology. (active / passive)*

2 We usually use the *active / passive* when we don't know, or don't want to say, who is responsible for an action.

Use of social networking technologies at work needs to be controlled.

3 We can also use it to sound more formal in emails, reports, research papers, newspaper articles and manuals.

Privacy is threatened. (formal / less formal)

Social networking sites threaten our privacy. (formal / less formal)

4 We usually use the *active / passive* when we want to sound more informal in emails and letters, text messages, notes, adverts, stories and newspaper articles.

Anyone could use this private information without permission. (formal / less formal)

Private information could be used without permission. (formal / less formal)

>> For more information on the passive form, see page 170.

5 Which form sounds best? Sometimes both the active and passive are possible.

1 a Researchers in Tokyo have developed Saya, the robotic receptionist.

   b Saya, the robotic receptionist, has been developed by researchers in Tokyo.

2 a A rescue team rescued two backpackers in the Italian Alps yesterday.

   b Two backpackers were rescued in the Italian Alps yesterday.

3 a Mix well until the mixture drops easily off the spoon.

   b The mixture is stirred well until it easily drops off the spoon.

4 a I'm afraid one of our employees has accidentally deleted the file.

   b I'm afraid the file has been accidentally deleted.

5 a A hacker infected the official website of the singer with a virus.

   b The official website of the singer was infected with a virus.

6 a Someone has trained our employees to use the latest new technologies.

   b Our employees have been trained to use the latest new technologies.

7 a Then repeat step 2 of the process.

   b Step 2 of the process is then repeated.

6 Where do you think the extracts in exercise 5 are from? An email, newspaper or manual? Anything else? What?

Speaking: A union meeting

7 What is the internet policy in your company or organization? Is the employee's internet access or use restricted in any way?

8 Work in small groups. Group A: You are a group of managers who want to restrict employee use of the internet. Brainstorm reasons why employees should have limited access. Group B: You are a group of employees. Brainstorm reasons why employees should have freedom to use the internet.

9 Managers, meet with your employees at a union meeting to discuss your differences of opinion and to come to a fair agreement.

Writing: Notes on a meeting

10 You are the union representative. Write an email to employees on the outcome of the meeting using these notes.

Main concerns:
Some employees are spending a lot of work time doing personal jobs and entertaining themselves on the internet.
The company is losing productivity.
Staff can write personal emails and go online at any time.
Employees might access inappropriate websites.

Points to consider:
Recent research shows that staff who take a break to surf are more productive!
We should encourage employees to improve their web skills.
We must allow staff some personal freedom.

Action to be taken:
We have to give staff set times for internet use.
We need to discipline employees when they misuse the internet.
We can't ban web use at work — this will be counter-productive.

TALKING POINT
• When did you last visit a social networking site? What did you do?

• How popular are these sites in your culture?

9 Telephoning

Word focus: Telephoning phrasal verbs

1 Which of these communication methods do you most/least prefer when speaking in English? Why? Something else, what?

email phone text messaging face-to-face webcam

2 2.12 What three tips would you give to someone for dealing with phone calls in English? Listen to these people and compare your ideas. Which of the telephoning tips do you find the most/least useful? Why?

3 Listen again to the tips and write down the phrasal verbs you hear. What do you think they mean?

Speaker 1 *If you know what you're going to say before you* 1 *p________ ________ the phone, it makes it easier.*

Speaker 2 *Take a deep breath before you* 2 *p________ someone ________ .*

3 *H________ ________ a minute, please.*

I'll look into it and I'll 4 *g________ ________ to you.*

Speaker 3 *I work in sales and I* 5 *________ ________ the phone all day.*

If someone 6 *r________ ________ , I ask a colleague to make an excuse.*

Most people don't 7 *p________ ________ .*

I 8 *h________ ________ because I didn't understand a word.*

Speaker 4 *I always ask the receptionist to* 9 *p________ the caller ________ to a meeting room.*

If I don't understand something, I 10 *p________ the caller ________ ________ .*

4 Choose the correct phrasal verb in these sentences. Which of the people are talking on the phone?

1 I'm sorry. Ted is at lunch right now. Could you *call up / phone back* later?

2 That phone keeps ringing. Someone should *pick it up / ring me up*.

3 I'm afraid we're unable to answer your call now. But if you leave your name and number, we'll *get back to / get through to* you as soon as we can.

4 When I mentioned the unpaid invoice, our client was very rude and *held on / hung up*!

5 I'm sorry. She's out of the office today. But I can *get through to / put you through to* her assistant.

6 When I *ring up / call back* their customer service department, they always *put on hold / put me on hold* for ages.

7 Could you keep the noise down, please? I *speak up / am on* the phone.

8 The reference number? *Hold on / Wait on* a minute, please, I'll just check it.

5 When was the last time you made or took a phone call in English? What happened?

Listening: Improving your phone manner

6 🔊 **2.13** Listen to four phone calls. What are the callers doing in each conversation?

a identifying herself/himself and explaining the reason for calling

b getting through to a voicemail

c confirming arrangements and ending a call

d leaving a recorded message

7 Which phone calls were the most/least effective? Why?

8 🔊 **2.14** Listen to the voicemail again. How could you improve it? A: Prepare a personal voicemail. B: Prepare a voicemail for your company/organization.

9 Compare your voicemail scripts with the ones in File 40, page 140. Record them if possible.

10 🔊 **2.15** How can you identify yourself on the phone? Listen again to calls two and three and complete what the callers say.

Call two

1 _____ , _____ Amrit _____ _____ Nano-tech Systems in Delhi.

2 _____ _____ _____ equipment we ordered from you last month.

Call three

3 I'd _____ _____ _____ _____ Steve, please.

4 _____ _____ Chloe Jones _____ Hydra Energies.

5 _____ _____ _____ the software you installed for us recently.

11 🔊 **2.16** Listen again to call four and correct Danny's text message. How did they end the call?

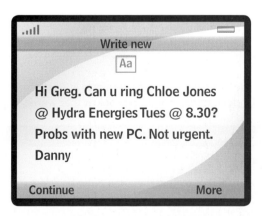

Hi Greg. Can u ring Chloe Jones @ Hydra Energies Tues @ 8.30? Probs with new PC. Not urgent. Danny

12 Put these telephoning expressions under the correct heading. All of them are from calls 1 to 4. What other expressions do you know?

a Could you call me back …

b Was there anything else?

c I'm afraid we're not available …

d This is Chloe Jones from …

e I'll tell him you called.

f Is that the IT department?

g Thanks for calling.

Telephoning
Voicemail
1 _____ right now. *Could you please leave a message after the tone/beep?*
Identifying yourself and explaining the reason for calling *Hello, it's Amrit here from Delhi.* 2 _____ *I'm phoning / calling about …*
Asking for someone 3 _____ *I'd like to speak to Steve, please.*
Leaving and taking messages 4 _____ *as soon as you can?* 5 _____
Ending a call 6 _____ *If there's anything else, just call me on my mobile, OK?* 7 _____ *It's good doing business with you.*

13 Test each other in pairs. Say the first two or three words of an expression and ask your partner to complete the sentence.

Speaking: Ring ring

14 Work in pairs. Prepare a better phone call between Chloe and Steve. Sit back-to-back and act it out.

15 Roleplay some phone calls in pairs. If you take a message, write down any important information. Give your real name and number when necessary. Student A: Turn to File 14, page 134. Student B: Turn to File 28, page 138.

TALKING POINT What's your biggest fear? Speaking on the phone in English? Speaking in public in any language? Spiders? Flying? Anything else? What?

93

Listening: Spoken requests

1 Look at the photos and read the situation for each one. What do you think the people are saying?

1 Directions
Alex, a Spanish business visitor, needs directions. He asks a company employee.

2 Snack Bar
Horst, a German tourist, is on holiday in the UK. He goes to a snack bar.

3 Class Trip
A teacher asks her students to help organize the class trip.

2 🔊 **2.17** Listen to the conversations. What was the communication problem in each situation, a or b?

1 **a** Alex sounds too direct.

 b The person doesn't understand Alex's request.

2 **a** Horst doesn't sound polite.

 b Horst sounds odd because he is being too formal.

3 **a** The teacher sounds rude.

 b Pieter doesn't give a reason when he says 'no' and sounds unhelpful.

3 Look at the audio scripts from exercise 2 on page 154. Make any necessary changes to the dialogues and then act them out in pairs.

4 🔊 **2.18** The level of directness in a request depends on the request and the relationship between the speakers. Listen to four pairs of requests. Which request do you hear first, a or b?

> **Situation 1: a coffee**
> **a** a regular customer to a waiter
> **b** a new member of staff to a work colleague
>
> **Situation 2: a technical problem**
> **a** a caller trying to get through
> **b** a supplier talking to a business contact
>
> **Situation 3: an arrangement**
> **a** someone talking to a business visitor
> **b** a husband talking to his wife
>
> **Situation 4: helping out**
> **a** two friends
> **b** a boss and employee

5 🔊 Listen again and complete the requests in the table.

> ### Requests
>
> **Making requests**
> The request forms we choose generally depend on the size of the request, but also who we are talking to.
>
> **People we know well and strangers**
> With people we know very well and have a close relationship with, and also with strangers, we tend to use short, simple requests.
> 1 *A caffè latte, _____ .*
> 2 *_____ one for technical assistance.*
> 3 *_____ leave around four, OK?*
> 4 *_____ _____ use yours?*
>
> **People in the middle ground**
> With people who fall in the middle ground, we tend to use longer requests.
> 5 *_____ _____ _____ _____ I help myself to coffee?*
> 6 *_____ _____ _____ OK to use the Canon projector for my presentation?*
> 7 *Do you _____ _____ at four?*
> 8 *_____ _____ _____ _____ could send me those pdf files?*

6 How did the people reply to the requests in exercise 5? Look at the table. <u>Underline</u> the expressions below that were used.

> ### Responding to requests
>
> **Saying 'yes'**
> *OK. / Fine. / That's fine. / That'll be fine. / No problem. / Certainly. / Coming up. / Sure. Go ahead. / Of course, that'll be fine.*
>
> **Saying 'no'**
> *Sorry, but… / I'm afraid + clause./ Actually, … / The thing is …*

7 Match these requests to the correct responses.

1 Oh dear, my computer's crashed again.
2 Do you mind if I leave early tomorrow?
3 Would it be OK to borrow your ID card?
4 Do you think you could go over that again?
5 Can I borrow that DVD?
6 Do you have a moment?
7 Is that a new networking site?
8 I'm feeling a bit tired. Shall we have a coffee?

a Sure, what's up?
b Yes, would you like to see it?
c OK, let's take a break.
d No problem. I'll bring it in tomorrow.
e Certainly. The code is XK-32W550-Q.
f Here, let me help you.
g Actually, we have a lot of work to do.
h Sorry, but security is very strict here.

Speaking: Making requests

8 Read the information. Work in pairs. Make requests starting with the ideas below.

> **Indirect requests**
>
> Sometimes people may avoid asking for something directly. They may hint and then the other person may offer to help.
> A: *The News is starting now on channel 6.* B: *Would you like to watch it?*
> It's easier to refuse an indirect request.
> A: *Are you watching the football match?* B: *Yes, I am.*

1 That book looks interesting. *(I want to borrow it.)*
2 I didn't have much for lunch. *(I want to have dinner now.)*
3 Is that dessert good? *(I'd like to try some of it.)*
4 Oh no, I've forgotten to bring a pen. *(I'd like to borrow your pen.)*
5 Oh no, I have a problem with the printer. *(I need someone to help me.)*
6 It's hot in here, isn't it? *(I'd like you to put the air conditioning on.)*
7 Are you busy? *(I've got some questions I need to ask you.)*

> **!** We say *I'm sorry but …* when we give a reason for saying 'no'. We can also say *Sorry* and then make a new sentence.
> *I'm **sorry**, but I'm very busy at the moment.*
> ***Sorry**. We're closed on Saturdays.*
> We use *I'm afraid (that)* + clause.
> *I'm **afraid** (that) I'm very busy at the moment.*
> *I'm **afraid** you'll have to come back tomorrow.*

9 Work in pairs. Roleplay these requests. Before you start, think about your relationship and the size of the request. Student A: Look at the information here. Student B: Turn to File 12, page 134.

> **Student A:**
>
> 1 You are a student in an English class. Agree to your friend's request.
>
> 2 You want to use a photo of your friend on your Facebook page. Ask for permission.
>
> 3 Ask your colleague to help you write a job application in English.
>
> 4 You are the Head of the R&D department. Your department is very busy this week. You need to send all monthly reports by Monday morning. It's also company policy to finish at 6 p.m. every day. Respond to your employee's request.
>
> 5 You are very good with computers but friends and co-workers are always asking you favours and you are getting fed up. Respond to your partner's request.

10 Think of two unusual requests. Act them out with your partner and respond to his/her requests.

Communication strategies

95

Reminder

Grammar reference page 170

We use the passive when we are interested in the action, not who does it.
The photos can be uploaded.
We use the passive when we don't know who is responsible for an action.
All the containers will be shipped back.

Small requests are generally short.
A cup of coffee, please.
Is it OK if I call you this evening?
Bigger requests are generally longer and may need explanation.
I know you're busy, but this is urgent. Do you think you could phone them?

Reading: Remote workers

1 Remote and virtual team management has become the norm for many organizations. What is a remote manager?

2 Quickly read these interviews from a college magazine for alumni. Where are they now and what do they do?

3 Work in twos or threes. Read about the alumni again and explain their work to your partner/group. How do they communicate virtually in their jobs?

4 What are the advantages and disadvantages of working remotely? Do you, or would you like to, work remotely?

Where are they now?

We interviewed some alumni* from all over the world who work remotely.

Tanya Wang, MA Art

I'm an artist and I have just been commissioned to coordinate a big project. The work is located on a big site based in Hong Kong, where we've put 50 freight* containers and invited 50 artists to paint on the surfaces of the containers. Later, the containers will be sailed around the world. Then all the containers will be shipped back to Hong Kong for another exhibition. I have to liaise with all the artists and arrange shipment of the containers via email and Skype. This is an ambitious project that involves a lot of virtual communication including video and teleconference.

Lauren West, BA Multimedia Studies

I work for Google Street View, the site where anyone can go online and look at images of streets and the people on them. I live in a small town in Canada but my remote manager is based in Toronto. My job is to change the photos that are taken. Individuals' faces and car licence plates have to be obscured by pixilation, that kind of thing. And then the photos can be uploaded. I mostly communicate with my supervisor and colleagues on the intranet and I'm left to get on with* the work, which is great. The only time we don't work remotely is when we have meetings or training in Toronto once a month.

Lidia Popescu, Bsc Information Technology

I'm a software developer and I work for a telephone company that's based in Oslo. My remote manager is currently working in India and I have colleagues in Paris, London and Frankfurt. Our manager trusts us and expects us to take the initiative. I communicate with him using email, Instant Messenger and the phone. Team meetings are held via videoconference. We're given a lot of autonomy.

alumni: former students of a college or university
freight: goods that are carried by ship
get on with: let someone do something on their own, without help

Listening: Working virtually

5 Read this report about managing remote teams and add these headings.

Using technology   Building teams   Management style

Managing and working remotely

1 _____

A high degree of trust is needed between the remote manager and the employee. Here are some of the main points:

- staff need to be informed of clear performance targets and short-term goals
- staff should be given regular and positive feedback
- remote teams need regular communication and team meetings – virtual and face-to-face, whenever feasible
- phone calls should include personal/social content and not purely business
- remote workers are in danger of developing the 'Superman' syndrome – a balance between control and autonomy is needed

2 _____

Electronic communication methods need to be user-friendly. New multimedia tools should be used, and adequate training provided.

3 _____

Too much use of technology can isolate people from their colleagues and business partners. Steps need to be taken to ensure teams meet together. When most day-to-day work is carried out virtually, face-to-face meetings can be sociable and highly productive.

6 🔊 2.19 The interviewees from exercise 2 were asked about the challenges of working remotely. Listen and underline in the report above the ideas they mention.

7 Who seems to enjoy working virtually the most/least?

Speaking: Do me a favour

8 🔊 2.20 It is Wednesday morning in Oslo and Lidia phones her boss, Erik in India. Listen to the call and tick (✓) the things Lidia does on her list.

Wednesday 21 April

1 Check Erik got the updated user manual
2 Tell Erik I won't have all proposals ready until Friday
3 Suggest face-to-face meeting with team
4 Confirm when Erik's back in Oslo

9 🔊 Listen again. What does Erik ask Lidia to do? What was the problem with their phone conversation?

Ask Lidia to ...

1 Send me project proposals today!
2 Phone project managers
3 Set up videoconference with team
4 Upload new software on intranet
5 Send me new user manual

10 Work in pairs and prepare and act out a better phone conversation between Lidia and Erik. Student A: You are Lidia. Student B: You are Erik. Turn to File 27, page 138.

11 Change roles and roleplay the phone call again. This time, Erik agrees to set up a face-to-face meeting with the team, including a discussion about working remotely. Which issues would you like to talk about? Prepare the call and then act it out.

Review 7–9

1 Complete this story. Put the verbs in brackets in the correct tense: either past simple, past continuous or past.

Shoppers in Canterbury were alarmed to see a 1.5m boa constrictor in the busy town centre on Thursday. One shopper, Esther Clark said, 'I ¹_____ (talk) to my sister when we ²_____ (notice) some people ³_____ (take) photos of something in the road. We ⁴_____ (cannot) believe our eyes'.

Police later ⁵_____ (discover) that the boa, called Snakespeare,⁶_____ (escape) from his cage in his owner's garage and ⁷_____ (get) under the car. When his owner, David Shaw, drove to work in the morning, the reptile ⁸_____ (go) into town with him.

Mr Shaw explained; 'While I ⁹_____ (drive) home from work, I ¹⁰_____ (hear) on the radio that something ¹¹_____ (happen) in the centre that morning, but I ¹²_____ (not catch) the details. Then, I ¹³_____ (get) home and ¹⁴_____ (see) that his cage was empty, but I ¹⁵_____ (not panic) at first. I ¹⁶_____ (look) around the garage for him when my wife ¹⁷_____ (come) home and told me that they ¹⁸_____ (find) a boa on the street. I ¹⁹_____ (have to) go to the police station to collect him. It ²⁰_____ (be) a bit embarrassing'.

2 Match the two parts of these famous proverbs to form zero conditional sentences.

1 If at first you don't succeed,
2 If a thing is worth doing,
3 If you want a thing done well,
4 When in Rome,
5 When the cat's away,
6 When one door shuts,
7 If you can't be good,
8 If you can't stand the heat,

a do as the Romans do.
b get out of the kitchen.
c the mice will play.
d try, try again.
e be careful.
f do it yourself.
g another one opens.
h it's worth doing well.

3 There is one extra word in each of these conditional sentences. Correct the sentence by crossing it out.

1 Call me if you will need anything.
2 You won't get good results unless if you work hard.
3 If the weather is be good this weekend, I might go away.
4 We won't have a holiday unless we don't save some money.
5 Where are you going to stay when you will go to London?
6 Life always feels better when unless you get a good night's sleep.

4 Complete these second conditional sentences with the correct form of the verbs in brackets. Use contractions when possible.

1 If I _____ (inherit) a lot of money, I _____ (buy) a big house.
2 What _____ (you change) if you _____ (be) the president?
3 If I _____ (can) have any car in the world, I _____ (love) a Ferrari.
4 He _____ (do) more sport if he _____ (have) more time.
5 I _____ (buy) a bicycle if I _____ (not have to) leave it in the street at night.
6 If I _____ (be) you, I _____ (not worry) so much all the time.

5 Look at what some people said. Then complete the written information using the passive form. Use two or three words in each sentence.

1 'Always keep this door shut.'

This door must _____ shut at all times.

2 'We have improved the production process.'

The production process _____ .

3 'They are making fluorescent light bulbs with low standards of safety.'

Florescent light bulbs _____ with low standards of safety.

4 'We pay monthly salaries on the 27th of the month unless that falls on a weekend.'

Monthly salaries _____ on 27th of the month unless that falls on a weekend.

5 'You can leave any valuable items in the hotel safe.'

Items of value _____ in the hotel safe.

6 'We asked all the staff to participate in the job satisfaction survey.'

All the staff _____ to participate in the job satisfaction survey.

6 Underline the word that is different.

1 Which of these is NOT an appliance?

fan cooker carton freezer

2 Which of these is NOT an eco-friendly description?

disposable reusable biodegradable energy-efficient

3 Which of these is NOT a form of packaging?

cardboard can carton battery

4 Which of these can you NOT do to an office?

soundproof bulb renovate refurbish

5 Which of these is NOT part of an office?

partition pollute cubicle screen

6 Which of these is NOT part of a car?

engine boot charge battery

7 Which of the letters <u>underlined</u> has a different vowel sound from the others?

1 rec<u>y</u>cled env<u>i</u>ronment pr<u>i</u>vate em<u>i</u>ssions appl<u>i</u>ance

2 s<u>u</u>rvey c<u>u</u>stomer m<u>u</u>lti-media c<u>o</u>mpany p<u>u</u>blic

3 st<u>a</u>ff l<u>au</u>gh c<u>a</u>r sh<u>a</u>re ch<u>a</u>rge

4 techn<u>o</u>logy c<u>o</u>st br<u>o</u>wser n<u>o</u>vel <u>o</u>ffice

5 m<u>u</u>sic b<u>u</u>lb red<u>u</u>ce h<u>u</u>mour re<u>u</u>se

6 scr<u>ee</u>n del<u>e</u>te spr<u>ea</u>d incr<u>ea</u>se sch<u>e</u>me

8 Complete the crossword about technology.

Across

1 computer program that finds information on the internet

4 information on a computer that you store under a particular name

8 move information or programs from a computer network to a smaller computer

9 eliminate something that has been put on a computer

10 sound made by a phone when someone is calling

Down

2 When a virus … , it affects more and more computers.

3 Facebook and MySpace are examples of social … sites.

5 The standard … that come with this mobile phone are a camera, mp3 player, FM radio and the internet.

6 opposite of 8 across

7 secret group of letters or numbers you type into a computer

[Crossword grid with numbered squares 1, 2, 3, 4, 5, 6, 7, 8, 9, 10]

9 Match each sentence 1–8 with a suitable response a–h.

1 Oh dear, I'm having trouble opening this file.
2 Do you mind if I help myself to a biscuit?
3 Would it be OK to smoke in here?
4 Do you think you could send me a copy?
5 Can I borrow some money?
6 Can I have a quick word?
7 How about if we run an anti-virus scan?
8 We've got another problem with the car.

a Certainly, I'll do that right away.
b I'm afraid not. The thing is it's banned.
c Here, let me help you.
d What if we sell it and buy a new one?
e That's an idea! I'll try that.
f Sure. Go ahead.
g Sure, what's up?
h No problem. How much do you need?

10 Complete these sentences. Choose the correct word.

1 We had a lot of *fun / funny* at the party.

2 Did you receive that hilarious *history / joke*?

3 Silvia *said / told* us an amusing anecdote about her holidays.

4 It was getting late *so / although* we decided to take a taxi.

5 We need to *work out / work for* how we're going to cut costs.

6 I'm too busy to *come up with / deal with* this problem at the moment.

7 Scientists think they've *come up with / solved* the solution.

11 Complete this anecdote with the words in the box.

> when   believe   told   time   so   funny   Anyway
> Really   Then   that   end   happened

A: Have I ever ¹_____ you about the time I got trapped in a flat in Madrid?

B: No, what ²_____?

A: Well, I was staying with a friend at the ³_____. He had an early flight to New York the next day. However, I didn't have to catch my flight to London until the afternoon ⁴_____ he didn't wake me when he left. ⁵_____ , I got up, had breakfast, packed my bags and was ready to leave ⁶_____ I discovered that he'd locked me in the flat.

B: You're joking! I don't ⁷_____ it! What did you do?

A: First, I looked calmly all over the flat for a key, but there wasn't one anywhere. ⁸_____ I tried his mobile but it was switched off and anyway he was flying over the Atlantic. What could he do? After ⁹_____ I started to cry.

B: ¹⁰_____? You poor thing.

A: Then I tried calling out the window, but I couldn't remember the Spanish word for 'help'. In the ¹¹_____ the neighbour came to his window and helped me climb over the balcony into his flat.

B: That's so ¹²_____ .

A: I know, but it wasn't at the time.

10

A Third conditional
B *should have*
C Collocations
D **Communication strategies** Saying sorry
E **Interaction** Doing the right thing

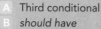

Right and wrong

Third conditional

Reading: Daily dilemmas

1 How up-to-date is your CV? What information does it contain? Do you have several versions of your CV? How are they different?

2 Read this newspaper column *Daily Dilemmas*. Who is Lee McQueen and what did he do?

3 What is your opinion of Lee McQueen's action? Do you agree with Rowan Manahan? Can you think of any acceptable reasons for lying on a CV?

4 Read these messages on the *Daily Dilemmas* message board. Who do you agree with?

One reader asks the question: 'Is it ever OK to lie on your CV?'

Readers will be familiar with the popular reality TV show *The Apprentice* in which candidates compete to become an apprentice to a top businessperson. One contestant, Lee McQueen, lied on his CV and was caught. He said he had spent longer at university than he had. Despite this revelation, McQueen wasn't expelled* from *The Apprentice* and actually went on to win the show.

It makes great reality TV but is lying to a potential employer acceptable in the real world? 'No, definitely not' says employment expert Rowan Manahan. 'The message you send if you lie on your CV is people can't trust* you, especially if you aren't telling the truth about something as fundamental as your education. It's very easy for recruiters to run a background check and verify most of the information on your CV. If you don't have the necessary experience or education, then don't apply for that job.

expelled: forced to leave
trust: believe, depend on

Today's question: Is it ever OK to lie on your CV?

MESSAGE 1 – POSTED BY KARL

I've told lies on my resume* before and it's actually worked. None of the lies were really crazy, but more an extension of the truth. Once I said I was an expert in Photoshop when I was just OK. I think we need to exaggerate a little and use a little marketing language to get an interview. What's important in the end is how well you do the job.

MESSAGE 2 – POSTED BY ROWAN MANAHAN

Karl – You were very lucky. If the interviewers had been good at their job, they wouldn't have given you the position. Imagine if they had asked a couple of in-depth technical questions, they would have discovered the truth. Or a quick test would have shown that you weren't as good as you claimed. You would have lost all credibility.

resume: CV – mainly used in American English

5 Which message in exercise 4 is talking about real past events? Which is imagining a different past?

Grammar: Third conditional

6 Read the information in the table and <u>underline</u> the examples of the third conditional in exercise 4.

Third conditional

We form the third conditional using *If* + past perfect + *would have* + past participle.

We use the third conditional when we want to imagine a different past from the reality, and to express criticism and regret about events and situations in the past.

*If I **had been** Lee McQueen, I **would have been** very embarrassed.*

*They **wouldn't have known** about his lie if they **hadn't phoned** the university.*

>> For more information on the third conditional, see page 170.

7 Read some more messages on the board and complete them using the third conditional form and the verbs in brackets.

MESSAGE 3 – POSTED BY ANON

If I ¹ _____ (be) in Karl's position, I ² _____ (do) the same. I'm sure recruiters know that smarter candidates exaggerate a bit on their CVs to get the job. If he ³ _____ (know) nothing about the software, he ⁴ _____ (have) problems doing his job.

MESSAGE 4 – POSTED BY SANDRA

My sister ⁵ _____ (not get) her first job in radio if she ⁶ _____ (not claim) that she already had some experience. She never got caught – and removed the false job from her resume as soon as she had real experience.

MESSAGE 5 – POSTED BY TARIK

I once read about a chief executive who lied about having an MBA. He lost his bonus but kept his job. My question is, ⁷ _____ the company _____ (fire) him if he ⁸ _____ (not be) the boss?

8 🔊 2.21 How would you pronounce the conditional sentences in exercise 7? Listen and repeat the pronunciation.

Speaking: What would you have done?

9 Read Vanessa's anecdote. Say what you would or wouldn't have done if you had been a) Vanessa, b) her friend, c) the HR manager, d) her boss.

I once applied for a job that required a degree but I didn't have one. I hadn't even been to university but I gave the name of a college and a fake telephone number on my resume. And I got the job. A week or two later, Human Resources called me at my new desk and told me that the number I gave wasn't working. So, I gave them the number of a friend of mine, Saskia. I told her that they were going to call and that all she had to do was confirm my attendance at the college and say I had a degree. Well, Saskia felt uneasy about lying for me but she agreed to help in the end. Then I felt bad about putting her in this position so I went to the HR manager and told him the truth.

10 🔊 2.22 What do you think happened to Vanessa in the end? Listen and find out if you are right.

TALKING POINT
- What makes a good resume?
- In what situations do you think it is OK to lie?

Word focus: Money

1 When was the last time you lent someone something? What was it?

2 Read this story about lending money to friends. Would you lend the money to Dan? Why?/Why not?

Money & Friendship

Kumar and Dan have been close friends since college. Kumar thinks that Dan has been a good friend in many ways. Kumar borrowed Dan's car when his broke down and Dan helped him move from one apartment to another. But Kumar has given similar help to Dan over the years.

Dan, who is manager of a small bookstore in the city, has been working on his first novel. Kumar is supportive of Dan's first major literary project. Dan has heard about a small house in a quiet area. He thinks the house would provide an ideal working environment for him.

Recently Dan asked Kumar to lend him $5,000 for the down payment* on the house. But the request surprised Kumar. Neither Kumar nor Dan has ever asked for a loan until now. Kumar and Dan never talk about their personal finances with each other.

Kumar, who works as a project manager for an engineering firm, can afford to lend the money to Dan. Kumar is not sure, however, exactly how Dan plans to pay a mortgage* when interest rates are so high, and repay the loan on his modest salary as a bookstore manager. Kumar feels uncomfortable asking Dan how he plans to repay the money, or when he hopes to pay it back.

down payment: the first payment made when you repay a large debt
mortgage: when you borrow money from a bank to pay for your home

3 Work in pairs. Which word is the odd one out? <u>Underline</u> it. Then compare and justify your answers with a partner.

1 saving up   spending   buying

2 borrow   take   return

3 interest   mortgage   debt

4 repay   lend   pay back

5 credit card   notes   cash

6 down payment   loan   deposit

7 can afford   can't afford   have enough money

8 bank   lender   finance

4 Complete the questions using words from exercise 3 in the correct form and then discuss them.

1 When was the last time you _____ something from someone? What was it?

2 What expensive item would you like to buy but _____ to?

3 What would you do if a friend borrowed €20 from you but didn't _____ it _____?

4 When do you have to pay a deposit or _____?

5 How much _____ would you lend to someone who you didn't know very well?

6 Are you _____ for anything special at the moment? What?

Listening: Different points of view

5 🔊 **2.23** Listen to Dan explaining his point of view to another friend. Tick (✓) the things Dan mentions. Has he paid back the money?

1 Dan got a loan from the bank for the down payment.

2 If Kumar had been in the same situation, he would have lent him the money.

3 Dan wasn't able to pay Kumar back after six months.

4 He found evening work to pay back the money.

5 Dan hopes to repay $2,000 by the end of the year.

6 Dan thinks he should have borrowed the money from his mother.

6 🔊 Listen again to Dan. What questions do you think his friend asks?

7 🔊 **2.24** Now listen to Kumar telling his side of the story to the same friend. How did the situation affect Kumar's relationship with Dan?

8 🔊 Listen again to Kumar. What questions do you think the friend asks?

Grammar: *should have/shouldn't have*

9 Look at the table and complete what Dan and Kumar said. Check your answers in the audio scripts on page 155.

---

should have

1 We use *should/shouldn't have* to express criticism and regret about situations in the past.

When we are less sure we often use words like *perhaps/maybe/I guess/ I suppose*.

2 We use the third conditional form: *should/shouldn't* + past participle of the main verb.

Dan: *I guess I _____ _____ _____ another year before buying the house. (regret)*

Kumar: *Some of my friends say I _____ _____ _____ him the money. (criticism)*

>> For more information on *should have*, see page 170.

---

10 Complete these sentences using *should/shouldn't* with the verbs in the correct form.

1 Kumar _____ _____ _____ (not/lend) his friend so much money.

2 Maybe Dan _____ _____ _____ (borrow) a smaller amount.

3 Dan _____ _____ _____ (not/ask) his friend for so much money.

4 Dan _____ _____ _____ (not/buy) a house in an expensive neighbourhood.

5 They _____ _____ _____ (agree) earlier how Dan planned to pay back the money.

6 I suppose Kumar _____ _____ _____ (ask) Dan to pay interest on the loan but he didn't.

Speaking: Asking for a friend's advice

11 Discuss these questions in pairs.

1 What do you think Dan and Kumar should or shouldn't have done?

2 Do you think Dan should have paid Kumar back sooner? How?

3 What would you have done if you had been in their position?

12 Work in pairs. Prepare what you are going to say before you begin the roleplay. Look at the story in exercise 2 or the audio script on page 155 again if you need to.

Student A: You are Dan. You think Kumar should apologize first. Explain your point of view to your friend and ask for advice.

Student B: You are the mutual friend. Listen to Dan and give him some advice. You are upset to see that your friends are not speaking to each other. Try to be fair.

13 Act out the roleplay again but change roles.

Student A: You are Kumar. You think Dan should apologize first. Explain your point of view to your friend and ask for advice.

Student B: You are the friend. Listen to Kumar and give him some advice. You are upset to see that your friends are not speaking to each other. Try to be fair.

Writing: Explaining your view

14 You are Dan and Kumar's friend. Write an email to one of them, explaining your view of the situation and why they should reconcile. Who should apologize and why?

TALKING POINT Have you ever lent something to someone and they didn't return it? What happened?

Word focus: *blame* and *fault*

1 Look at these definitions and complete the article *The Blame Game* with the correct forms of *blame* and *fault*.

> *blame (n):* responsibility for a mistake or for something bad.
>
> *blame (v):* to say or think that someone or something is responsible for something bad.
>
> *fault (n):* If something bad that has happened is your fault, you should be blamed for it, because you made a mistake or failed to do something.

The Blame Game

Most people have heard the words 'It's your
1 _____' more than once in their lifetime.
The suggestion that they have done something wrong
is usually annoying. It seems that no one likes to get
the **2** _____ for something. Putting the
3 _____ on other people seems to be a
very common human characteristic. The Blame Game
isn't isolated to relationships between couples. It's
also played by family members, between friends
and in workplace relationships. No one wants to be
the person at **4** _____ in any situation.
Generally, people find it difficult to say they made a
mistake, didn't do something they should have or did
something they shouldn't have. So what do we do
instead? We either make excuses or point the finger at
someone else and say, 'It's not my **5** _____
it's yours!' Why is it so difficult for people to accept
that they may be to **6** _____ in a situation
that has an unfortunate outcome*? Perhaps it has
something to do with the other game that is played
by many people. Taking the **7** _____ is
accepting the fact that they are not perfect. In the
end, the most important question to ask yourself is
does it really matter who is right and who is wrong in
any given situation. Does **8** _____ someone
else ever improve a relationship? Probably not; in
fact, it probably causes more problems than it solves.
Choosing integrity* is better than playing The Blame
Game.

unfortunate outcome: bad result
integrity: the quality of being honest and strong about what you
believe to be right

2 <u>Underline</u> the combination that is NOT possible with each verb. Look at the article in exercise 1 to help you.

1   make   an excuse / a mistake / something wrong
2   be   at fault / fault / to blame
3   take   my fault / responsibility / the blame
4   do   a serious mistake / something wrong / the right thing
5   get   the blame / your own fault / annoyed
6   blame   someone else / the government / responsible

3 Discuss these news items. Who or what do you think is to blame? Give reasons for your opinion.

> Obesity is rising significantly among children in Europe. As many as one in four are affected in some regions.

> It's time to stop drug-taking in sport. It threatens the image and integrity of sport. One cause of the increase in doping is the growing pressure from sponsors and promoters.

> Who was to blame for the financial and economic crisis which started with the sub-prime mortgages in 2008? Bankers, government ministers, regulators or people who borrowed too much?

> It's easy to blame the fashion industry for anorexia. Just look at all the ultra-thin models and digitally-enhanced images of celebrities in magazines and newspapers every day.

Word focus: *make* and *do*

4 Put these words and expressions with the correct verb.

> a mistake   something wrong   some work
> a complaint   a good job   a mess   a decision
> a suggestion   some housework   a noise
> a lot of money   business with someone   the shopping
> the best you can   your duty   an excuse

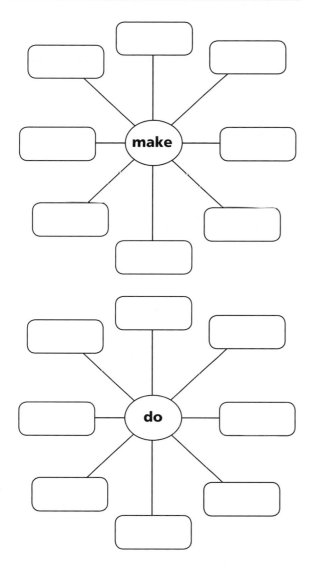

Speaking: The Blame Game

6 Read the rules. Then play The Blame Game.

RULES

- Your colleague(s) will try to blame you for these situations.
- Think of as many reasons as possible why it isn't your fault.
- You get one point for each excuse you make.
- Use these expressions to help you make excuses and blame your colleague(s):

  It wasn't my fault because …

  It was your fault because …

  I blame it on …

  You should/shouldn't have …

  I shouldn't get the blame because …

  You're to blame because …

Student A:

- You have no money in the bank.
- You've been caught cheating on your taxes.
- Your computer at work has crashed.
- You didn't do your English homework.

Student B:

- You pay for a gym membership each month but never go.
- You can't find your mobile phone.
- Your desk at work is very untidy.
- You've been on a diet for a month but you haven't lost any weight.

Student C:

- You've received a fine for parking illegally.
- You were caught smoking in a no-smoking area.
- You didn't reply to an important email from your boss.
- You've burnt the dinner.

5 Complete these questions with the correct forms of *make* and *do*. Discuss them with your partner.

1 If you had a lot of work to _____ , what would you do about it?

2 If a colleague has _____ a mistake or _____ something wrong and your boss thinks it was you, what would you say?

3 If a friend invites you out one evening and you don't want to go, what excuse would you _____?

4 Have you ever _____ a complaint in a restaurant, shop or hotel? What about?

5 If you think your friend has _____ a bad decision about something, would you say something?

6 When and where do you _____ your food shopping? Why?

7 When do you _____ the housework? What do you hate _____ most?

8 Who _____ the most mess in your family?

TALKING POINT   Who or what do you usually blame for things that are really your fault?

Listening: When sorry isn't enough

1 Have you ever had a company apologize to you about its products or services? What and why? How did you respond? Can you think of any recent public apologies by companies in your country?

2 A new company has recently had problems with customers ordering products. It decides to put a public apology on its website. What seems to be the issue? Do you think customers will respond well to this apology? Why?/Why not?

K CLOTHES

We've made some mistakes – too many in our mind.

We want to say that we're sorry for any complications you have had while shopping with us online or over the phone in the last few weeks.

We are making some improvements to our website and call centre and, unfortunately, there have been some hiccups* along the way. We know it's not perfect. Please bear with us.

We appreciate your patience.

hiccup: small problem or delay

3))) **2.25** Listen to a podcast on the internet about two companies that made public apologies. Complete the chart.

Name of company		
Apologized for		
Apologized to		

4 What is your reaction to these apologies? Are the apologies effective in your opinion? Why?/Why not?

5 What would you say in the following situations? Why is it sometimes difficult to say sorry?

a You accidentally bump into someone in the street.

b You jump the queue in a shop and another customer points it out.

c Your partner was recording a TV programme and you wipe it by mistake.

d You haven't finished some work by the deadline you agreed with your boss.

6))) **2.26** Listen to four conversations and match them to the situations in exercise 5.

7))) Listen again to each conversation and correct what was said.

Conversation 1

Please forgive me, Alicia. You know that progress report you wanted today? I'm afraid I haven't had time to finish it. It isn't my fault; a few people are off sick. I'll get on to it first thing tomorrow.

Conversation 2

I'm sorry. I didn't mean to do that. Are you all right?

Conversation 3

Jin: *I'm such an idiot, Werner. I did something silly and wiped that match you were recording.*

Werner: *What?*

Jin: *You're right to be angry. I know you love your tennis.*

Werner: *Jin! It was the Shanghai Open final. I really wanted to watch that later.*

Jin: *I know, I know. I'm sorry. Look, I'll pay for the damage.*

Conversation 4

Customer 1: *Pardon me, I was here before you.*

Customer 2: *Oh, so sorry. I feel awful about pushing in.*

8 Which situation in exercise 7 do you think was the most serious? Which would be the most embarrassing for you? Why?

9 Which of the strategies in the table does each speaker in exercise 7 use? Add more example phrases from the conversations.

Saying sorry			Responding to apologies
1 Expressing regret	*I'm sorry.*		*Not to worry.*
2 Asking for forgiveness	*Please accept our apologies.*		*Don't worry about it.*
3 Giving an explanation	*The traffic was terrible.*		*No problem.*
4 Taking responsibility	*It's my mistake.*		*Thanks for letting me know.*
5 Not taking responsibility	*It isn't my fault.*		
6 Showing concern for the other person	*I hope I didn't upset you.*		
7 Offering to put things right	*I'll pay for the damage.*		

10 Match the two halves of the apologies below. Which strategies from exercise 9 are used in each apology?

1 Sorry we're late.	**a** morning. I forgot we said we'd meet at 10.
2 Sorry I forgot your book.	**b** interrupt your meeting, but you have a visitor.
3 I'm so sorry about this	**c** your birthday. I've got a terrible memory.
4 I'm so sorry for	**d** The bus was slow. Have you been waiting long?
5 I'm sorry for forgetting	**e** I'll bring it next week.
6 I'm very sorry to	**f** wiping those files. I didn't mean to.

Speaking: I'm so sorry

11 Work in pairs. Student A: Look at the information on this page. Student B: Turn to File 32, page 139.

1 You have a tendency to always arrive a few minutes late. Most people don't mind, but one of your friends gets very upset when people aren't punctual. You arrive 15 minutes late at the restaurant where you agreed to meet. What do you say?

2 An important client phones to ask about an order that hasn't arrived as promised. This has happened before to this particular client. There will be a one-week delay because there were some problems with some new machinery, but everything is working fine now.

3 You asked your boss to look at a report you prepared a week ago and give you some feedback. Your boss hasn't said anything about it. Find out if he/she has finished reading it.

4 You are having a meal in an expensive restaurant. You've already been waiting for 15 minutes when your waiter / waitress brings you some ice cream instead of the dessert that you had ordered.

12 Look at the situations in exercise 11 again. When do you think a) you were right/wrong? b) both of you were to blame?

Reminder

Grammar reference page 170

We use the third conditional when we want to imagine a different past from the reality.
If he'd told us, it would have been different.
What would you have done?

We use *should/shouldn't have* to express criticism and regret about situations in the past.
He shouldn't have listened to her.
He should have asked me for advice instead.

Word focus: Personal characteristics

1 Match the adjectives with the definitions. What are the opposites of these adjectives? What are the nouns?

> honest   thoughtful and kind   brave   consistent
> open-minded   rational   wise   sensitive

1 always telling the truth and never cheating or stealing
2 always behaving in the same way and having the same attitudes and standards
3 prepared to consider and accept other people's ideas and opinions
4 always thinking of things you can do to make other people happy
5 able to understand other people's feelings and problems
6 thinking calmly and sensibly
7 dealing with difficult situations with courage and confidence
8 making good decisions and giving good advice

2 Which three characteristics from exercise 1 are the most important for you in a friend, a partner and a boss?

3 Who is the wisest person you know? Who is the most consistent, the most thoughtful, the most rational? Give reasons for your answers.

Listening: Telling right from wrong

4 🔊 2.27 This is the Rossini family. Listen to their conversation at dinner one evening. Make a note of the anecdote Tom tells his parents.

5 How would you describe Raul and Tom? What do you think they should have done?

6 🔊 2.28 Listen to the rest of the Rossinis' conversation. Did you say the same?

Reading: Challenges at work

7 Read Susan Rossini's email to a friend. What sort of person do you think Susan is? What dilemmas did she face last week? How would you reply to her?

Hi Angie

How's it going? The family are all well but I'm really busy at work these days. You know, when I went into business with Anton I had no idea how hard it would be mixing work and friendship. We have a major project to finish right now, and yesterday he told me he's planning a two-week holiday in the middle of it. I didn't know what to say. He's leaving me to do all the work. What would you have said to him?

And last week I needed to find someone to do Karen's job while she's on maternity leave. Her friend Paula wanted to do it, but there was also someone more qualified than her. I wanted to be rational, but I was worried about how Karen would react if I rejected her friend, so I gave her the job. Was I right, do you think?

Susan

8 Read her friend's reply. Do you agree with her opinions? Why?/Why not? What would you have said?

Hi Susan

I think you should have said something to Anton. If it's a busy time, it's not very wise to take a holiday right now. Perhaps he should have renegotiated the deadline with your client so you're not left with all the work. Maybe his heart isn't in the business any more. I think you should talk to him when he gets back and discuss where your partnership is going.

As for Karen's substitute, maybe you should have employed the other, better-qualified candidate. At the same time, it's only a short-term contract and you would have upset Karen if you hadn't given her friend a job for a few months. I think you did the right thing there. I hope she does a good job for you.

Bye for now

Angie

Speaking: More dilemmas

9 Student A: You are Susan. Read the information and roleplay the conversation on Anton's return from holiday. Student B: You are Susan's business partner, Anton, turn to File 38 page 140.

Student A:

Anton has just come back from a two-week Caribbean cruise with his wife. He looks incredibly relaxed and tanned. But you're feeling ill and stressed out.

- Ask Anton about his holiday.
- Ask him why he took time off when it was a busy period.
- Tell him that you haven't had a decent holiday for two years now and you'd like to spend more time with your family.
- Tell him that the project is behind schedule now and you don't know what to do about it.

10)) 2.29 John and Susan are out shopping one day. Listen to their conversation and put the four pictures in order.

11)) Listen again and answer the questions.

1 Who was the man in the café?
2 What dilemma does John face?
3 Where does John want to go next?
4 Why does he argue with the driver?

12 What would you have done in these situations?

13 Read another email from Susan to her friend. Which dilemma(s) had an unexpected ending?

Hi Angie

Great to hear all your news, as always. I'm afraid I've been ill recently with flu. Remember Anton went away on holiday in the middle of a big project for us. Well, it was very stressful doing the work by myself and I got sick. I know, I should have said something to him. You were right. He apologized to me when he got back and said I worked too hard, but if he doesn't help out more, I can't take it easy.

And yesterday we thought we saw Michelle's boyfriend with another woman. But then she phoned us last night and told us they split up last week. I was so relieved. That was one dilemma solved.

Interaction

11

A Relative pronouns
B Writing emails 2
C Present perfect continuous
D Communication strategies Networking
E Interaction Team-building

Working together

Relative pronouns

Reading Aid

1 What are charities, non-governmental (NGO) and non-profit (NPO) organizations? Match each one to the correct definition.

1 An organization that doesn't distribute its profits to shareholders. For example, a charity, a trade union or a public arts organization. _____

2 An organization which gives money, goods or help to people who are poor or sick. For example, The Red Cross, Save the Children, Médecins Sans Frontières. _____

3 An independent organization that is not controlled by a government. For example, Amnesty International, Scouts, Greenpeace. _____

2 Think of more examples of charities, NGOs and NPOs. What do they do?

3 Look at the title of the article. What do you think it means? What do you think the article will be about?

4 Read the text very quickly. What does Clowns Without Borders do?

a It runs workshops that teach people how to be a clown.

b It performs for volunteers who work in areas of conflict.

c It performs for people who have experienced difficult situations.

d It teaches children that live in disadvantaged areas.

Clowns Without Borders

Clowns Without Borders is a non-profit NGO which travels around the world bringing smiles and laughter to those in crisis. It works in natural disaster areas, war zones, refugee camps and disadvantaged areas. Its aim is to work mostly with disadvantaged children and refugees, watching over and improving their psychological condition.

Payasos Sin Fronteras, which is its original Spanish name, was founded in Barcelona in 1993. It was after the success of a project in a refugee camp in Croatia where the Catalan artist Tortell Poltrona performed in front of 700 children. The performance proved that humour provides great psychological support* to people in need. Since then the number of clown projects sent to crisis areas around the world has gradually increased. There are now Clowns Without Borders teams that are based in France, Belgium, Sweden, Canada and the States.

The clowns are volunteers from all areas of the performing arts* who are neither educators nor social commentators and that work without any political or social agenda*. They perform with an awareness* of the local environment and tolerance of different cultural values. They are also sensitive to the difficult and traumatic situations the children have experienced. Their motivation is simply to bring smiles to the faces of those who need it most. And as we all know, laughter is always the best medicine.

support: help and being kind to someone
performing arts: arts such as dance, music or drama
political/social agenda: ideas that a political party thinks are important
awareness: knowledge or understanding of something

A

Grammar: Relative pronouns

5 Read the information in the table and choose the correct options. Can you find any more relative pronouns in the article?

Relative pronouns

Defining

1 We use **which** or **that** when we define *people / places / things*.

*Clowns Without Borders is an NGO **which/that** travels around the world bringing smiles and laughter to those in crisis.*

2 We use **who** or **that** when we define *people / places / things*.

*The clowns are volunteers from all areas of the performing arts **who** are neither educators nor social commentators and **who/that** work without any political or social agenda.*

3 We use **where** / **when** to give information about places and **where** / **when** to describe situations.

*… in a refugee camp in Croatia **where** the Catalan artist Tortell Poltrona performed.*

*A flood is **when** there's a covering of water in an area that is normally dry.*

Non-defining

4 When we give extra information, we can't use *who / which / that*.

*Payasos Sin Fronteras, **which** is its original Spanish name, was founded in Barcelona in 1993.*

>> For more information on relative pronouns, see page 173.

6 Complete these definitions using *who/that*, *which/that*, *when* or *where* and then find the words in the text.

1 Someone _____ wears a red nose and makes people laugh.

2 A person _____ does a job willingly without being paid.

3 An organization _____ helps people and is not run by the government.

4 A situation _____ someone performs a play or piece of music.

5 Someone _____ has been forced to leave their country for political reasons.

6 A place _____ refugees go to be protected.

7 A child _____ has social problems or doesn't have any money or education.

8 A situation _____ something very bad happens which can cause a lot of damage.

7 Match these sentence halves and <u>underline</u> the relative clauses. Say whether they are giving extra information, or defining something or someone.

1 My friend volunteered to go to the disaster area
2 My friend, who's a nurse,
3 Clowns without Borders is an NGO
4 Tortell Poltrona, whose real name is
5 His famous trick is the one that he does
6 That's the circus
7 I don't like going to circuses

a whose aim is to make children smile.
b where I saw him perform.
c Jaume Mateu Bullich, is a clown.
d while balancing a chair on his nose.
e which was affected by floods.
f which exploit animals.
g volunteered to go to the disaster area.

Speaking: A fund-raising event

8 Work in groups of three. You are wealthy philanthropists who would like to organize a fund-raising event at your company/organization. Agree on these points. Student A: Turn to File 23, page 137. Student B: Turn to File 33, page 139. Student C: Turn to File 44, page 141.

- a charity that you would all like to donate to and which doesn't have a political agenda
- a marathon event that you could organize and which will be good fun
- a place where the event can be held and which is easy to get to
- a person who could coordinate the event and who is enthusiastic

TALKING POINT Have you ever worked as a volunteer? What did you do?

Reading: A TV charity marathon

1 Roughly how many emails do you have in your inbox at the moment? Approximately how many of them are from people who want you to do something for them? What are some of the things they want you to do?

2 Brenda works for TV4us, a regional Australian television channel that is organizing a marathon in aid of a children's charity. Read some messages from her inbox and sent items. Think of a suitable subject line for each message.

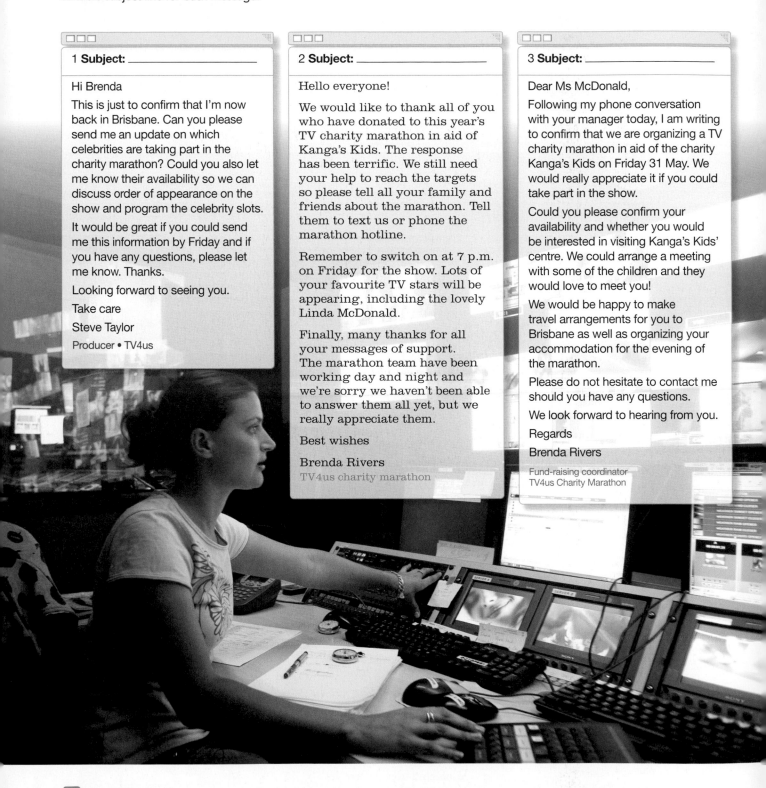

1 Subject: _____

Hi Brenda

This is just to confirm that I'm now back in Brisbane. Can you please send me an update on which celebrities are taking part in the charity marathon? Could you also let me know their availability so we can discuss order of appearance on the show and program the celebrity slots.

It would be great if you could send me this information by Friday and if you have any questions, please let me know. Thanks.

Looking forward to seeing you.

Take care

Steve Taylor

Producer • TV4us

2 Subject: _____

Hello everyone!

We would like to thank all of you who have donated to this year's TV charity marathon in aid of Kanga's Kids. The response has been terrific. We still need your help to reach the targets so please tell all your family and friends about the marathon. Tell them to text us or phone the marathon hotline.

Remember to switch on at 7 p.m. on Friday for the show. Lots of your favourite TV stars will be appearing, including the lovely Linda McDonald.

Finally, many thanks for all your messages of support. The marathon team have been working day and night and we're sorry we haven't been able to answer them all yet, but we really appreciate them.

Best wishes

Brenda Rivers

TV4us charity marathon

3 Subject: _____

Dear Ms McDonald,

Following my phone conversation with your manager today, I am writing to confirm that we are organizing a TV charity marathon in aid of the charity Kanga's Kids on Friday 31 May. We would really appreciate it if you could take part in the show.

Could you please confirm your availability and whether you would be interested in visiting Kanga's Kids' centre. We could arrange a meeting with some of the children and they would love to meet you!

We would be happy to make travel arrangements for you to Brisbane as well as organizing your accommodation for the evening of the marathon.

Please do not hesitate to contact me should you have any questions.

We look forward to hearing from you.

Regards

Brenda Rivers

Fund-raising coordinator
TV4us Charity Marathon

3 Match these subject lines to the correct message. Why is it important to write a suitable subject line on emails?

a Availability for TV charity marathon   **b** Charity marathon celebrities   **c** Donations for Kanga's Kids

4 Read the messages again. How many requests can you find? <u>Underline</u> them.

5 Look at the formal written expressions in the table and match them to less formal expressions in the messages.

Writing: Formal and less formal expressions

		Formal	Less formal
Opening	1	Dear Ms McDonald	_____
	2	I am writing to confirm*	*This is just to confirm …*
Requests	3	Could/Would you please	_____ / _____ / _____
	4	We would really appreciate it if	_____
Ending	5	Please do not hesitate to contact me should you	_____
	6	Thanks in advance for your help	_____
	7	We look forward to hearing from you	_____
	8	Best regards / Regards / Best wishes	*Best wishes / See you soon. / _____*

*We generally use *Following our phone call, …* to confirm in writing something that was agreed orally.

Speaking: Formality in emails

6 Look at the expressions in exercise 5 and discuss these questions.

1 Think of someone you could write to using the informal expressions. What would this person think if you used the formal expressions instead?

2 Think of someone you could write to using formal forms. What would this person think if you used the informal expressions instead?

7 Work in pairs. Brenda has written a reply to the TV producer Steve. She knows Steve quite well. Read the email. Is it too formal or informal? Why?

8 How could Brenda improve her email? Work with your partner to make improvements. Consider these points.

- use shorter requests
- use contractions where possible
- keep the email short, concise and accurate

To: Steve Taylor
From: Brenda Rivers
Re: Interview with Linda McDonald

Dear Mr Taylor

I am writing to confirm that Ms McDonald is available for the charity marathon. I was wondering if it would be at all possible for you to confirm her appearance time as she has a busy schedule that week. Please do not hesitate to contact me should you have any questions. Thanks in advance.

I look forward to seeing you soon.

Regards
Brenda Rivers
Fund-raising coordinator
TV4us Charity Marathon

Writing: Making requests

9 Write an email to the celebrity, Linda McDonald. How formal/informal should your email be? Write between 120–150 words and include this information.

1 Confirm her appearance times: 7.00 p.m. then at 7.45, 8.45 and 9.45 p.m.

2 Ask Linda to perform during the marathon. Think of different types of performances, e.g. dance, sing a song, etc.

3 Ask Linda to attend three rehearsals before the show.

4 Ask her to donate some of her designer clothes in aid of the charity.

TALKING POINT   In what situations do you prefer to ask people to do things face-to-face, on the phone or by email?

Listening: The newsletter

1 Does your organization have a newsletter? Do you receive other newsletters and webzines? Which do you read?

2 🔊 **2.30** Listen to the editorial team for Barkington Hospital's newsletter. Put the articles in the order they talk about them. Listen again and make some notes about each of the articles mentioned.

a fund raising

b a letter from the chief executive

c employee of the month

d special events

Grammar: Present perfect continuous

3 🔊 **2.31** Listen and complete these questions and answers from Daniel's interview with employee of the month, Sandra Harzog.

1 How long have you _____ at the hospital, Sandra?

2 I've _____ at Barkington for almost two years now.

3 Have you _____ in the UK long?

4 I've only _____ here since 2007.

5 I've _____ on the new digital records scheme for six months.

6 I've _____ to play since then.

4 Complete the table. Which use of the present perfect continuous are the examples in exercise 3?

Present perfect continuous

To form the present perfect continuous we use *has/have* + _____ + _____.

1 We use the present perfect continuous with *for* and *since* to talk about unfinished activities that started in the past and continue up until the present time.

*I've been working at Barkington **for** almost two years now.*

2 When we talk about unfinished actions, the present perfect continuous and the present perfect simple have a similar meaning:

*I **have** only **lived/been living** in the UK since 2007.*

3 We also use the present perfect continuous to talk about recent activities that have a consequence in the present.

*Hospital staff **have been helping** to raise funds for improvements to the park and they've collected £5,000 already.*

>> For more information on the present perfect continuous, see page 162.

---

5 Look at the pictures and complete the sentences using the present perfect continuous of these verbs. Which use of the present perfect continuous are these examples?

| lift plant carry reorganize do look for write |

1 A: Why is there furniture everywhere?

  B: They _____ the department. It'll be like this for another week.

2 A: Your clothes are all dirty. What _____ you _____ ?

  B: We _____ trees in the local park. It's the official opening tomorrow.

3 A: What's wrong with your back?

  B: I _____ and _____ heavy boxes of dental records and I've strained it.

4 A: Is this month's newsletter nearly ready?

  B: Not quite. I _____ all day but I'll need a few more hours tomorrow.

5 A: What are you doing?

  B: I can't find my glasses. I _____ them everywhere.

  A: They're on your head.

6 Complete this second part of the interview with Sandra Harzog using either the present prefect simple or present perfect continuous, or both.

SPOTLIGHT ON …

This month we talk to dental nurse Sandra Harzog.

I hear you got engaged recently. Congratulations!

Thank you. We're getting married in the spring. My partner, Rick, and I
¹ _____ (plan) the wedding for months now and everything is almost ready.
We ² _____ (tell) friends and family not to buy us presents because we've got everything we need for the house.

My mother ³ _____ (get) more and more excited about it and says she ⁴ _____ (not sleep) very well at night, but I ⁵ _____ (not have) too many wedding nerves yet. We ⁶ _____ (not decide) where to go for the honeymoon yet.
Rick ⁷ _____ (talk) about going to Peru, but I'd like to go back to Australia to spend some time with the family. I ⁸ _____ (not see) them for a couple of years and most can't come to the wedding in the UK.

Speaking: Special occasions

7 Match the special occasions below to the related words and expressions. Add two more words or expressions of your own to each group.

a	b	c	d	e	f
promotion	retirement	wedding	moving house	public holiday	having a baby

1 maternity leave   be pregnant   due date   paternity leave

2 parade   festival   fireworks   day off work

3 mortgage   new furniture   house-warming party   removal firm

4 new office   get promoted   pay rise   career move

5 get engaged   get married   reception   honeymoon

6 collection   leaving do   retire   company pension scheme

8 Discuss these questions.

1 How much does an average wedding cost? Are customs changing?

2 How much maternity leave do you get in your country? How much paternity leave?

3 How old can people retire? Do you know anyone who has taken early retirement?

4 How often have you moved house? Did you find it stressful?

5 How easy is it to get a promotion in your organization?

6 What are your favourite public holidays? Why?

9 You are going to interview your colleague for the company/class newsletter. Complete these questions. Then add some questions of your own and interview your colleague.

1 How long/you/learn English?

2 How long/you/work/at (company, organization, etc.)?

3 What/you/do/at work/recently?

4 You/have/any celebrations at work or at home lately?

5 What do you do in your free time? How long/you/be interested in (hobby or sport)?

6 Are you a member of a social group or gym? How long/you/be/a member?

Writing: Newspaper article

10 Write a short article about your colleague based on your interview in exercise 9.

TALKING POINT
- What have been the most memorable special occasions in your life? How did you celebrate these events?
- Are you going to celebrate any special occasions this year?

Reading: Career success

1 Networking is the process of establishing a mutually beneficial relationship with other professional people and building alliances. How important is networking in your job? Who do you network with, when and where?

2 Do you think networking has a bigger impact on men's careers than women's? Why?/Why not?

3 Look at the article: *Networking behaviour* and find out if you're right.

4 Look at the five types of networking behaviour mentioned in the article. Which ones do you engage in?

Networking behaviour

Recent research by Forret and Dougherty (2001) identified five types of networking behaviour: maintaining contacts, socializing, engaging in professional activities, participating in the community and increasing internal visibility in the company.

Further research by Forret and Dougherty (2004) indicates that only some forms of networking behaviour were related to longer-term career outcomes. In this study, the two most career-enhancing types of networking behaviour were increasing internal visibility and engaging in professional activities.

But these networking behaviours were related to career success for men only. Their results show that networking behaviours are not as advantageous for women as for men.

5 Look at this question in a forum and the reply. What reasons does the writer give for socializing at work? Do you agree? Add two more reasons to the list.

Is socializing at work really important?

Well, it does depend on what type of work you are in, but I think socializing is a good skill to have. I'm not surprised when the people person* type of employees get promoted. I mean, in most jobs you have to liaise* with other people – have good interpersonal skills. While some people spend little time at their desks, they have solid relations with other departments, customers, co-workers, etc. Very useful to have! I find troubleshooting* easy because I'm fully aware of what's going on in the organization. While I leave my desk only for short breaks, I'm visited all the time by other people for a chat. It's really made my life easy knowing everyone and getting the inside gossip* on what's going on. OK, some of it is pure entertainment but work-related info is always useful.

people person: someone who likes being with other people
liaise: exchange information with someone who works in another department or place
troubleshooting: finding solutions to serious problems
inside gossip: talk about people's lives and things that have been happening at work

6 Read another message to the forum. How would you respond to this person?

As part of my job I am expected to attend a lot of functions, receptions and award dinners. I am expected to circulate and meet potential business contacts. But, to be honest, sometimes I just don't want to talk to strangers. Can you give me a few suggestions on feeling more comfortable networking at these events?

Listening: Making connections

7 🔊 **2.32** Listen to a conversation at a company social event and answer the questions.

1 Do Michaela and Dev know each other?

2 What are their jobs?

3 What news and gossip do they exchange?

4 What doesn't Michaela want to talk about?

5 Do they manage to network effectively?

8 Here's the first part of their conversation, but it's in the wrong order. Put the parts of the conversation in the correct order.

☐ Are you? Congratulations!

[1] Hi, I don't think we've met before. I'm Michaela Perry.

☐ Me, I'm taking over from her next month.

☐ Nice to meet you, Michaela. I'm Dev Sharma.

☐ Oh terrific. So who will be in charge when she goes on maternity leave?

☐ Oh yes, I hear she's expecting.

☐ PR. I'm the Assistant to the Events Coordinator, Amrita Krishen.

☐ Really? That's cool! How's it going?

☐ So, tell me about yourself Dev. Which department are you in?

☐ Things are pretty quiet at the moment. It's going to be hectic next month though. And Amrita's going to be away.

☐ That's right. Twins!

9 🔊 **2.33** Read the conversation in exercise 8 with a partner. Then listen to part one to check your answers.

10 🔊 **2.34** Work in pairs. Here is the second part of their conversation, but some parts are missing. With your partner try and remember what they said. Then listen again to check your answers.

Dev: So, how about you Michaela? ¹_____ ?

Michaela: Well, I work in IT. ²_____ Head of Special Projects, and I'm still finding my ³_____ .

Dev: Wow! Sounds ⁴_____ ! Doesn't Massimo work in your department?

Michaela: Well, yes, he did. Actually, ⁵_____ .

Dev: No! I'm ⁶_____ to hear that.

Michaela: It's probably best not to talk about it.

Dev: I see. So, Michaela ⁷_____ sort out a new database for the PR department.

Michaela: ⁸_____ Hey! ⁹_____ at the same time you could give me some ideas for some team-building activities for my new staff.

Dev: Um, It's not my area, ¹⁰_____ , but I know just the man to help you. ¹¹_____ Stefan. He's just over there.

11 Match the news you heard in exercises 8 and 10 to the responses.

News and Gossip	Responses
1 I'm the Assistant to the Events Coordinator.	a Are you? Congratulations!
2 I hear she's expecting.	b I see.
3 I'm taking over from her next month.	c No! I'm sorry to hear that.
4 I've just become Head of Special Projects.	d Really? That's cool! How's it going?
5 Actually, he left under a cloud.	e That's right. Twins!
6 It's probably best not to talk about it.	f Wow! Sounds interesting.

12 In what ways might these expressions help people build alliances? Think of more expressions to add to the table.

News and gossip
Tell me about …
So, Michaela perhaps you could help me …
Maybe at the same time you could give me some ideas for …
I know just the man to help you.
Let me introduce you to …

Speaking: Network your way to success

13 Work in pairs. You are socializing with someone from another subsidiary or organization at a party. Prepare a dialogue including the following.

- greet your partner

- say what has been happening in your department recently

- include two items of gossip

- respond to each other's news and gossip

14 Listen to another pair's dialogue. What gossip and news did you hear that was useful to know?

15 You are at a conference and you want to make some useful contacts. Student A: Turn to File 9, page 133. Student B: Turn to File 17, page 135. Student C: Turn to File 18, page 136. Student D: Turn to File 36, page 140.

16 Were you able to network successfully with the other people at the party? Did you make any good contacts? Were you able to help each other?

Communication strategies

Reminder

Grammar reference
pages 173 and 162

We can use *which* or *that* when we define things.

A team-building event is one which/that encourages a group of people to work well together.

We can use *who* or *that* when we define people.

Time penalty points are deducted for any teams who/that are late.

We use the present perfect continuous to talk about unfinished activities that started in the past and are continuing now.

We've been organizing this year's event.

We can also use it to talk about recent activities that have a consequence in the present.

People have been complaining that the party's cancelled.

Reading: Special events

1 Have you ever been on a team-building event? If not, what do you know about them? How do you feel about them?

2 Read these adverts for team-building events and match the events (A, B, C or D) to these statements.

1 This event can be adapted to the needs and interests of your group. _____

2 It includes an opportunity to do some water sports. _____ _____

3 This event will take you to see a unique geographical feature. _____

4 It is probably only suitable for the very fit. _____

5 This team-building event is competitive. _____

6 This one can develop problem-solving skills. _____ _____

A Pureoutdoors

Are you looking to bond, build or develop your team? We have been organizing customized, innovative team-building events for many years.

Challenges are a mixture of physical and non-physical activities designed to encourage an increased sense of trust in one another as well as self-confidence.

Physical challenges may include: Abseiling, River Rope Traverse, Raft Building, Archery, Mountain Biking, Kayaking, climbing glaciers.

Non-physical challenges may include: Trivia, Brain Teasers, Puzzles, Jigsaws.

This event can be designed around your location. Long or short events are available.

B Perfect Day Ocean Cruise

This recipe for a Perfect Day cannot be matched anywhere! Perfect Day deliver eco-cruises to New Zealand's most beautiful islands. Experience the dramatic scenery, the world's largest sea cave and unique wildlife. Activities range from relaxing and sunbathing, to kayaking, snorkelling, or even diving for the first time! The Perfect Day Ocean Cruise is great for team-building, incentives and events with a difference.

CLIENT TESTIMONIAL
I've been attending annual team-building away days for 14 years and your event was the best ever!
Becky Hamilton

C Forest Challenge

We have been providing custom-made outdoor team-building activities since 1992. In this activity, participants working in small teams have to use their strategic and time-management skills to find different points in a forest. There is no set route. It's good fun and a great way to let off steam. Learn how to read a map and develop that teamwork ethic at the same time.

The winners are the team who get the most points. Time penalty points are deducted for any teams who are late! This event suits* all ages/abilities and is set in the stunning* Hanmer Heritage Forest.

D Bridge Climb

The perfect team-building event, the Bridge Climb is an unforgettable adventure that takes people under, up and over Auckland Harbor Bridge. Allow your team to stretch their legs and breathe some fresh air and clear their minds while they experience Auckland from a whole new perspective. The Auckland Bridge climb is great for any team event, social club, conference groups, youth groups, educational groups or incentives. It's recommended that all team members have a record of some physical training before applying for this event.

suits: is suitable for
stunning: extremely beautiful

3 Work in two groups. Group 1: Look at adverts A and C again and find the words or expressions that match the definitions. Group 2: Look at adverts B and D again.

Group 1

1 develop a special relationship with someone

2 tests of strength, skill or ability

3 made for a particular group (two possible words)

4 strong belief in the goodness of other people

5 release anger, excitement or energy in a safe way

Group 2

6 rewards that encourage you to work harder

7 time spent out of the office on team-building events

8 go for a walk, after sitting for a long time

9 stop worrying or thinking about something

10 different way of thinking about something

4 Explain your words and expressions to the other group using the correct definitions.

5 Which event would best suit these groups of people? Give reasons for your answers.

a a group of six, mainly male, software engineers

b a board of directors and their families

c a choir of 100 people, mostly female but of all ages

d a local rugby team

e all 50 staff in an engineering company, men and women of all ages

6 Which event would you like to do with other students, friends or your work colleagues? Why?

Speaking: Planning an event

7 🔊 2.35 Kiwi Projects is an engineering firm with a staff of 50 based in Auckland, New Zealand. Listen to this conversation between the CEO Aidan and his assistant Marama. What is Aidan proposing? What does Marama suggest?

8 🔊 2.36 Listen to some opinions from staff and take notes to summarize their comments.

9 Work in small groups. What is the best option for Kiwi Projects? Think about the comments and complaints you have been receiving from staff and discuss these points.

1 Should you cancel or adapt the annual family barbecue?

2 Define the objectives and outcome of your team-building event.

3 Should you plan a competitive or non-competitive event?

4 Which team-building company can best cater for your needs? Why?

5 What sort of customized programme would you have? e.g. How long should the event be? Should it be inside or outside working hours? What would the programme be?

6 What ongoing activities could the company organize to continue the team-building process?

10 Summarize your main points. Present your plan to the other teams and give reasons for your decisions.

11 Compare your ideas with those of the other teams. Which of their ideas would you incorporate into your plan?

12

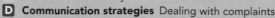

A Reported speech
B Embedded questions
C Consumer vocabulary
D Communication strategies Dealing with complaints
E Interaction Online entrepreneurs

Trial and error

Reported speech

Reading: Views on mistakes

1 What kinds of mistakes could these people make?

> a civil engineer   an athlete   a trader on the stock exchange
> a journalist   an architect   an opera singer   a civil servant   a sales assistant

2 Read the article quickly and say if these ideas are true or false, or not mentioned.

1 The writer says it's only natural that people make mistakes.
2 Peter Drucker was a successful managing director.
3 Drucker said we shouldn't trust a person who never makes a mistake.
4 Drucker changed his mind about management theory in the 1950s.
5 The writer thinks Drucker was brave to admit to making mistakes.

3 Which of the ideas in the article do you most/least agree with? Why?

We learn by making mistakes

When was the last time you made a mistake? If you're honest with yourself, it was probably recently. Mistakes are part of life; they are part of business. But too many companies try to cover them up rather than admit* to them. Management guru* Peter Drucker wrote, in *The Practice of Management*, he would never promote a man into a top-level job who had not made mistakes.

Drucker argued that there are different kinds of talent in any organization. He believed there are two kinds of 'performers'*. Drucker said one type of employee does consistently well but isn't exceptional. He added, 'Another man will perform only adequately under normal circumstances but will then perform like a true star.' Drucker continued, 'The one man to distrust*, however, is the one who never makes a mistake'.

In the 1950s, Drucker thought there was only one way to manage people correctly: believing that everyone will be responsible and motivated. In the 1960s a competing theory argued that managers should treat every employee as if they are basically lazy and resistant to change.

But then psychologist Abraham Maslow said it was silly to talk about a single management theory. And Drucker was quickly persuaded. He agreed that different people had to be managed differently. In fact Drucker later admitted that he was wrong. Imagine, if more people had the courage* to say they were wrong, and learn from it, a lot more things would go right.

admit: say you have done something wrong
guru: someone who knows a lot about something and gives advice to others
performer: someone who does a job well or badly
distrust: believe people aren't honest and usually do bad things
courage: being brave when you are in a difficult situation

Grammar: Reported speech

4 Look at the table and fill in the gaps.

Reported speech

Tense changes

1 When we're reporting what someone has said we sometimes change the tense of the verbs.

'Mistakes are part of life.' → *The writer says mistakes are part of life.*

2 We don't always change the tense when something was said recently, or if something is still true in the present.

Present simple → Present simple or ¹ _____

Present continuous → Present continuous or ² _____

Past simple → Past simple or ³ _____

Present perfect → Present Perfect or ⁴ _____

3 Modal verbs change when we're reporting.

will → *would*   *have to/must* → *had to*   *can* → *could*

4 Pronouns also change when we're reporting.

'I almost never learn from my mistakes.' → **She** *told me she almost never* **learns/learnt** *from* ⁵ _____ *mistakes.*

>> For more information on reported speech, see page 174.

5 Change these sentences into reported speech. Use *say* or *tell* in your answers.

1 Your CEO: 'It is important to celebrate failure as well as success.'

2 Your colleague: 'Oops, I've made a mistake. I've sent you the wrong file again.'

3 Your supplier: 'Don't worry. The technician will come tomorrow.'

4 A football manager: 'We've just lost this match but we'll win next time!'

5 Your friend: 'I'm sorry, but I thought you said Tuesday. I can't come on Thursday.'

6 A designer: 'There are lots of faults in the design so we're going to start again.'

Speaking: Embarrassing mistakes

6 Work in pairs. Which of these mistakes do you think are the most embarrassing? Have similar things ever happened to you or someone you know?

1 You send an email with holiday photos to a client by mistake.

2 You mispronounce the Managing Director's name various times in a meeting.

3 You want to demonstrate a new product but it isn't working properly.

4 You have prepared a great presentation but can't find your pendrive five minutes before your talk.

5 You invite your boss to your home but forget he is vegetarian.

6 You work as a trader. You make a mistake which costs your company about US $100,000.

7 Report what the people said in the situations in exercise 6 to your partner. It is not necessary to report 'word for word'. Student A: Turn to File 25, page 137. Student B: Turn to File 41, page 141.

He said he was sorry and told me to …

She apologized and offered to …

Tacoma Narrows Suspension Bridge, (Washington State, USA, 1940.)

> **!** After *tell* we say who was told something. So we tell someone something.
> This doesn't happen with *say*. We say something (to someone).
> *She* **said she** *didn't agree.*
> *She* **told the teacher/him** *she didn't agree.*

TALKING POINT   In your job is it more important to be careful or to take risks?

Listening: Celebrity gossip

1 Discuss these questions.

1 Which famous people are most admired in your country? Why?

2 Do you like reading about celebrities in newspapers and magazines? Why?/Why not?

3 Why do you think we often enjoy seeing people in the public eye making mistakes?

2 Read some headlines below about different celebrities and answer these questions.

Who do you think:

a is planning to divorce?

b was taken ill during a show?

c may have a new girlfriend?

d has accused a newspaper of telling lies?

e has been involved in a scandal?

3 Find words in the headlines that mean:

1 will separate or stop living together

2 suddenly fell down because he/she was ill or weak

3 will make a legal claim against someone because they have harmed you

4 left a job, etc. especially without finishing it completely

4 🔊 2.37 Listen to a news interview about one of the celebrities in exercise 2. Which one are they talking about?

5 🔊 Listen again and complete the newsreader's questions.

1 Could you tell us _____ _____ _____ this morning?

2 Do you know _____ _____ _____ _____ _____ like this?

3 _____ _____ still a possibility?

4 _____ _____ _____ to her daughter yet?

5 So _____ _____ _____ _____ the possibility that this was a heart attack?

ANGIE COLE TO SUE EVENING POST

JAKE CRUZ LEAVES LONDON CLUB WTH CO-STAR

SHAMED RICHARD WATSON QUITS TV SHOW

Paul and Kate Morgan to Split

STELLA DELAINE COLLAPSES ON STAGE

Grammar: Embedded questions

6 Compare the word order in the direct and embedded questions in the table. How is it different?

Embedded questions	
Sometimes we do not ask questions directly. Instead we start with phrases like *Do you know …?* or *Could you tell me …?*	
Direct questions	**Embedded questions**
Why did he quit the show?	***Could you tell me*** *why he quit the show?*
Are they planning to get married?	***Do you know if*** *they're planning to get married?*

>> For more information on embedded questions, see page 175.

7 Look at the questions in exercise 5 and answer these questions.

1 Did the embedded questions come at the beginning or the end of the interview?

2 Find a question where the interviewer is asking for confirmation. Does it contain a question form?

8 Look at some more questions about the celebrities in the headlines. Change them to embedded questions. Start: *Could you tell me …?* or *Do you know …?*

1 Will Richard's career survive?

2 What time did they leave the club?

3 Which law firm is Angie consulting?

4 Have they found a new presenter yet?

5 Are they living apart now?

6 What sort of financial settlement does Kate want?

7 Have we received a statement from the *Post*?

8 Which direction did their taxi go?

Speaking: Celebrity interviews

9 Work in pairs. Choose one of the following types of celebrities and one of the headlines. Then tell your partner which celebrity you are and which headline is about you.

> Film star   Politician   TV chef   Singer   Top model
> Reality TV contestant   Entrepreneur

_____ CHECKS INTO WEIGHT LOSS CLINIC*

_____'S SON ARRESTED* AFTER PARTY

_____ QUITS CABINET

_____ SELLS RESTAURANT CHAIN

_____ STORMS OFF* TV INTERVIEW

_____ TO TAKE TRIP INTO SPACE

_____ ACCUSED OF LIBEL* ON BLOG

Weight loss clinic: place where you go to get thinner
Arrest: when the police take a person to a police station because he/she has done something illegal
Storm off: leave a place very quickly because you are angry
Libel: when someone writes untrue statements about someone

10 Take a few minutes to prepare to interview one another about the news in your headlines. Be ready to talk about these points.

- what the celebrity did or what happened to them (and why)
- what their plans for the future are

11 Take turns to interview each other. Reporters: begin the interview with embedded questions like *Could you tell me …?* As the interview progresses, ask your questions more directly.

12 Report back to the class. Talk about these points.

a which celebrity your partner was and what they did

b why they acted as they did

c what their plans are for the future

> **TALKING POINT**   If you saw your favourite celebrity in the street, what would you ask them?

Listening: Consumer stories

1 🔊 **2.38** Listen to four podcasts. Match each extract to the description.

a   News report about builders

b   Advert for a consumer service

c   Anecdote about an angry customer

d   Problems with payment

2 🔊 **2.39** Listen to the first story again and complete this note. What lesson did the speaker learn?

Complaints Form

A man phoned today to report an online

¹ _____ _____ company. When he

received his ² _____ _____ bill they

had charged him an extra ³ _____

euros. They promised to return the money

within ⁴ _____ days but didn't. Can you

call him back and get more details? Then

find out if the company is still operating, get

their ⁵ _____ and write to them?

3 🔊 **2.40** Listen to the second story again and correct this newspaper article. There are five errors.

People prefer cheap builders

A survey reveals that 16% of UK homeowners prefer to pay cash to builders to avoid taxes. 20,000 adults were interviewed for the survey, commissioned by the National Federation of Architects. At the same time, Trading Standards* figures show that over 10,000 complaints are made about unprofessional builders and tradespeople each month.

Trading Standards: UK government agency responsible for protecting consumers

4 🔊 **2.41** Listen to the third speaker again and complete her story.

This shop assistant works in a ¹ _____ . When this incident happened yesterday the shop was especially ² _____ . A customer gave her a prescription and she asked him to return ³ _____ minutes later for it. Unfortunately, she later found out that the medication was not ⁴ _____ _____ . When the man returned and heard this, he was very angry and demanded to speak to her ⁵ _____ .

Word focus: Consumer vocabulary

5 Look at these extracts from the podcasts in exercise 1. What do the words and phrases in italics mean? Use the context to help you. Then match them to the definitions.

1   But this one time I was nearly *ripped off*. c

2   … they'd *overcharged* me by 500 euros.

3   … and they'd *refund* my money within 15 days.

4   … I *reported* them to the trading standards people.

5   I'll only give my details online to well-known, *reputable* companies.

6   … there are a lot of internet *scams* about these days.

7   60% of UK homeowners prefer *cash-in-hand* builders.

8   Over half of Britons would risk hiring a *cowboy* builder to carry out work on their home.

9   There are over 100,000 complaints made about *rogue tradespeople* each year.

a   complain about someone to people in authority

b   clever but dishonest ways to make money

c   charged too much money for something (two possibilities)

d   payment made in notes and coins so that there is no record

e   someone who is dishonest in business or produces very bad quality work (two possibilities)

f   money that is returned to you if you are not satisfied with the goods or services

g   respected for being honest or for doing good work

6 Which tradespeople would you call in each of these situations? How would you choose a person/company to do some work for you, e.g. personal recommendation?

1 You want to install some lights.	a	plumber
2 You've decided to repaint your home.	b	electrician
3 You have to prune some trees.	c	mechanic
4 Water is leaking from your bathroom taps.	d	gas engineer
5 You want to install gas central heating.	e	gardener
6 You'd like to knock down a wall.	f	carpenter
7 Your motorbike won't start.	g	decorator
8 Some old doors need to be replaced.	h	builder

7 Can you think of other situations when you need expert help?

Speaking: This is what happened

8 Read and memorize your information. Tell your group your story using some of the expressions from exercise 5. What lesson(s) did you learn from the experience? Student B: Turn to File 34, page 139. Student C: Turn to File 42, page 141.

Student A:

You once hired some decorators.

- they were recommended to you
- they wanted to be paid cash-in-hand by the day
- they didn't work very fast
- you suspected that they were wasting time
- many days you got home early from work and they had already gone
- one day they just never came back again
- lesson(s) you've learnt …

9 Which experience in exercise 8 was the worst? Why?

TALKING POINT Do you remember a time you, or someone you know, had a particularly good or bad consumer experience? What? What lesson(s) did you learn?

Speaking: Common complaints

1 Look at a list of situations when you might complain. Add two more of your own ideas.

- waiting to be served in a shop
- an incorrect or late delivery
- a faulty product
- the service in a restaurant
- noisy neighbours
- delays on public transport
- colleagues who take long breaks
- being overcharged for something
- _____
- _____

2 Work in pairs. Which situations in exercise 1 do you find most annoying and why?

3 When was the last time you complained about some of these things? What happened?

Listening: A customer complaint

4)) **2.42** Claire works in Customer Service for Ritchie's, a retail store that sells clothes both instore and online. What type of complaints do you think Claire might receive? Listen to two conversations. What are her customers complaining about?

5 Work in pairs. Roleplay the two phone calls between Claire and the customers. Student A: Turn to File 31, page 139. Student B: Turn to File 45, page 141.

6)) **2.43** Listen to the rest of Claire's phone call with the first customer and discuss these questions.

1 What happened? How was the conversation different from yours?

2 How professionally did Claire deal with the customer's complaint?

3 How would you feel if you were Claire?

7)) Claire has to complete this online form about the complaint. Listen to Call 1 Part 2 again and complete the form.

Ritchie's Ltd Customer Services Incident

Name of Customer Service rep:

Claire Simpson

Name of customer:

Neil Jackson

Order No:

#582/107-94036

Complaint:

The customer had misread the 1 _____ and thought he had been 2 _____ .

Explanation given:

I told him the online offer only applies to orders for 3 _____ and confirmed he had been charged correctly.

Action taken:

I asked the customer to complete the online 4 _____ .

Customer satisfied? Yes / No. If not, please specify.

The customer thought the website was 5 _____ because he had to scroll down to see the 6 _____ .

8 Look at these expressions for responding to complaints. <u>Underline</u> the ones that a customer service representative would say. What is wrong with the other ones?

Dealing with complaints

Asking about the complaint
What's your problem?
What seems to be the problem?

Showing empathy
Don't worry my dear.
Oh dear, I'm sorry to hear that.
Yes, I see/understand.
That must be very annoying.
I know what you mean.

Apologizing
We're really very sorry about this.
Oops, sorry.
I do apologize.
I'm afraid we've had some trouble with the system.
The system doesn't work properly.

Correcting and explaining
No, you're wrong.
If you look at our website, I think you'll find …
There seems to have been a mistake.
You've made a mistake.

Putting things right
You could complete our questionnaire.
You must complete this form.
You'll need to complete this form.
I'll see what I can do.
I'll pass on your complaint.
Thanks for letting us know.

Speaking: Putting things right

9 Work in pairs. Look again at exercise 1 and roleplay some of the other situations. Use some of the expressions in exercise 8.

10 Work in pairs. A customer has sent this email to your customer services department. Read the email. What seems to be the problem? What should you say to this customer to put things right?

To: Ritchie's Customer Services
From: Amy Henderson
Subject: Unsatisfactory delivery

Dear Customer Services

I am writing to complain about my order number: # 5821/304-973478.

I am a regular customer with your store, but I was very concerned to find that my last online order was delivered to my neighbour by mistake. What's more, the parcel was left in my neighbour's back garden in the rain for a few days with no note or explanation so no one noticed it. The parcel was wet through and the items, two T-shirts and a pair of trousers, were damaged because of the rain.

I called your customer service line and one of your employees told me that I can't have a refund because the goods are damaged. That is unacceptable. Please note that I will not place any more orders with Ritchie's if I don't receive a full refund immediately.

Regards

Amy Henderson

Writing: Replying to a complaint

11 Write an email in reply to Amy's complaint. Include these ideas.
- thank the customer for writing and express sympathy
- admit that a mistake was made: explain the local mail service sent the parcel, not Ritchie's
- offer a free replacement or refund
- say you will add €5 of credit to the customer's account on her next order
- apologize for any inconvenience caused

12 When you have finished, show your email to your partner. Would he/she be happy with your reply? Why?/Why not?

Reminder

Grammar reference page 175

Sometimes we do not ask questions directly. Instead we start with sentences like these:

Do you have any idea where you hope to be in five years' time?

But be careful with word order.

Could you tell me what you're working on at the moment?

When dealing with complaints we usually ask about the problem, show empathy, apologize, correct someone or explain and offer to put things right.

What seems to be the problem?

Oh dear, I'm sorry to hear that. I'll see what I can do.

Reading: Starting up

1 What kind of business could you run from home? What are the advantages of setting up your own business?

2 Read about the entrepreneur, Lauren Luke. What does she sell? How did she become successful?

3 Do you think online social networking will continue to grow rapidly? Do you think the success of businesses like panacea81 will last? Why?/Why not?

4 Read this interview with fashion entrepreneur, Dominic Fendius. What do you think the questions were?

Entrepreneurs use social networks

A young mother goes from selling make-up on Ebay to launching her own beauty range and newspaper column. She owes her popularity to social networks such as MySpace and YouTube. Enthusiastic amateurs are turning professional by using web tools to achieve popularity.

As panacea81 has shown, online social networks can be powerful marketing machines for young entrepreneurs. But will the volume of people online make it harder to stand out*?

stand out: be different and noticeable

Dominic Fendius

Founder of **Stitsh.com**

1 It's a style blog, a street fashion site based in London.

2 We take pictures of fashionable members of the public and link their clothing to online retailers, where you can buy the items at great prices. When you scroll over the photos, a speech bubble appears with the details of the clothes. When you click on the speech bubble, you are taken directly to the retailer where you can buy it.

3 We earn a commission every time someone buys through Stitsh.

4 We're currently working on a New York version.

5 After studying business at university I started a free magazine in London, although this didn't work out. I then worked in the City for a US investment bank and saved some money to start my next business.

6 The first person I go to for advice is my mother who runs her own business.

7 I work very hard and really enjoy it. I'm careful to know when to stop and get away from work. But I find it difficult to stop thinking about it.

8 In five years we hope that Stitsh will be the first site people visit globally when shopping for new clothes.

5 Think of three more questions you could ask the founder of Stitsh.com. Roleplay the questions in pairs.

Board game: Online business

6 Work in pairs. A: You are Trisha. B: You are the other people in the game. Read the situation and the rules.

TRISHA BARON

Trisha Baron is a graphic designer who is trying to expand her business. Six months ago she started designing electronic greeting cards for friends and then started selling them on social networking sites. She now wants to sell other products online and is designing her own brand of stationery (notebooks, pens, etc.).

Rules

Play this game in pairs. You each need a coin to play. Move two squares if it is heads and one square if it is tails. Take it in turns to throw the coin and answer the questions, or act out the situations with your partner. Stay on the square if your partner is satisfied with your response. If not, go back to the previous square.

1 Start
You are recording a video for your website but the neighbours are doing building work. Ask them to stop.

2
Your business is going well but you don't have time to update your blog. Ask a friend to help you.

3
You do a short interview for a local radio station. Roleplay three questions from the interview.

4
You have an important meeting with a new client. Just before the meeting, you get the flu. Phone your client to cancel.

5
Your friend is interested in becoming your business partner but you don't think it's a good idea. Talk to him/her and explain your reasons.

6
You discover a competitor has been copying your ideas. You record a short podcast for your site to complain.

7
A design magazine invites you to write a monthly column. You accept. Role-play the phone call.

8
You have been having problems with your internet connection. Phone the server to complain.

9
You haven't had time to answer all your emails recently. Customers are complaining. Record a short podcast for your site, apologizing. What do you say?

10
You employed your cousin to help in the office but he makes a lot of mistakes. What do you say?

11
You produce new samples of greetings cards. Your mum loves them and gives them away to her friends. You complain. What do you say?

12
You return from the printers with some new notebooks but the cat spills a cup of coffee on your desk. Phone the printers. Ask them to print 50 more by the end of the week.

13
You decide to diversify your product range. Decide with your partner whether you should: a) produce a clothes range. b) do something else. What?

14
A TV channel does a documentary about you. Someone stops you in the street and asks for your autograph. Roleplay the conversation.

15
You decide to start producing a designer clothes range and move to a new office but you need more capital. Ask your bank manager for a loan. Roleplay the conversation.

16
A retailer accuses you of copying their clothes range. You ask your father, who's a lawyer, for advice. What do you say?

17
The press accuse you of copying the ideas of your competitors. You give a one-minute TV interview. What do you say?

18 Finish
You win the case against your competitor. Your company is a success. You are invited to go on a celebrity reality show. Congratulations!

1 Read the story and choose the correct options.

2 Complete the sentences about the story in exercise 1. Put the verbs in the correct form for talking about hypothetical situations in the past. Use *should/shouldn't have*, where necessary.

1 This _____ (not happen) if they _____ (had) lunch in the canteen.

2 If she _____ (not be) so interested in office gossip, someone (not steal) _____ her handbag.

3 If she _____ (be) wiser, she _____ (put) so much cash in her bag.

4 It _____ (not be) so bad if she _____ (have) her keys and mobile phone in her pocket.

5 She _____ (not leave) her bag on the back of the chair.

6 Her friend _____ (not notice) the thief take the handbag.

7 The CCTV cameras _____ (not catch) the thief on camera.

8 The waitress in the café _____ (not see) anything suspicious if she had _____ (be) busy.

The day my bag was stolen

I was having lunch the other day with a colleague in a café near the office. I had put my handbag across the back of my chair but when I stood up to leave, I found that it had gone. I'd been so interested in office ¹ gossip / chat that I hadn't noticed someone had ² stolen / stole my expensive, designer bag.

Inside were my keys, mobile phone, mp3 player, €300 in ³ money / cash (I had just been to the bank), ⁴ loan / credit cards, my make-up bag and my security pass. At first, I was very ⁵ upset / annoying. But later, I decided the thief ⁶ gave / had given me five reasons to be grateful:

- Being without your mobile phone is great. People can't phone you up so easily and have to make an effort to talk to you face-to-face.
- People have ⁷ bought / spent me things so far, a coffee, some chocolate and a free lunch. I lost €300 but at least I'll ⁸ save / afford some money until I get my new cards.
- It's not your ⁹ fault / blame. Once, when I lost my mobile phone, I was to ¹⁰ fault / blame and felt guilty. This time I was a victim, and people have been very sympathetic.
- We shouldn't worry about CCTV watching us. The ¹¹ waitress / camera in the café failed to catch anything suspicious.
- I now have a story to ¹² say / tell.

3 Complete the crossword about right and wrong.

Across

4 Some people never learn from their … .

5 Mistakes have been … .

7 say you have done something wrong

10 the noun from honest

12 say sorry

Down

1 Who's to … for this situation?

2 a moral problem

3 You should have listened to me. It's your own … !

6 someone who is dishonest in business or produces bad quality work (BrE)

8 People should … responsibility for their actions.

9 behave dishonestly in order to get an advantage

11 opposite of tell the truth

4 Put the words and expressions in the box into the correct group.

wedding electrician apology
builder mortgage wise loan
retirement promotion overcharge
thoughtful refund sensitive borrow
public holiday plumber replacement
down payment dishonest mechanic
pay back damaged goods irrational
decorator anniversary

Banking	Special occasions	Tradespeople	Complaints	Adjectives of personality

5 Choose the correct relative pronouns in these sentences. Sometimes more than one answer is possible. Which of them are defining or giving extra information?

1 That's the woman *whose / who's / that* bag was stolen.

2 They finally replied to my complaint, *which / that / when* I'd written months ago.

3 She's that famous singer *who / which / that* is always in the news.

4 It's a social networking site *where / which / when* you can meet people.

5 They regularly donate money to charity, *that / which / who* is very kind of them.

6 He's the man *which / that / who* runs his own construction business.

7 The woman *who / that / which* I met at the conference knows my boss.

8 Victor, *who's / whose / that* son goes to the same school as my boy, is our supplier.

6 Complete the sentences for apologizing and dealing with complaints with these expressions.

> a can't give you a refund
> b Sorry, I forgot
> c I'm very sorry to
> d letting us know
> e forgetting our anniversary
> f The traffic was terrible
> g very annoying for you
> h There seems to have been a mistake

1 I'm really sorry about ___ .

2 I'm so sorry I'm late. ___ .

3 ___ call this late but have you got a minute?

4 ___ to phone you but something urgent came up.

5 I'm sorry to hear that. It must be ___ .

6 I'm afraid we ___ without a receipt.

7 ___ with the reference number.

8 Thanks for ___ . We'll look into it straightaway.

7 Complete the interview questions with a Turkish retailer. Put the verbs in brackets in the correct tense: present perfect simple or present perfect continuous. If both are possible, use the present perfect continuous.

1 Could you tell me how long _____ (you run) your own business?

2 Do you know how many stores _____ (you open) so far?

3 How many online visitors _____ (you have) this month?

4 What _____ (you do) recently?

5 _____ (you find) the right person yet?

6 You look a little tired. _____ (you get) enough sleep lately?

7 _____ (you celebrate) anything special recently?

8 How many awards _____ (you win)?

8 Match these answers to the questions in exercise 7.

a 35,000.

b No, not yet.

c For over two years now.

d No, I haven't. But I've been going out a lot recently with my sales team.

e I've been interviewing people for the marketing department.

f Only one so far.

g Yes, we've just won a business award.

h We've opened five stores to date: two in Ankara and three in Istanbul.

9 Complete this conversation at a college reunion with these expressions.

> a did you hear about   b Congratulations!   c We've known each other
> d getting engaged   e How's it going?   f he's been going out with
> g I'm really sorry but   h What are you doing these days?

Sharon: Hi, didn't you use to work for Bingley Insurance in accounts?

Amanda: That's right. Hello. ¹___ I've forgotten your name.

Sharon: It's Sharon.

Amanda: Yes, of course. Sharon. ²___ ?

Sharon: Oh, I'm pretty busy. We've got twins now!

Amanda: ³___ .

Sharon: But I'm back at work at Bingley's.

Amanda: That's great. ⁴___ ?

Sharon: Not too bad. The little ones have been sleeping all through the night.

Amanda: And the job?

Sharon: Fine. Listen, ⁵___ Vladimir?

Amanda: No. What?

Sharon: Well, ⁶___ Francine. I hear they're ⁷___ !

Amanda: Really? I don't believe it!

Sharon: Oh, sorry. Hi Gina. Amanda, this is my friend, Gina. ⁸___ since college.

Amanda: Nice to meet you, Gina.

Information files

File 1

Student A:

Look at your information and answer questions about dining in someone's house in Russia. When you have finished, change roles. Ask your partners about dining in Argentina and India.

Dining Etiquette in Russia

- Dress smartly in clothes you might wear to the office.
- Remove your outdoor shoes – host may give you slippers.
- Guests are treated with honour and respect.
- Offer to help the host with the preparation or clearing up after a meal is served.
- Do not start eating until the host invites you to start.
- Men pour drinks for women seated next to them.
- You will often be encouraged to have second helpings.
- Leave a small amount of food on your plate to show you have finished eating.
- Do not get up until you are invited to leave the table. But at formal dinners, the guest of honour is the first to get up from the table.

File 2

Student A:

Rafael Nadal plays left-handed. Nadal's main rival has been 1_____ since 2004. Many people have described this special rivalry as the greatest in tennis history. Nadal was World No. 2 behind Federer for 3_____ weeks before he earned the top spot.

Cate Blanchett has lived with her family in Sydney for the last few years in a mansion built in 1877, which they renovated in 5_____ to be more eco-friendly. Since 2007 she has been ambassador of an Australian conservation campaign for climate change. Blanchett has appeared in a special edition of 7_____ featuring Australian actors.

Haruki Murakami has collected over 7,000 vinyl records including jazz, pop and classical music. An enthusiastic marathon runner, he did not start running until he was 9_____ . He has written an autobiographical book called *What I talk about when I talk about running*.

File 3

Student A:

Imagine you are sitting next to someone during a meal and you start making conversation. Choose two or three of these topics and tell your partner a one-minute story. Prepare your stories any vocabulary you don't know before you start.

1 a day you lost something important
2 a good friend
3 a time you were ill
4 a moment of bravery
5 your best sunset
6 a long wait

File 4

Answers:

1 It's often tempting to skip breakfast, but it's an essential meal for maintaining blood-sugar levels and getting us functioning well in the morning.

2 a) and b) are true. c) and d) are false – sugar contains the same calories as other carbohydrates but it does not provide any nutrients. Experts recommend that people cut down on sugar and sugary foods.

3 When we are busy or stressed, we tend to make bad nutritional choices and eat too much fast food. But eating badly only adds to our stress levels.

4 c) 15–22 grams. It all depends on the amount and type of ingredients. Experts say women should eat less than 20 grams of saturated fat per day and men should eat less than 30g.

5 These foods are high in saturated fat:

    a butter and margarine

    b milk and yoghurt

    c meat and meat products

    d biscuits, crisps and cakes

    g cheese

Nutritionists say few people are clear about where saturated fat comes from in their diet. And there is little information on food labels to help consumers make healthy choices. Anything containing more than 20g of fat per 100g is a lot.

6 Three-quarters (75%) of the salt we eat comes from processed foods, such as bread, breakfast cereals, soups, sauces, ready-made meals, biscuits and lots and lots of other foods. In fact, manufacturers add so much salt to our food that there is no need to add any extra salt, because most of us are already eating too much.

7 b) 6g: Most people eat too much salt, on average about 9.5g of salt a day. We should try to cut this down to less than 6g of salt a day.

File 5

Results:

Mostly a's: You like to think ahead, prepare things in advance and do things in an orderly way. Your colleagues probably admire and appreciate your organizational skills.

Mostly b's: You may sometimes seem disorganized and even a little crazy to your colleagues. But when the unexpected happens, they probably appreciate your ability to improvise and adapt.

Mostly c's: You like to be organized up to a point but can also be creative, depending on the situation. Your colleagues probably appreciate your flexibility.

File 6

Student B:

You are Oskar, a&k's training manager. You think Karen should pay for one of her courses because this is what you agreed previously and you are cutting the training budget this year. Persuade Karen that your point of view is right.

Make some notes before you begin. Make sure you summarize what you have agreed at the end of the meeting.

File 7

Student A:

How did Ricky Cash become successful? Use these pictures and notes to write Ricky's life story. Memorize it and then tell it to your partner.

The Life of Ricky Cash

- Ricky / 16 / start / sell electronic goods / markets / London
- Ricky Cash / leave school / 14, by 27 / become / managing director / electronics group
- 28 / marry / wife, Christine / knew since 21
- 45 / make / £830 million / become Sir Ricky Cash
- 50 / start appearing / successful TV business show, *How to Make Money*
- prize winner / get / opportunity / manage one / Ricky's companies
- once / say / interview / owe / success to hard work / have tough childhood / growing up / London

File 9

Student A:

Complete your role card. Introduce yourself and network with another person. Then move on and meet someone else.

You are a TV presenter and have worked for several TV channels (…) and hosted TV shows including (…). You have interviewed many famous people, such as (…).

Your hobbies and interests are (…).

You want to produce a new documentary series about unusual people.

You'd like to write a book, maybe with a co-author.

File 8

Student A:

Read your information and put your proposals to the group. Complete the 'Outcome' column and add some proposals of your own to the table.

Situation	Proposal	Outcome
The company has no recycling scheme.	Introduce recycling bins for paper, electronics, batteries, plastics, etc.	*Make recycling part of everyday life and engage staff.*
Electricity bills are high.	Install solar panels and/or wind turbines on the roof.	
Staff buy water in plastic bottles because the tap water is poor quality.	Introduce a water fountain with filtered water.	

Information files

File 10

Student A:

You deal with market research and handle a lot of statistics in your job. You are also a musician and can play the piano and classical guitar.

Student B:

You are very good at giving presentations and know a few magic tricks. The day of the visit will be very busy for you because you are going on annual leave the following day. You don't want to stay late in the evening.

Student C:

You are good at design and often have good ideas for how publicity should look. You are a basketball coach in your free time and your wife is a prize-winning chef.

Student D:

Your job mainly consists of presenting products to clients. You like the human contact. You are a natural comedian and also run a local drama group.

Student E:

You have lots of contacts with local clients. You know the head of marketing because you worked for her five years ago. You didn't like the way she managed people and left the job after six months. She probably doesn't realize who you are because you changed your name by marriage, but it's best if she doesn't recognize you.

Student F:

You are the marketing assistant. You are young and inexperienced but very enthusiastic. You are an aerobic instructor in your free time.

File 11

Student B:

You are Oskar, the Training Manager at a&k. Persuade the employee that one of the courses is the most suitable for him/her. a&k will pay for one course per employee but possibly more if the employee can prove there will be benefits to the company. Consider these points before you begin. When you have finished, change roles with your partner.

1 Employee's motivation

2 Benefits of the training to the company and the participant

3 Cost – (The company's average training budget per employee is about €1,000 but it depends on their interests, needs and job position. Do not tell this to the employee.)

4 Length and time, e.g. A&K prefers employees to attend courses in the evenings and at weekends. If the course is in company time, will the participant be able to make up for lost time in the office?

5 Attendance, e.g. Will he/she be able to attend all of the course? Why?/Why not?

File 12

Student B:

1 You want to borrow your partner's English notes before the test next week.

2 You would prefer not to have photos or any other personal information about you on websites or on friends' Facebook pages. Respond to your partner's request.

3 Agree to your partner's request.

4 Your boss has asked you to finish a report by Friday afternoon. It's now Thursday. You haven't had time to finish it but you want to leave work at 3 p.m. on Friday because you're going away for the weekend. Ask your boss if you can send it on Monday.

5 You're having problems downloading some computer software. Ask your colleague, who's an expert, to help you.

File 13

Student B:

Rafael Nadal plays left-handed. Nadal's main rival has been Roger Federer since 2004. Many people have described this special rivalry as 2_____ . Nadal was World No. 2 behind Federer for 160 weeks before he earned the top spot.

Cate Blanchett has lived with her family in 4_____ for the last few years in a mansion built in 1877, which they renovated in 2007 in order to be more eco-friendly. Since 2007 she has been ambassador of 6_____ for climate change. Blanchett has appeared in a special edition of postage stamps featuring Australian actors.

Haruki Murakami has collected over 8_____ vinyl records including jazz, pop and classical music. An enthusiastic marathon runner, he did not start running until he was 33. He has written an autobiographical book called 10_____ .

File 14

Student A:

1 Call your colleague. Tell him/her you can't make lunch today – suggest Friday. Ask him/her to buy you a sandwich when he/she goes out. You need to eat at your desk today.

2 It's Friday evening and you are working late, finishing a report, when suddenly the phone rings. The HR Manager said he never wanted to speak to this person again. Be brief and polite and take a message.

3 This is an urgent call. If you can't speak to Stella Morris in the legal department, you have to leave a detailed message. The copy of the contract has been received but not signed. You will email her a copy. She needs to sign it and scan it for you and then send you the original by ordinary mail.

4 You pick up the phone. Maria Piccolo is out of the office – she's gone to the doctor's. Take a message.

2

File 15

Student B:

Look at this information about David Horn and Carla D'Silva and answer your partner's questions. Then ask your partner questions to complete the two profiles for Sally Warren and Jamie Barnes.

Name: David Horn
Company: Top Note Orchestra (TNO)
Started: ten years ago

Main achievements:
- TNO aims to develop aspiring talent, especially young people who can't afford music lessons.
- TNO has trained 400 young musicians from poor city areas.
- The orchestra has given concerts all over the country. The musicians play with an energy and passion that audiences love.
- TNO uses the money from concerts to buy more instruments and set up new projects.
- TNO gives music workshops to people with learning difficulties.

Name: Carla D'Silva
Company: D'Silva Arts Centre
Started: four years ago

Main achievements:
- Carla, who graduated from art school in 2005, has won several awards for her art.
- She opened an arts centre with her prize money and government grants.
- D'Silva Arts Centre has helped thousands of mentally ill people change their lives through art therapy.
- The Centre organizes public exhibitions and raises money through sales of art to continue the project.
- The Centre runs street art courses for children having problems at school.

Name: Sally Warren
Company: City Leisure Unlimited (CLU)
Started: eight years ago

Main achievements:
- CLU started as a local council sports centre. After cuts in the service, employees ⁹_____ and have reduced costs by 10%.
- CLU operates ¹⁰_____ policy, with reduced prices for customers on a low income.
- CLU now has three centres and has created ¹¹_____ jobs in the local community.
- CLU provides financial support for ¹²_____ people. Sally Warren, who used to be an Olympic runner, remembers how hard it was getting money to continue training.

Name: Jamie Barnes
Company: Barnes Apprentice Restaurants
Started: six years ago

Main achievements:
- Jamie runs ¹³_____ high-quality restaurants in fashionable parts of London.
- He has written ¹⁴_____ cookbooks and some of the money from sales goes into his apprentice restaurant chain.
- The restaurants create opportunities for people who have been unemployed for a long time.
- Professional staff in the restaurants work with and train new apprentices for ¹⁵_____ months.
- ¹⁶_____% of the apprentices who graduate have found permanent jobs.

File 16

Student B:

1 Ask your partner questions to guess what he/she used to do.

Did you use to work in an office?

2 You are now a famous actor, but you used to work as a cleaner. Complete these sentences about your former life. Then answer your partner's questions.

- I used to own _____ . (form of transport)
- I used to earn _____ . (salary)
- I used to work _____ . (working hours)
- I didn't use to have _____ . (possessions)
- I used to spend my holidays in _____ . (places)
- I used to / didn't use to _____ . (free time and social life)

File 17

Student B:

Complete your role card. Introduce yourself and network with another person. Then move on and meet someone else.

You are an adventurer. You have travelled around the world for (…) years and visited all these places (…). You have climbed Everest as well as (…)

Your hobbies and interests are (…).

You'd like to find sponsors for your next big adventure to sail around the world.

One day you want to set up sports and education programmes for young people.

File 18

Student C:

Complete your role card. Introduce yourself and network with another person. Then move on and meet someone else.

You are a former sports star (sport?…).

You have won (…).

You have retired from professional sport and now you (…).

Your hobbies and interests are (…)

You are thinking of becoming a TV sports presenter.

You give a lot of money to children's charities.

File 19

Student B:

Read your information and put your proposals to the group. Complete the 'Outcome' column and add some proposals of your own to the table.

Situation	Proposal	Outcome
Staff complain that the air quality isn't very good.	Put plants in the office to freshen up the air.	*Improve air quality and staff feel better.*
Office equipment is often on all night.	Set policies on shutting down computers, copiers and appliances out-of-hours.	
Water consumption is high in the office.	Change the taps in the washrooms.	

File 20

Student B:

How did Penny Winner become successful? Use these pictures above and notes to tell Penny's life story. Memorize it and then tell it to your partner.

The Life of Penny Winner

- Penny start working / fast food chain / 17 / leave college / 16
- 18 / marry / husband, Cliff / met / at work / 24 / have three children
- one day / win / short story competition / win $500,000 / not have to work
- get bored / miss her workmates / go back / same job
- get promotion / start training new employees / be / something / always want to do
- continue / live / modest lifestyle / spend most / money / new home / donate rest to charity
- once / say / interview / owe / success to good luck / family / always support / decisions

3

File 21

Quiz answers:

Mostly a's: You're probably not very good at remembering jokes or stories and appreciate good conversation more than practical jokes. Although you have a fun side, you don't like jokes at other people's expense and sometimes criticize others for joking too much. Remember, a good sense of humour can often relieve stress and tension at work.

Mostly b's: You have a good sense of humour and enjoy listening to other people's jokes and amusing anecdotes. You are not a natural comedian but you probably enjoy watching TV sitcoms and telling funny stories about yourself when you are socializing with people.

Mostly c's: You have a very good sense of humour and are good fun to be with. You already know laughter can help to reduce stress. You often enjoy telling jokes or funny stories when you are socializing with people. You might not enjoy practical jokes in the office, but are happy for others to have fun while working.

Mostly d's: You have a strong sense of humour and are good at breaking the ice and helping others feel more relaxed with your amusing comments. You probably love watching TV sitcoms, playing practical jokes and poking fun at authority figures. But be careful not to make comments that may be too critical or personal – not everyone may share your particular sense of humour.

File 22

Student B:

Imagine you're sitting next to someone during brunch, lunch or dinner and you start making conversation. Choose two or three of these topics and tell your partner a one-minute story. Prepare your stories and check any vocabulary you don't know before you start.

1 your best holiday
2 a favourite relative
3 a time you moved house
4 a big disappointment
5 the day you got a scar
6 your first love

File 23

Student A:

Your preferred NGO is an organization that helps victims of natural disasters who have experienced earthquakes, floods or hurricanes.

You would like to organize a nine-hour line-dancing marathon where you work. You volunteer to be the coordinator but need two dancing instructors.

File 24

Score:								
1	a	3	b	1	c	4	d	2
2	a	1	b	3	c	4	d	2
3	a	3	b	2	c	2	d	4
4	a	4	b	1	c	3	d	2
5	a	3	b	1	c	2	d	4

17–20 points: You are either a 'green warrior' who is making significant changes in lifestyle to be more environmentally friendly or you have always used resources carefully. Perhaps sometimes your attitude is hard for people around you.

14–16 points: In general you try to recycle and the environment concerns you, but you don't want to make too many sacrifices. You'd prefer to find quick, easy solutions and don't mind paying a bit extra if necessary. You think it would be good if the government did more but you're also prepared to do your bit.

8–13 points: You are probably suffering from 'green fatigue'. You know all the environmental messages but you're tired of the contradictory information, and the fact that the effort you make is not having much impact. The ice caps are still melting and polar bears are disappearing. You think businesses and governments talk about the issues but there's no real action behind the words.

7 points and below: Clearly environmental issues are not a priority for you. It's someone else's problem and you're probably not convinced there is such a thing as global warming. You could try to consume less and save yourself some money.

File 25

Student A:

Read these conversations and report what the people said to your partner.

1 You: I'm very sorry but I sent you some personal photos by mistake.
   Client: Ah yes, the holiday photos. Don't worry, I've already deleted them.

2 MD: Actually, my name's pronounced, *Leigh Murray*.
   Employee: Oh, I do apologize.
   MD: That's all right. People often get it wrong. But it's my name.
   Employee: Yes, of course. I'm really sorry.
   MD: Just carry on, please.

5 You: Would you like some roast turkey?
   Guest: Not for me, thanks. I'm vegetarian, remember?
   You: Really?
   Guest: I'm sure I mentioned it to you.
   You: I'm so sorry. I completely forgot. Can I make you a cheese omelette or something?
   Guest: That'll be nice, thanks.

File 26

Student C:

Read your information and put your proposals to the group. Complete the 'Outcome' column and add some proposals of your own to the table.

Situation	Proposal	Outcome
Many walled offices have no natural light or outside views.	Redesign the offices and use glass walls.	*Improve staff well-being and productivity.*
People use a lot of disposable coffee cups.	Staff use their own cups and mugs.	
Office photocopiers are getting old.	Replace them with energy-efficient equipment.	

File 27

Student A: Lidia	Student B: Erik
Phone Erik and make some small talk.	
	Answer the call and make some small talk.
Ask if he received the latest user manual for the new software.	
	Confirm you got the user manual. Ask for the project proposals today – it's urgent.
Tell Erik you won't have all the project proposals until Friday – two missing.	
	Ask Lidia to phone the project managers to remind them about the proposals.
Agree to Erik's request.	
	Ask if the new software has been uploaded on the intranet.
Say you don't know but you'll look into it. Mention you'd like a face-to-face meeting with the team this year – to discuss some of the difficulties of working remotely.	
	Refuse Lidia's request – the travel budget has been cut. Confirm the videoconference for next Monday.
Ask Erik to send you the details of the videoconference.	
	Say you'll confirm the details in writing.
Ask Erik to confirm when he's going to be back in the office in Oslo.	
	Say you don't know. Thank Lidia and tell her she's doing a great job.

File 28

Student B:

1 Your colleague phones you. You want to go to the gym at lunchtime today and don't have much time. You are free Friday lunchtime.

2 You want to speak to the HR Manager. Your friend, Jeanne Malan, said you should call him about a job opening. This is the second time you're calling. Insist on talking to the manager.

3 You pick up the phone. Stella Morris is on a business trip. You are a student doing work practice in the legal department. Take a message.

4 This is an urgent call. If you can't speak to Maria Piccolo, you have to leave a detailed message. Your flight has been changed. Instead of arriving at 6.30 a.m. at the airport, you are arriving at 5.30 a.m. You need to know if Maria can still meet you at Milan airport, or if you should take a taxi. She can send you a text message, you'll have your mobile phone.

File 29

Answers:

1 Germany
2 Japan
3 Turkey
4 Saudi Arabia

File 30

Student B:

Ask your partners about dining in someone's house in Russia and India. When you have finished, change roles. Look at your information and answer questions about dining in Argentina.

Dining Etiquette in Argentina

- Dress well.
- Arrive 30–45 minutes later than invited for a dinner party. Arriving on time is not the norm.
- Wait for the host to tell you where to sit.
- Do not begin eating until the host does so.
- Keep your hands visible when eating but do not place your elbows on the table.
- It is considered polite to leave a small amount of food on your plate when you have finished eating.
- When you have finished eating, place your knife and fork across your plate facing to the right.
- Avoid pouring drinks – there are many cultural taboos about pouring wine.
- Telephone your hosts the following day to thank them.

File 31

Student A: Call 1

You are Claire, a customer service representative for Ritchie's. An angry customer calls you. He/She thinks he/she has been overcharged. Take the call and deal with the customer politely and professionally. Consider these points:

1 Take the customer's personal details and order number.

2 Explain that free delivery only applies to orders of over €50, (customers often misread the website).

3 Confirm that the customer has been charged correctly.

4 Be professional and sympathetic if the customer gets annoyed.

5 Thank the customer for calling.

Student A: Call 2

You placed an online order with the retailer Ritchie's. You have received an incorrect item. You wanted a brown top, not a blue one. You also ordered some brown trousers. Phone customer services to complain. Consider these points:

1 You will need to give your personal details and order number. Your order number is: # 582/412-97227*.

2 Explain that you wanted the brown top to go with the brown trousers. You don't want either of these items if one is not available.

3 Complain there was no note with the delivery.

4 Anything else? What? How annoyed are you? Will you say you won't place any more orders with Ritchie's if this happens again?

1 # = hash, / = slash, - = hyphen

File 32

Student B:

1 You are waiting in a café for a friend who is notoriously unpunctual. As usual he/she arrives 15 minutes late. It is a habit that really annoys you. Today you've decided you must tell him/her how it makes you feel always having to wait for him/her.

2 One of your suppliers hasn't sent an order on time as promised. They regularly deliver a week late and you are a bit frustrated by having to constantly phone them to follow up on orders. You want them to let you know in advance if there are going to be delays in future.

3 A member of your staff gave you a report to look at and feed back on a week ago. You haven't read it yet. What's more, it was sitting on your desk but now you can't find it.

4 You are a waiter/waitress in an expensive restaurant. It's a very busy night. You bring a customer the ice cream he/she eventually ordered for dessert after changing his/her mind several times.

File 33

Student B:

Your favourite charity is an organization based in your country that provides free veterinary care for the sick and injured pets of people who can't afford vets' fees, including guide dogs for the blind. Five per cent of donations go to administrative costs.

You would like to organize a 12 km marathon run in your town or city. You volunteer to coordinate it and would like your colleagues to run with you.

File 34

Student B:

You had a bad experience once at the hairdresser's.
- you went to a new hairdresser
- you wanted to have your hair dyed
- the hairdresser offered to straighten your hair as well
- he started by applying the lotion to the ends of your hair
- there was a strange smell and smoke started rising from your hair
- your hair started to disintegrate and the hairdresser started crying
- he quickly washed your hair to remove the lotion and you only lost the ends of your hair
- lesson(s) you've learnt …

Information files

File 35

Student B:

1 The first call on a mobile phone was made by Dr Martin Cooper of Motorola, in April 1973. He called his rival at AT&T's Bell Labs in New York.

2 In December 1992 _____ (what) was sent on Vodafone's network.

3 Around one billion text messages are sent worldwide each day.

4 Chatting on your mobile is forbidden _____ (where).

5 The train's windows are covered with a hi-tech material that blocks phone signals.

6 The world's most expensive mobile phone number is 666 6666. It was sold for 10m riyals ($2.75m) _____ (where).

7 The ring tone was first launched in Finland in 1998.

8 _____ (what?) on mobile phones was introduced in 1999 and was called i-Mode.

9 As early mobile phones were too large to carry they were installed in vehicles as car phones.

10 A standard charger for mobile phones was agreed in February 2009 by _____ (who?)

File 36

Student D:

Complete your role card. Introduce yourself and network with another person. Then move on and meet someone else.

You are a writer. You have written books about (…) and articles for various publications including (…). You have lived in different countries (…).

Your hobbies and interests are (…).

You aren't sure what to write your next book about.

You are looking for someone interesting to speak at your children's school.

File 37

Student B:

The finalists for the award are all staying in the same hotel. There is a party at the hotel for them to socialize the evening before the award ceremony. Decide if you are David Horn or Carla D'Silva. Make small talk with one of the other candidates. Talk about your travel experiences and the food and ask the other student questions.

File 38

Student B:

You are Susan's business partner Anton. Read the information and roleplay the conversation on your return from holiday.

You've just come back from a fantastic Caribbean cruise with your wife. You look tanned and feel relaxed. When you get to the office, Susan is looking stressed out.

- Tell Susan about your wonderful, relaxing holiday.
- Say sorry to Susan, but remind her that you haven't had a decent holiday for two years and you needed to dedicate some more time to your family.
- Ask her how work's going.
- Offer to phone the client to apologize and explain the situation.

File 39

Student C:

Ask your partners about dining in someone's house in Russia and Argentina. When you have finished, change roles. Look at your information and answer questions about dining in India.

Dining Etiquette in India

- Dress modestly and conservatively.
- Although Indians are not always punctual they expect foreigners to arrive at the appointed time.
- Take off your shoes before entering an Indian's house.
- Politely turn down the first offer of tea, coffee or snacks. You will be asked many times. Saying no to the first invitation is normal behaviour.
- There are meat restrictions for religious groups: Muslims do not eat pork and Hindus and Sikhs do not eat beef.
- It's best to wash your hands before and after the meal.
- It is impolite to eat or pass food with your left hand.
- Guests are served in a particular order: the guest of honour is served first, followed by the men and the children are served last. Women typically serve food and eat later.
- Leave a small amount on your plate to show you are satisfied. Finishing all your food means you are still hungry.

File 40

Suggestions:

You have reached _____ (your name) at _____ (name of company/organization). I'm sorry I can't take your call right now. But please leave a message (with your name and number) after the tone. And I'll get back to you as soon as I can.

Or:

You have reached _____ (name of company/organization). I'm afraid we can't take your call right now. Our office hours/ hours of operation are Monday to Friday from nine to five. Please leave a message after the tone/beep.

File 41

Student B:

Read these conversations and report what the people said to your partner.

3 Supplier: Oh dear, this toy doesn't seem to be working properly.

Buyer: Really? What seems to be the problem?

Supplier: Actually, I think the batteries are flat.

Buyer: Never mind. Here, use these.

4 Presenter: Erm, Today I was going to show you our sales figures for this quarter, but we seem to have a technical problem, so, instead, I'm going to tell you about our excellent sales team.

6 Trader: Have you got a moment?

Boss: What's up?

Trader: It's just that, er … I've made a terrible mistake. I'm really very sorry, but I've bought shares in olive oil from Italy.

Boss: You what?

Trader: I bought shares in olive oil, instead of the other kind of oil from the Middle East.

Boss: I don't believe it! How much will that cost us?

Trader: Maybe about uh … $100,000.

Boss: $100,000! Right, you're on trial until the end of the month. Another mistake like this, and you're out. Do you understand?

File 42

Student C:

You are a qualified electrician and take pride in your work.

- you worked for a company a few years ago
- they charged the customer €45 an hour
- you earned €20 an hour and they kept €25
- they insisted that every job had to take at least two hours
- you were instructed never to have the right tools or parts with you so you could leave the client's home and return later
- you weren't happy and left the company after a month
- lesson(s) you've learnt …

File 43

Congratulations! Your team won! Which prize will you choose?

- Tickets for a comedy show for all the team.
- A special day out for the team – where?
- €50 for each member of the team.
- Something else, what?

File 44

Student C:

Your favourite charity is a charity called Child's Play that provides toys, games and books for sick children in hospitals around the world. All contributions go directly to Child's Play.

You are interested in online games and would like to organize a Multiplayer Marathon in which gamers will play only multiplayer games for 36 hours non-stop. You volunteer to coordinate the event but need two helpers that are skilled in online games.

File 45

Student B: Call 1

You placed an online order with the retailer Ritchie's. You think you have been overcharged. You thought there was no delivery charge and that delivery was free for all orders. Phone customer services to complain. Consider these points:

1 You will need to give your personal details and order number. Your order number is: # 582/107-94036*.

2 Complain that you have been overcharged for your order: you thought delivery was free but you have been charged €8.50 for delivery.

3 Anything else? What? How annoyed are you? Will you ask for a refund, refuse to pay for delivery or say you won't place any more orders with Ritchie's?

* # = hash, / = slash, - = hyphen

Student B: Call 2

You are Claire, a customer service representative for Ritchie's. An angry customer calls you. He/She complains he/she has been sent the wrong items. Take the call and deal with the customer politely and professionally. Consider these points:

1 Take the customer's personal details and order number.

2 Explain that there are no brown tops in stock at the moment.

3 Point out there was a note with the delivery explaining that Ritchie's were offering the customer a 50% discount for the blue top.

4 Be professional and sympathetic if the customer gets annoyed.

5 Thank the customer for calling.

Audio scripts

1A, page 5, Exercises 7 and 8

1

What a journey! It always takes longer to get home on Tuesdays. And there's a meeting at the kids' school tonight. It starts at eight. I'm feeling exhausted but I'd better go. I'm taking the minutes this evening. I'd love to have a personal assistant or maybe a butler.

2

I think I'll get these ones … or the other ones. No, the other ones were hurting my toes. Ted's been complaining for the last half hour. Why can't he give me some advice? I'm going to leave him at home next time. I'd love to have a personal shopper. They could help me decide what to buy.

3

Oh dear. Well, that new diet didn't work. I've never been good at dieting … or exercise. I haven't had a chance to get to the gym this week. If I had someone to help me, I'd feel more motivated. I think I need a personal trainer.

1B, Page 6, Exercise 2

I = Interviewer, **M** = Mario, **A**= Alissa, **S** = Steve, **W** = Wanda

I: Commuting! For many people it means delays, overcrowding and stress. The average British commuter spends nearly an hour travelling to and from work every day, and for some it's two, three or more. So how do they survive their daily journeys? Today we're talking to travellers on London's commuter trains to find out. With me now is Mario, that's right, isn't it?

M: Yes, I'm Mario.

I: And what do you usually do while you're commuting?

M: I generally work on my laptop – check emails on my mobile phone – and I read.

I: Ah. What book are you reading at the moment?

M: Well, I'm not actually reading this book. I'm people watching today.

I: People watching?

M: Yeah, I'm writing a novel in my spare time so I'm looking at the other passengers and trying to imagine where they're going and what their life is like.

I: Well, let's speak to one of them and find out. OK, here we have …

A: Alissa. Nice to meet you.

I: Does it take you long to get to work, Alissa?

A: Yes. I don't usually take the train but my car's broken down.

I: So you're taking the train today.

A: Yeah.

I: What's the traffic on the roads like normally?

A: Terrible, so I'm enjoying the train ride today. I can close my eyes and relax.

I: Well, you can't do that in your car! And here's someone else enjoying the ride …

S: Steve. Hi.

I: Hi, Steve. I see you have an mp3 player. Do you listen to music while you're commuting?

S: I mostly listen to podcasts or if I'm not doing that then I daydream.

I: What are you daydreaming about at the moment?

S: Oh the usual – winning the lottery.

I: No wonder you look so happy. And sitting next to you is …

W: Call me Wanda, though my real name is Wendaline. I usually study on the train.

I: Uhuh.

W: I have to use my time productively because I'm taking an MBA course.

I: Are you studying for any exams at the moment?

W: Yes, I am. It's a stressful time. … I'm doing breathing exercises at the moment. You know, to help me relax.

I: How does that work then?

W: I'm focusing on breathing … in … out …

I: And there you have it. London's commuters are all finding ways to survive their journeys. So how do you manage to survive yours? Phone in and tell us about it …

1D, Page 10, Exercises 4 and 6

V = Valerie, **J** = Jay

V: Hi, Jay. Have you got a couple of minutes?

J: Sure Valerie. Is it about the new website?

V: Yeah, I got your email, thanks. So, we're two weeks behind schedule on this project. That's bad news!

J: Afraid so. There were lots of changes to the design and some people sent us new content very late. It's just one of those things.

V: I know, I know. Is there any way we can have the site ready for the first of May? It's very important.

J: How about asking someone to help us? What do you think?

V: Well, it's an interesting idea. Do you mean getting someone from another department?

J: No, I mean hiring an external contractor. We could have the site ready in time then.

V: Oh, I see.

J: My brother-in-law's a very good web designer. Why don't we ask him?

V: Um, I don't know. It sounds expensive.

J: I could talk to him today if you like.

V: Let's look at some other options first.

J: Oh, OK.

V: What about meeting a bit later to discuss this again?

J: Sure. I'm free after lunch.

V: Thanks Jay.

1E, page 12, Exercises 2 and 3

P = Presenter, **N** = Nancy

P: Nancy Bailey is here with us today to talk about life coaching. Nancy, I'm sure many of our listeners want to know what this is.

N: Well, to put it simply, it's called coaching because in many ways it's similar to sports coaching. People often know they want to make changes in their lives, but then usually don't do anything about it. We help people to be clear about what they really want out of life, and we help them to make the changes they need to make.

P: So, who are your clients?

N: Coaching started out as a service for company executives, but now it's basically for anyone who wants to make changes in their lives. I work with small business owners, people who want to change careers, people who are planning for their retirement and managers who want a better balance between work and home life.

P: How much time do you spend with a client?

N: It's very flexible. We do all our coaching over the phone. Typically, we talk to clients once a week for 30 or 40 minutes and also communicate by email. The client can be anywhere in the world. Of course, most of the real action happens between the calls. Our clients can do as much or as little as they want to make those changes.

P: So how long do you work with clients?

N: It depends. I generally work with clients for three to six months and most see results in that time. It's a very fast process. The bottom line is when you work with a coach, you can identify clearer objectives and get results faster than if you work alone.

1E, Page 12, Exercise 4

1
N = Nancy, **J** = Joe

N: Hi, Joe, how are you?

J: Hi, Nancy, very well thanks. And you?

N: Fine thanks. So, what do you want to talk about today? Shall we discuss your progress this week?

J: Yeah, sure. Things are definitely improving a lot at work. I'm feeling more relaxed and in control. The interruptions are becoming less of a problem – I'm using the strategies you suggested. And I'm learning to say 'no' nicely, when people ask me to do jobs that aren't a priority for me and my department.

N: Great! Tell me about the relationships with your team this week.

2
N = Nancy, **K** = Kim

N: Good evening, Kim. It's Nancy here.

K: Hiya, Nancy. Good to talk to you.

N: Do you want to talk about your homework for this week?

K: I'd love to. It was a really busy week, but I found the time to phone around a few colleges and get the information about courses.

N: Have you looked at it?

K: Yeah, I am so excited thinking about this. I really know I don't want to work in my parents' business forever, but it's taken me the longest time to decide what I really want to do. You know, the idea of being an interior designer really excites me.

N: That's great news, Kim.

1E, Page 13, Exercise 10

Vikram

I took Nancy's advice and hired an assistant to deal with the day-to-day business. She's doing a good job, very efficient. The only problem is that, er … she doesn't have the same personal touch as me. You see, she doesn't get on with staff at all levels in the company.

Ruth

I talked to my boss at the advertising agency as Nancy suggested. I asked if there was anything more interesting I could do. He thought I was bored and he's just given me more admin work. It wasn't what I wanted at all!

2A Page 14, Exercises 2 and 3

1
HL = Hong Li, **W** = Woman

HL: Excuse me, My name's Hong Li. I'm doing a passenger survey for the airport. I wonder if I could take a few minutes of your time.

W: Sure.

HL: Thank you. First of all, where are you travelling to today?

W: To London.

HL: For business?

W: Yes.

HL: Is business travel important for your job?

W: It is. I often travel for work. I'm going to meet the sales and marketing managers for my publishing company.

HL: Where are you going to stay in London? Near the airport?

W: No, in a hotel close to the city centre.

HL: What are you going to do at the airport today?

W: Well, there's free wireless internet access, so I'll probably check my email. Then, I'm going to charge my cellphone in the Business Centre. I forgot to do that last night.

HL: Technology follows us everywhere! Will you buy anything special for yourself?

W: Anything special! No, but I think I'll get a head and shoulder massage. I'm going to need it.

HL: Why's that?

W: Well, because my plane leaves early in the morning at around 5.30 and it's about 12 hours to London. I like to be relaxed on the flight.

HL: Thank you for talking to me today. Here's a complimentary voucher for the duty-free shops.

W: Thank you.

2
HL = Hong Li, **M** = Man

HL: Hello, my name's Hong Li. I'm doing a passenger survey for the airport. Can I ask you a few questions?

M: Yeah, sure. Why not?

HL: Thanks. So, where are you travelling to today?

M: To Malaysia, Kuala Lumpur.

HL: And what is the purpose of your trip?

M: See my family. I'm doing medical research in New York City, and I've been away from home for a year.

HL: Where are you going to stay?

M: Mostly with my parents and I'll probably visit other relatives, too.

HL: How long are you going to be there?

M: A whole month. It's a trip home. You know, I'm really looking forward to some home cooking.

HL: What are you going to do at the airport this evening? Will you buy anything special for yourself?

M: No! I am too tired. I'm in transit and my flight to KL doesn't leave until the morning. I don't want to pay for the round trip in to town and a room, so I'm going to stay here in the airport all night. Some restaurants are open 24 hours, so I'll get dinner. And I've found a lounge with comfy seats, and no armrests, near gate 61. But the airport's quite cold. I think I'll ask one of the airline staff for a blanket and pillow.

HL: Thank you very much for your time. Here's a complimentary voucher for the duty-free shops.

2D, Page 21, Exercise 6

K = Keith, **B** = Beatrice

K: I don't believe it! The queue for boarding is already a mile long. We're never going to get a good seat.

B: Oh, no. That's what you get when you travel with a budget airline.

K: Absolutely. You get what you pay for.

B: Still, the tickets were really cheap.

K: That's right. We got a great deal.

B: Well … maybe. But, is it really cheaper? There are all those extras we have to pay for – the extra bag, the credit card charge …

K: Yes and sandwiches on the plane.

B: Good point. I think these airlines should provide a better service.

K: Yeah, they should.

B: Shall we get in the queue?

K: It's twenty minutes till boarding. I think I'll buy a sandwich.

B: Good idea. I'll come with you.

2D, Page 21, Exercises 8 and 9

A: We need a simple clear rule that everyone can understand.

B: Mmm.

A: So from now on, everyone has to take the cheapest flight they can find …

B: …Yes?

A: So? … What do you think?

B: Well … erm … I'm not sure. What if the cheapest flight has several stops?

A: They should take it. It's the cheapest flight.

B: Yes, but what if it takes ten hours instead of three?

A: It doesn't matter. We have to get our flight costs down.

B: That's true, but productivity's important, too. If people spend a day travelling, they're not going to be working.

A: Everyone has laptops and most airports have wifi.

B: How about setting a limit? They take the cheapest flight available, but not if it adds more than six hours to their journey time.

A: That makes the rule more complicated.

B: I'm sorry, but I think this rule could cost us more money in the long run.

A: The cheapest flight is the cheapest flight.

B: Yes, but what I'm saying is it won't always save us money.

A: It's a simple rule that everyone can understand. It has to save us money.

B: I don't think that's true.

2E, Page 22, Exercises 3 and 4

M = Martin, **F** = Fay

M: So, while you interview your local business contacts, I'll go on the desert trip then, right?

F: Mmm, I'm not sure. Don't you think Thursday would be better for the desert trip? I mean together. I've got interviews all day Wednesday but we're both free on Thursday. I'd love to see the desert.

M: Well, I wanted to try sandboarding and maybe some er … dune bashing.

F: Dune bashing? What's that?

M: It's when you crash into sand dunes.

F: But won't you get a lot of sand in your eyes?

M: No, it's not like that, Fay. You're in a car, like a jeep or a four-by-four.

F: Oh, it sounds fun. I'd love to do that!

M: I don't know if that will be a good idea, Fay. I don't think it's your kind of thing. You know, you usually hate snowboarding and adventure sports.

F: No, I don't. Anyway, this is different. It's the desert! I'd love to go on a camel ride – you could take pictures of me. And we'll spend the night in a tent.

M: Well, all right then. But don't complain to me when you get covered in sand. There won't be any luxury bathrooms or hairdryers or anything.

F: Don't worry. I'll manage. So, will you change the booking to Thursday for two?

M: I suppose so. And I might do some more sightseeing on Wednesday.

F: Great. You know, Martin, we're visiting the Burj Al Arab hotel on Friday. It's seven stars and it's a fantastic building that looks like a sail. Shall we have dinner there?

M: Yeah, but it's very pricey. To be honest, I don't think we'll be able to afford it. I've already got permission to take photos inside, remember? But I'd love to get some shots from the beach at sunset.

F: Mmm, I see they do afternoon tea. We don't need to have dinner there.

M: Well, you can schedule it in but let's see how it goes when we're in Dubai. I don't want to pay a huge bill just for a cup of tea!

F: All right. I'll pencil it in, OK?

M: Fine.

F: Friday – tea and watch sunset at the Burj Al Arab hotel.

3A, Page 24, Exercise 2

I was applying for a really good job with a great company. My potential boss wanted to meet me at a restaurant for lunch. The interview was going well until they brought our food. This man had the most awful table manners I have ever seen. He was dropping food on his shirt, eating with his fingers and making a terrible mess! I was shocked. I didn't get the job and I'm sure it was because I couldn't speak. I was too distracted by his table manners.

3A, Page 24, Exercise 3

There's no tidy way to eat lobster. You have to break the shells and to work at it to get all the meat out. So I take job candidates to a seafood restaurant, order lobster and show great enthusiasm eating it. Then I watch their reactions. If they dislike my way of eating a lobster, I know I don't want to work with them. I want people who roll up their sleeves and get the job done. A lobster meal is a great way to find out who to hire.

3B, Page 26, Exercises 2 and 3

B = Barbara, **R** = Richie, **V** = Street vendor

B: Isn't this night market great?

R: Yeah. Hey, I've heard we should try the balut.

B: What's balut, Richie?

R: It's a popular snack here. Just look out for a street vendor selling them.

B: But what IS balut?

R: Ah look, here you go!

B: Ah, they're big eggs. What sort are they?

V: These are duck balut. Want to try? It's very tasty.

B: Are they cooked? I can't eat raw egg.

V: Yes, they're boiled. You want 12-day, 16-day or 18-day?

B: Sorry? What do you mean?

R: Look Barbara, I think I should warn you, it's a fertilized egg with an embryo inside.

B: What! Oh, no, not for me, thanks.

V: It's a local delicacy. Please, try it.

R: I'll give it a go. Which would you suggest?

V: 18-day is the king of balut. You crack open the shell like this and then eat it with a pinch of salt. …

R: OK, here we go. …

B: So, what's it like?

R: It's very good. It's quite chewy. It's like a normal boiled egg cooked with a bit of meat. Not bad at all for a midnight snack.

3B, Page 26, Exercises 4 and 5

R = Richie, **E** = Enrique

R: This is one of my favourite restaurants in Sydney. I hope you like it.

E: The location is fantastic. I really wanted to see Bondi Beach and it's nice to eat outside on the terrace. This menu looks interesting. I've never eaten crocodile or kangaroo before. What would you recommend?

R: For the entrée I usually have the crocodile carpaccio with a side order of green salad.

E: OK, that sounds good. I think I'll have the same.

R: For the main course, you could try the grilled emu or the kangaroo steak if you want to try something new.

E: What's emu?

R: It's a sort of big, funny-looking bird we have here. It can't fly. It's similar to an ostrich.

E: What does it taste like? Chicken?

R: No, it's like beef, only it's healthier. Apparently, it has, er … fewer calories and less fat.

E: Really? And what about the kangaroo?

R: That kind of tastes like beef, too, only it's tougher. The emu's more tender.

E: OK, I'll have the emu then.

R: Do you want to order any side dishes?

E: I don't know. What does it come with?

R: Um, you know, I don't remember. Let's get the waitress over and ask her.

E: What are you having for the main course?

R: Well, I've had a lot of red meat recently so I'm going for the white fish. Excuse me, hello …

3B, Page 26, Exercises 6 and 7

R = Richie, **E** = Enrique, **B** = Barbara

R: Glad you could make it to the barbie, Enrique.

E: Thank you for the invitation. I've heard a lot about the traditional Australian barbecue. People eat lots of meat, don't they?

R: Yeah, well, it's changed. It's more prawns than steak these days, mate.

E: Why's that?

R: Everyone's getting more health conscious. Hey, I'd like you to meet my wife. Barbara this is Enrique. He's here from the Philippines on business.

B: Hi, Enrique.

E: Pleased to meet you.

B: Did Richie tell you about the time we went to the Philippines and he tried that duck egg?

E: Balut? Did you like it?

R: Yeah, it was great. Listen guys, I'm going to check on the barbie.

E: Can I help you with anything, Barbara?

B: No, I'm fine thanks. Help yourself to the salads. Is there anything you don't eat?

E: Well, I'm not allergic to anything, but is there any onion in the salads? I can't eat it, you see, it repeats on me.

B: No worries, there isn't any.

E: This looks good. What's in it?

B: Ah, I wouldn't eat that with your salad, Enrique, it's the chocolate mousse for dessert. …

E: OK, thanks for warning me.

3D, Page 30, Exercise 4

Conversation 1

G = guest, **H** = host

G: Is that the check? Let me get that.

H: Oh no. This is on me.

G: No, no. Why don't we split it?

H: No, no. I insist. You're our guest.

G: Are you sure?

H: Yes, the company's paying.

G: Well, that's very kind of you.

H: It's our pleasure.

G: Well, thank you very much. It was a terrific meal.

H: I'm glad you enjoyed it. Don't forget your doggy bag.

Conversation 2

H = host, **G** = guest

H: Have some more paella.

G: No, no. It was terrific, but I couldn't manage any more.

H: Some more shrimps then?

G: No really, I'm full. I'm trying to diet.

H: You don't need to lose weight!

G: I do!

H: Just a few more?

G: Well … maybe just a few then.

H: Good, and a little more paella?

G: No really. I'll have to pass on that, but thank you.

3D, Page 31, Exercise 8

G = Gabriella

G: Hello.

G: Sandy! Great to hear from you. How are you?

G: Not too bad. How's Peter?

G: Oh, nothing exciting. I've got some exams coming up so I'm studying all weekend.

G: Oh … I don't think I can. Sunday, you say?

G: It sounds great, but I have two exams the next day – Marketing and Accounting.

G: I'm really sorry but I have to study.

G: Thanks for thinking of me. Look, when my exams are over, perhaps you and Peter can come over to my place for a meal?

G: OK, choose a restaurant you want to go to and it'll be my treat.

G: No, no, I insist. It'll be your birthday present.

G: OK, I will. And have a lovely birthday on Sunday.

G: Bye.

3D, Page 31, Exercises 10 and 11

G = Gabriella, **S** = Sandy

G: Hello.

S: Hi, Gabriella, it's Sandy.

G: Sandy! Great to hear from you. How are you?

S: Pretty good thanks and you?

G: Not too bad. How's Peter?

S: Oh, same as ever. Listen, what are you doing this Sunday?

G: Oh, nothing exciting. I've got some exams coming up so I'm studying all weekend.

S: Can you take a break? It's my birthday and I'm having a party.

G: Oh … I don't think I can. Sunday, you say?

S: Yes, we're just inviting a few close friends and Peter's cooking lasagne.

G: It sounds great, but I have two exams the next day – Marketing and Accounting.

S: Oh, what a pity.

G: I'm really sorry but I have to study.

S: It's OK, I understand.

G: Thanks for thinking of me. Look, when my exams are over, perhaps you and Peter can come over to my place for a meal?

S: That'd be nice. Or we could all go out to a restaurant together.

G: OK, choose a restaurant you want to go to and it'll be my treat.

S: Oh, no. We'll pay for ourselves.

G: No, no. I insist. It'll be your birthday present.

S: No, you don't have to do that. Let's talk about it later. Go and get on with your studying and make sure you pass the exams.

G: OK, I will. And have a lovely birthday on Sunday.

S: I will. Take care. Bye now.

G: Bye.

4B, Page 38, Exercises 2 and 3

RS = Recruitment specialist, **A** = Job seeker 1, **B** = Jobseeker 2

RS: We all know that employers are looking for job-specific skills when they advertise a vacancy. But there are also certain skills that they're looking for in all their staff. They're what we sometimes call 'soft' skills or 'people' skills. Can anyone suggest what some of these might be?

A: Good communication?

RS: That's exactly right. One of the most important soft skills is communication. Employers want people who are able to express their thoughts well, both when speaking and when writing. They don't want someone who can't spell or speak coherently. And let's not forget, the other part of communication is being a good listener. Any other ideas?

B: Getting on with people is important.

RS: Yes, isn't it? You know, there are all kinds of personalities in a work environment and you need to be able to communicate with all of them to work as part of a team. We're talking about good interpersonal skills here.

A: I think they'd want someone to be organized.

RS: I agree. Organizational skills are also essential. Employers rarely want someone who is messy or disorganized. If you're able to maintain a tidy workplace without leaving piles of paper everywhere, they know your work habits and time management will be more efficient. Great!

There are three more soft skills I would add: firstly, the ability to do research. If you can find out about the company and make a good impression at the interview, it can help you to get the job. But that's not all. In most jobs you'll need to be able to research answers to questions as well as find data for your manager. Companies basically want people who are self-sufficient when they get a task like this to do.

Next comes analytical skills and the ability to think logically. Being able to look at routine problems and using your common sense to make good decisions is a part of most jobs.

Finally, you know, employers want people who have thought about their career growth. I mean, someone who is prepared to improve professionally by learning new things. The good news is that if you think you're weak in some of these areas, you can always get some training to help you improve. Any questions so far?

4C, Page 40, Exercises 2 and 3

Mark

I never enjoyed studying when I was at school. I failed most of my exams and left at sixteen. I became a driving instructor and I've never needed many qualifications. But when my children started going to school, I wanted to be able to help them with their homework, so I started studying again.

I studied on my own at first. I got into computers, and taught myself how to do some programming and how to upgrade the hardware for the business.

Going from that to studying online was a natural progression. I've always been fascinated by law, so I signed up for a law degree with the Open University two years ago. I can't take time off work and studying online is much more flexible than attending full-time classes.

I can choose how much I want to study every year, which is a big advantage. It's also a bit cheaper than a traditional course.

Last year, our oldest son, Nathan, got a place at one of the best universities in the country to study law as well. We're very proud of him. So, you see, there are two students in our family at the moment!

Nathan says the worst part for him is all the exams. My course is less stressful because it's mostly continuous assessment.

I don't learn as quickly as him, as you can imagine. Let's face it, studying for a degree when you're young is easier than at my age. Fortunately, I can take it more slowly. I'll probably retire before I graduate.

It would be easy to give up. I'm just doing it for fun and to encourage my kids to be good students. But I'd like to carry on. I hope Nathan completes his course, but if he does drop out, he knows he can study online, like his dad, if he wants to.

4E, Page 44, Exercise 2

Karen

I work in the R&D department. I think I'm very hard-working, but my boss tells me I'm a bit shy and lack confidence. She says I need to improve my communication skills. I always get nervous when I have to attend meetings. Actually, my boss doesn't speak very good English, so she always wants me to go with her when she has to negotiate product requirements with our clients. I prefer writing emails, although I know I need to be more confident when talking to people.

Ricardo

I help staff with any IT problems they have. I get on with everyone at work and I'm pretty good at what I do, but the job's getting a bit boring. The trouble is, I don't have any formal qualifications. I'm basically self-taught. But I'm 30 now and my girlfriend says it's a good idea to get a university degree. That way, I could get promoted and earn more money. I suppose I could work part-time and study but I'm not sure. If I study, I won't have time to do sports – and I love skiing and playing golf.

Nadia

I think I have quite a lot of work experience at 46. I also speak fluent Swedish, Russian and German, but I really need to improve my presentations skills in English. I have to travel a lot for work, and I sometimes give presentations at international conferences in the languages I know. The thing is, the company has now asked me to go to China for six months and I don't speak Chinese! But I'm worried that if I say no, I might lose my job.

4E, Page 45, Exercise 4

O = Oskar, **K** = Karen

O: Hi, Karen. As you know, I'm talking to everybody about their training needs and the courses you're interested in. Have you had any thoughts?

K: Well, I would like to do something to, er … improve my confidence and er … my communication skills.

O: Uhuh, so, which course do you want to sign up for?

K: Uh, my boss recommends the Assertiveness course, but I'm also interested in Presentations Across Cultures.

O: Yes, but do you have to give presentations in your job now, Karen?

K: No, not really.

O: Then it might be better to do a simpler course.

K: Yes, but I'd like to be able to participate more in meetings and be more confident when speaking in public, you know.

O: So you don't feel comfortable in meetings?

K: To be honest, I find it difficult but I know it's something I need to improve. Actually, I think it might be a good idea if I do both courses.

O: Two courses?

K: Yeah, if that's OK with you. Assertiveness and er … Presentations Across Cultures.

O: The thing is, a&k will definitely pay for one of the courses, but I'm afraid we won't be able to pay for both courses. You see, the situation is they're cutting the training budget this year and they're only going to pay for one course per employee for members of staff at your level.

K: Oh, so what happens if I want to do another course?

O: Well, one option is that you pay for the course yourself. Another possibility is that you wait until next year and do the presentations course then. What I'm saying is, you don't really need to do the presentations course at the moment, do you?

K: Not right now, no. I don't know. Maybe I could pay for the course myself?

O: Yes. That could be the best solution if you'd like to do both courses.

K: Yes, and it will benefit the company, too, because I think I'll be able to contribute more in meetings.

O: Great. So, we've agreed that you'll sign up for both courses, and we'll pay for one of them. I don't think there will be a problem with that. But let me check with the Human Resources Director and I'll get back to you.

K: Will you able to let me know soon, Oskar?

O: Yeah, sure. I'll put that in writing to the director and copy you in, OK?

K: Sounds good.

O: And if you have any more questions, Karen, you know where I am.

K: Thanks.

5C, Page 50, Exercises 5 and 6

1
Are you going to watch the match on Saturday?

2
Can you believe the rain we're having this week?

3

Have you heard the news about the physics experiment in Switzerland?

4

I hear that the big boss is coming from France next week.

5

What do you think of that new shopping centre?

6

Have you seen the beautiful spring flowers outside the office?

5C, Page 50, Exercises 9 and 10

Conversation 1

P = Paul, M = Marco

P: Hi, Marco, it's Paul. Sorry to call you first thing on a Monday morning. It's about a problem we're having with this new database.

M: I'm sorry to hear that. What seems to be the problem?

P: You see we can't get access to all the fields. Is some of it password protected?

Conversation 2

M = Marco, P = Paul

M: Hi, Paul, it's Marco here. How are you? I hear the weather's been bad up north recently.

P: That's right. It's been snowing heavily, and apparently some villages had no electricity.

M: Did it affect you?

P: No, not much, happy to say. Didn't play football on Saturday, that's about all. And yourself? Did you have a good weekend?

M: Fine, thanks. Just relaxed with the family, and I had lunch with my in-laws on Sunday. Anyway, Paul, I was just phoning to check if you've tried out the modified version of that database.

P: Yes, we're working on it now in fact. It all seems to be working fine.

5D, Page 52, Exercise 2

1

Hi! How's it going?

2

You must be Günter. I'm Miriam from R&D. It's nice to finally put a face to a voice.

3

Hi. I don't think we've met before. I'm Sandra Mendelssohn.

4

Hey, what's up?

5

Hi, you're David, Carla's assistant, aren't you?

6

Hello, Irina. Mind if I join you?

5E, Page 54, Exercises 1 and 2

Part one

P = Presenter, Z = Zahir

P: Zahir Rahman has received many social enterprise awards. I spoke to him earlier today. Zahir, what is a social enterprise?

Z: It's basically an organization that provides goods or services like any other business, and uses the same business strategies.

P: So, how are social enterprises different from a commercial business?

Z: Well, like the name suggests, they focus on social causes and needs. It's central to what we do. But er, one of the main differences is that er, with social enterprise the profits generated are put back into the business rather than going into the pockets of owners or shareholders.

P: Can you give me some examples?

Z: Sure. For instance, it can be a company that promotes better health. There are lots and lots of examples all over the world. It could be a company that helps old people. Another example is a company that provides transport for remote communities. Some people talk about 'not-for-profit' organizations, but I prefer to call it 'more-than-profit'. It doesn't mean not for money, but the money's going back into the quality of service.

5E, Page 54, Exercise 3

Part two

P = Presenter, Z = Zahir

P: You started selling solar panels to poor communities in your native Bangladesh ten years ago, and today you have more than 180,000 customers. You call yourself a social entrepreneur. What does that mean exactly?

Z: I like to think I'm an innovator. A social entrepreneur is someone who identifies a social problem and then organizes and manages a business that will make change.

P: You studied economics. So, what made you want to be a social entrepreneur?

Z: I wanted to do some good, something ethical. Just making money isn't enough for me. When I left the US twelve years ago and came back home, I had very little money. I moved to a rural area, and lived in a house without electricity because I wanted to find out what it was like in those conditions. That gave me the idea for my first business. Having very little money helped me to be more innovative.

P: What projects are you working on now?

Z: Well, I've just started a low-cost mobile phone company. The batteries are solar powered. It's a very exciting project.

5E, Page 55, Exercise 9

David Horn

We're hoping to get a contract with a music company. The idea is that sales from our music will go back into the orchestra. I also plan to set up similar projects in poor communities in other parts of the country. But the most immediate project for us is to give concerts in other countries. Can you imagine how exciting this travel experience will be for these youngsters?

Carla D'Silva

I would like to create sculpture gardens on neglected land, something the local community can be proud of. If I win this award and get publicity, the local council will be more interested in working with us. I would also like to expand the art therapy to prisoners and I've already had a lot of interest from the prison service. And I want to open a café at the arts centre to get more people coming here.

Sally Warren

This award will bring us a lot of prestige. We want to negotiate with other local councils to run their sports and leisure facilities for them. We have shown our ability to run a profitable business and cut costs without cutting quality in three centres already. But most of all, we want to take sport to everyone in the community.

Jamie Barnes

I want to continue expanding the chain of restaurants in London. And set up a catering service for companies and individuals. It will be run as a commercial business just like the restaurants, and we'll also train apprentices at the same time. I'm also thinking of selling my own range of food. This will create more jobs.

6B, Page 58, Exercises 2 and 3

1

My first boss was a doctor before she went into hospital management. I was only an admin assistant in the department, but she sometimes mentioned my research and contribution to her reports when we were in meetings with other managers. She didn't have to do it but she often thanked her staff and always shared the credit with us.

2

Our office manager encourages us to work independently so he's not keeping an eye on what we do all day long. The only problem is that my co-worker is really lazy and she keeps chatting on the phone to her friends and spending too much time on Facebook. Last week, we needed to prepare a presentation and I had to do most of it. I'm tired of doing her work as well as my own, but our manager doesn't seem to notice.

3

I once worked for a small marketing company and I shared an office with my boss, who just loved sending me emails. It was a bit strange. I could understand it when she was out of the office, but she didn't need to email me when she was sitting opposite me. Why didn't she just tell me the information I needed to know?

4

I once worked in a large open-plan office, but our section head put lots of partitions and plants around himself – to hide from us I think. He only spoke to the supervisors and not the rest of his staff. And he had some strange rules. Like, we had to speak to each other very quietly, and we weren't allowed to laugh because he said it was unprofessional. As you can imagine, they didn't keep staff for long in that department.

5

My boss has young children herself and values her free time. She knows how to keep her team happy. We don't need to work late often, but when there is something urgent or really important, like the monthly sales figures, nobody minds too much staying to get the work done.

6B, Page 59, Exercises 7 and 8

M = Marianne, **N** = Nicole

M: Did you watch *Mad Men* last night?

N: Is that the show about some advertising executives?

M: Yeah, that's the one. It's set in New York in the 60s.

N: Why's it called '*Mad Men*'?

M: They work in an ad agency on Madison Avenue.

N: Oh, yeah, I've heard of it. But I haven't seen it yet.

M: You must! It's great. It took me a few episodes to really connect with the show, but I love it now.

N: Why do you like it?

M: Lots of things; brilliant dialogues, amazing acting and it feels really authentic. You see what society was like in the sixties. In those days people were allowed to smoke at their desks, and everybody smokes a lot. And all the men had to wear smart suits, ties and hats to the office. The women's clothes and make-up are amazing, too. They're so glamorous.

N: Sounds interesting.

M: It is. The most interesting part is the lives of the female characters. You know, women were basically second-class citizens and had to fight a lot harder then. They usually had to work as telephone operators or secretaries, or be the perfect housewife and stay at home with the kids. And at work, the secretary had to make the coffee, and give the boss his hat and coat when he left for the day. It makes me realize how far we've come in society.

N: I'm glad those days are over!

6D, Page 62, Exercises 2 and 4

Conversation 1

K = Kelly, **R** = Robert

K: Robert, I have a question. I want to ask Kristof for a few days off next month but I think he'll say no. It's one of our busy periods. I wonder what I should say to him.

R: Maybe you could just tell him why you need to have the time off.

K: OK, I'll try that.

R: And you might want to make sure your work is up-to-date before you go away.

K: Yes, that's a good idea. And I'll tell Kristof I'll do that.

R: And what you could do is leave information with me, you know, so I can cover for you. Tell Kris I'll take care of things, no problem.

K: Really? That's excellent. Thanks Robert. I'll do the same for you some day.

R: You're welcome. What do you need time off for, by the way?

K: I'm going away with my husband, without the kids. We need a break.

R: Well, good luck with Kristof.

Conversation 2

K = Kelly, **J** = Jake

K: You know that job interview I went for last week.

J: Yeah, did you get the job?

K: Well, I dunno. I haven't heard from them yet. But I thought the interview went really well. Do you think I should phone them?

J: No, don't do that yet. It'd be better to send them a thank-you note first.

K: A thank-you note? You must be joking!

J: No seriously, that's pretty standard in the States. An email will do. Then you follow up with a phone call.

K: Oh, no. I don't think that would work. We don't do that here.

J: Oh, OK. I think you should phone them then.

K: Yeah, perhaps. I'll give it another couple of days.

6D, Page 63, Exercise 9

Conversation 1

A: If you want to improve your English, I think you should study abroad for a couple of months. Maybe in San Diego. I know a family there you could stay with.

B: That's a great idea!

Conversation 2

A: What you could do is go on holiday in November. You can get really good deals at that time of year.

B: Yeah, perhaps we should do that.

Conversation 3

A: Ask someone to check your resume for you. It might help to get a second opinion.

B: Maybe, but I'm not sure who to ask.

Conversation 4

A: Well, it'd be better to get a laptop. You can take it with you wherever you go. No one uses PCs these days.

B: That sounds like a good idea.

Conversation 5

A: Maybe you could move to a better area if you want your kids to go to a good school.

B: Yeah, but I don't think we can afford to move house.

Conversation 6

A: You might want to write the report in French, seeing that it's a French client.

B: Mmm, my French isn't very good. I'll think about it.

6E, Page 64, Exercises 3 and 5

Julia

I was really excited about my first day and a bit nervous, too, because I'd never had a job before. When I got there I was shown to my desk and given things to do, but I wasn't really shown around or introduced. It was a busy office so I decided it was up to me to get to know everyone. To break the ice I went round asking the people in my team if they wanted a cup of tea. We soon got chatting and my nerves disappeared! I think that the key to a good first day in a new job is to make sure people know who you are. Don't be afraid to introduce yourself. It means you're included from the start, and even if not everybody's friendly at first, at least it's a start.

Saul

I could hardly sleep the night before my first day at the engineering firm. I was so tired that I kept getting things wrong when I was left to do something. Getting stuff wrong made me even more nervous and I couldn't really take in what was being said to me. I thought I was in trouble when my boss called me into his office, but he actually said that he could see I was nervous and that he would team me up with somebody the next day. Being partnered with someone more experienced was just what I needed. After that, it got loads better. Because I was being shown what to do by somebody I felt more included and learned a lot more.

7C, Page 73, Exercise 6

P = Presenter, **A1** and **A2** = Members of the audience

P: We asked everyone coming to the website to tell us which country they were from. Then we studied the data from the ten countries that rated the highest number of jokes.

There were some interesting differences between nations in terms of the jokes they found funny. For instance, people from The Republic of Ireland, the UK, Australia and New Zealand liked jokes involving a play on words – you know – where a word has two meanings. Americans and Canadians preferred jokes which make fun of someone's sense of superiority – so jokes where someone looked stupid, or was made to look stupid.

Many European countries, such as France, Denmark and Belgium, liked jokes that were a bit surreal. Do you know what I mean? European countries also enjoyed jokes about topics that often make us feel anxious, such as death, illness and marriage, like this one:

A woman told her friend, 'For eighteen years my husband and I were the happiest people in the world! Then we met.'

The other interesting thing about humour is that it's all about timing. … Our computers recorded the time that each person rated the jokes. We then looked at the data and examined how the way people found jokes funny changed over the course of the day. It seems people find the jokes funniest at six in the evening …

A1 and A2: Really? At six?

P: Yes, and they found a joke is least funny at half past one in the morning. People also found jokes funnier at different times during the month. They were the funniest on the fifteenth and less funny towards the end or start of the month. … So, if you want to make people laugh, tell a joke on the fifteenth of the month, at six in the evening!

And finally, many of the jokes people sent were about animals. We found that jokes about ducks are funnier than others. Why do you think that is?

A1: Perhaps it's because of their feet, and their funny walk.

A2: Or the funny sound they make?

P: That's right. Anyway, if you are going to tell a joke about an animal, make it a duck. *Quack, quack.*

7C, Page 73, Exercise 7

A couple of hunters are out in the woods when one of them suddenly falls to the ground. He doesn't seem to be breathing and his eyes are rolled back in his head. So the other guy quickly takes out his cellphone and calls the emergency services. He shouts to the operator: 'My friend is dead! My friend is dead! What can I do?' The operator says: 'Calm down. I can help. First, let's make sure he's dead.' There is a silence, and then a shot is heard. Bang! The hunter's voice comes back on the line. The guy says: 'OK, now what?'

7D, Page 74, Exercises 2 and 4

Part one
B = Ben, **G** = Georgia

B: Mmm, did I tell you about the time I went on a bike ride at night?

G: No, what happened?

B: Well, I have a friend who's really into cycling and he once said, 'Come on, Ben! Go on a night ride with us.' My wife has a bike so I took it out that night. Three of his friends were there who were sort of super jocks.

G: Really athletic, huh?

B: Yeah, but they immediately started laughing. Apparently, I have a girl's mountain bike …

G: Really?

B: Yeah, I didn't know … Anyway, they started putting on elbow pads and all this protective clothing … and I was dressed in my shorts and T-shirt … and then they started putting on their helmets, like those helmets that have lights on them …

G: Like the ones you use for camping.

B: That's right. So, we started going along this road by the ocean and it was great. The moon was out … We'd gone three miles and I was getting kind of tired but I was enjoying it, …

G: So, what happened next?

7D, Page 74, Exercises 3 and 5

Part two
B = Ben, **G** = Georgia

B: After we'd gone five miles, we got to the top of this hill and everybody got off their bikes. I was thinking, 'Yes! We did it'. But then they started checking their bikes and gear and pulling out Powerbars, you know, those high energy cereal bars. And I said, 'What's going on?' and they said, 'Well, we're ready to start now'.

G: You mean, you'd just started!

B: Uhuh. And one guy, who's super-serious, just looked at me and said, 'Whatever happens, don't fight the mountain.'

G: Don't fight the mountain? You're kidding!

B: I had no idea what it meant but it scared me … And as they were going down the hill, I was falling behind.

G: They were too fast for you.

B: That's right, but I got this adrenaline rush and I was doing OK and I could hear them up ahead, shouting 'Come on, Ben!' and I suddenly heard one of them yell out, 'No brunch! No brunch!' And I think, this is some kind of biking term. I mean, we're going so well, we're not gonna stop to eat the Powerbars now. So I'm thinking, 'Yeah! No brunch! No brunch!' Then I look up and suddenly there is this great, big tree in front of me!

G: Oh no!

B: And you know they say when an accident happens everything slows down, you go in slow motion and you do whatever it takes to save yourself in that moment?

G: Yeah.

B: That didn't happen! So I slammed right into it … and as I came to, they were all looking at me saying, 'Ben, didn't you hear? We were shouting low branch!'

G: Oh, I see! Low *branch*, not *brunch*! … That's so funny … Actually, that reminds me of the time I went for a midnight swim with some friends …

7E, Page 76, Exercises 3 and 4

Sam Harris
Part one

Let me tell you a bit about myself. I have a problem: I can't stop setting up online businesses. I'm basically a serial e-commerce entrepreneur, which is my real passion. In 1998, I started one of the UK's first price comparison websites. Then I became a co-founder of a clothing online retailer.

But today I'd like to tell you about Instant Desks. We can make a desk appear like magic. It's our new business venture and it's already profitable. Well, we haven't lost any money … yet. Don't you think that's great? Most start-ups don't make any money in their first year.

7E, Page 77, Exercise 5

Part two

At Instant Desks we bring together businesses with spare desks with people who want to rent desks. If your mum is an entrepreneur, consultant, graphic designer or any other kind of freelancer, and she would like to rent some desk space with similar kinds of people – then she should use our site. Professionals, who we call 'deskers', can move into an office with interesting colleagues, where they'll have access to not only a desk, but also a broadband connection, a meeting room and other facilities. We can also help companies who are hoping to make a bit of extra money and want to rent out some spare desks.

So, how does Instant Desks work? The site has a really simple search engine. Enter the city or postcode of the area where you need desk space and how far you want to travel. You'll then get descriptions of desk spaces that are available in that area, complete with photos and maps. And if you're an advertiser, you just need to fill in details of where your office is, how much you want to charge for the work space and add anything else like descriptions of printers, the type of people who work there, tea and coffee facilities, that kind of thing. Don't worry, it doesn't take long – the site is incredibly user-friendly.

Right. You're probably thinking, 'How much does it cost?' The great thing about Instant Desks is it's absolutely free. It will always be free for people looking for desk space. And there's only a small fee for advertisers. We charge according to the number of completed forms or phone calls a company receives from people who might become deskers or customers. Any questions?

8A, Page 78, Exercises 3 and 4

Part one
P = Presenter, **E** = Erik

P: Has your organization gone green? If so, it is one of a few. According to a recent international survey, 80% of the world's businesses are still trying to work out what sustainability means to them. Earlier today I spoke to Erik Andersson, a consultant and expert on green business.

E: Now is the perfect time for businesses to go green. The typical first action to take is to work out how to use less electricity and reduce energy costs. If you replace your old light bulbs with low-energy ones, it can cut your electricity bills drastically and make the Finance Officer very happy.

Switch to more eco-friendly, fuel-efficient cars if you have a fleet of company vehicles. Many companies now buy energy efficient equipment as well.

Another typical move is to do something with all that stuff in the wastepaper bins. If you launch a recycling scheme, it probably won't save you money, but it will help to engage your employees and to win the all-important approval of your customers. Companies are also starting to buy part of their electricity supply from renewable sources, such as wind and solar power. Unless you have a lot of time and money, it makes sense to start with these simple initiatives.

8A, Page 79, Exercise 9

Part two
P = Presenter, **R** = Robyn, **K** = Kevin

P: The experts agree that easy measures such as energy-efficient lighting or recycling schemes can only produce limited results. The search engine Google is one corporation that is taking green initiatives to the next level. Robyn Beavers leads the company's Green Business and Operations Strategy team in California. I spoke to her by phone.

R: We use a lot of electricity and it just seems like the responsible thing to do, to show that a corporation can make a positive impact on the environment, but also that we can do it in a way that makes sense for our business. For instance, our large solar installation was a major project. Nine thousand solar panels now cover the rooftops of our headquarters Googleplex. These produce renewable energy without greenhouse gas emissions and provide 30% of the power we need at peak times. It makes good business as well as environmental sense. We'll earn our investment back in seven and a half years, and after that, we'll have cheap power for decades.

P: The company finds ways to engage its staff, too. Google donates money to charity if employees ride their bikes, walk or skateboard to work. It manages shuttle buses to carry Googlers to and from work and provides benefits for those who car share or take the train. And if they must use a car, the company encourages them to use an eco-friendly version, offering a cash incentive to staff who drive fuel-saving hybrid cars.

And it's not just large corporations that are making the transition to sustainable business. PB Copy, a two-man digital printing operation in Surrey, Canada, has found an innovative way to go green. The owners, Kevin LaHay and Shane Fortune, have connected an exercise bicycle to a battery pack to generate power for their office equipment. I spoke to Kevin LaHay.

K: We put in a couple of hours a day on the bike in the winter months. On days with lots of sunshine, our solar panels are able to generate most of the power to charge the batteries. If you pedal for ten minutes, it'll power 100 copies on the digital printer. When the battery is full, it can power three to four hours of printing. We ask customers to participate by riding the bike for a few minutes while they're waiting for their copies. They usually think we're joking but most people agree when they see we're being serious.

P: Combining this with two solar panels means 90 per cent of the company's print jobs now use renewable energy. LaHay believes this gives his company a competitive advantage.

8D, Page 84, Exercises 7 and 8

Conversation 1
A = Andy, **B** = Beth

A: Can I have a word?

B: Sure, what's up?

A: We've got a little problem with the photocopiers. They keep jamming.

B: Oh no!

A: I think it might be the new recycled paper. It's a bit of a pain.

B: Perhaps we should go back to using normal paper. It's not very eco-friendly though.

A: I called the paper manufacturers and they say their paper isn't the problem.

B: But you think it is.

A: Don't know. Maybe.

B: Do we know how often the copiers jammed before we used the recycled paper?

A: Well, no, not really.

B: So, what if we do a little experiment. Er, we could use normal paper in, say, half the copiers and the recycled stuff in the others. And record any paper jams over the next month, say.

A: Um. Why's that?

B: Well, then we'll know if it's a problem with the copiers or the recycled stuff.

A: OK. I like that idea. It's a start.

B: That's right and we can see what happens.

A: Good. Well, we haven't figured it out yet, but I think I know what to do now.

B: Great!

A: That was useful. Thanks!

8D, Page 84, Exercise 10

Conversation 2
S = Sophie, **B** = Bill

S: My car's broken down again.

B: What's the problem this time?

S: Oh, I don't know. It's a real headache.

B: It's so unreliable. You need a new one.

S: Have you seen the prices of new cars?

B: Yeah, I know. But you can't do your job without it.

S: Mmm.

B: If we buy one second-hand, it'll be cheaper.

S: What? Get one that's just a few years old?

B: Yes.

S: We'd still need a loan to pay for it. Interest rates are terrible.

B: Not if we borrowed against the house.

S: That's an idea! I'll call the bank tomorrow.

B: So we have a plan of action now.

S: Yeah, I'm glad you thought of that.

6

8E, Page 87, Exercises 6 and 7

Environmental considerations play an important part in office design today. And we're not just talking about new projects, but also existing buildings. So, what makes an office 'green'? Well, there are various things that can reduce the negative environmental impact of a building. And improve the well-being of its occupants.

Firstly, let's take the location of the building. It's important to ask the question 'Can staff easily walk, cycle or take public transport to the office?' A second consideration is the use of water and a commitment to saving water wherever possible. Thirdly, in order to help reduce the organization's carbon dioxide emissions, offices should be designed to use less energy, for instance, through the use of energy-efficient equipment.

A fourth factor is materials selection. Is it an office that's been built using recyclable materials and organic non-volatile paints? We now realize that chemical emissions from certain paints and materials aren't good for our health. Fortunately, there are organic products which offer healthier, eco-friendly alternatives.

The fifth area is indoor environmental quality; for instance the use of glass walls and doors to make the most of natural light. And also improved ventilation systems. The green office doesn't just look nicer, it makes people feel better, too. Better quality of air and access to natural light make a huge difference. Studies show that access to daylight improves worker productivity by between five to twenty-five per cent.

Organizations are naturally concerned about the cost of all this. But there is a strong business case for the green office. Many examples show that over time, it actually saves money because energy bills are lower and staff productivity is higher. One recent example in the US, is the case of the software maker Adobe Systems. The company spent $1.4 million on a green office project at its San Jose headquarters and earned that investment back in energy savings in under 10 months.

To conclude, I believe that the sustainable office is both good for the environment and good for business, too.

9C, Page 92, Exercises 2 and 3

1

I always prepare what I'm going to say before I make a phone call in English. I write down something like, 'Hello, it's Martine here. I'm phoning about the email you sent me. I have a few questions about ...', and so on. If you know what you're going to say before you pick up the phone, it makes it easier.

2

I'm a trainer in communication skills. I often tell people, take a deep breath before you phone someone up or when you hear the phone ringing. Breathing really helps because the caller can hear it in your voice – they can tell if you're prepared or not. You can also use neat little phrases like, 'Hold on a minute, please. I'll just check that for you'. You can use the time to check the information, or think about what you're going to say next. It's also good to end the call on a positive note saying, 'Thanks for calling. It's good doing business with you', or, 'I'll look into it and I'll get back to you'.

3

Well, I work in sales and I'm on the phone all day, but I avoid making calls in English. If someone rings up, I ask a colleague to make an excuse and say I'm in a meeting or out of the office. Most people don't phone back. Once, I didn't understand anything a guy was saying. He had a funny accent and spoke too fast and I kept saying, 'Could you repeat that, please?' But in the end I hung up because I didn't understand a word.

4

We work in a busy open-plan office, but I prefer to take my phone calls in English in a quiet place, so I always ask the receptionist to put the caller through to a meeting room. And I usually ask my colleague to come with me. She's good at listening, so we put the speaker phone on and we can both listen at the same time. And if I don't understand something, I put the caller on hold and check with my colleague. But you can't do that very often.

9C, Page 93, Exercises 6, 8, 10 and 11

Call 1

Could you erm ... we're not available right now, sorry. Could you please leave a message after the tone ... oh, and our hours of operation are nine to five, that's Monday to Friday, but not Saturday. Bye.

Call 2

Hello, it's Amrit here from Nano-tech Systems in Delhi. I'd like to speak to the laboratory manager, Isabel Fernandez. It's about some equipment we ordered from you last month. I sent you a couple of emails last week, Isabel. Could you call me back as soon as you can? Thank you.

Call 3

S = Steve, **C** = Chloe

S: Hi.

C: Oh, uh, hello. Is that the IT department?

S: Yep. ... How can I help you?

C: Oh, I'd like to speak to Steve, please.

S: That's me.

C: Right, well, this is Chloe Jones from Hydra Energies. I'm phoning about the software you installed for us recently. I'm afraid we're still having a few problems with it.

S: Oh, you want to speak to Danny about that.

C: Danny?

S: Yep, he's the boss.

C: The thing is, it's a bit urgent and I was wondering if you could ...

S: Yeah, sorry. It's his day off. He'll be in tomorrow. I'll tell him you called. Bye.

Call 4

D = Danny, **C** = Chloe

D: OK, Chloe, so one of our engineers will come round on Thursday morning to reinstall the programme.

C: The thing is, we're working on a big project at the moment.

D: Yes, I understand. I'm sure we'll be able to fix it on Thursday. And I'm really sorry again about not calling you sooner but, you know, I only got the message this morning. Was there anything else, Chloe?

C: Yes, just one thing. What's the name of the engineer who's coming?

D: Er, let's see ... Greg.

C: Oh, fine. Not Steve then?

D: No, it's Greg. He's our software specialist.

C: Great. I'll see Greg on Thursday at eight then.

D: Yes, Thursday at eight a.m. And if there's anything else, Chloe, just call me on my mobile, OK?

C: Thanks a lot, Danny.

D: Thanks for calling. It's good doing business with you. Bye.

C: Bye.

Audio scripts

9D, Page 94, Exercise 2

Conversation 1

A = Alex, **R** = Receptionist

A: Hi.

R: Hello. Can I help you?

A: Yes, tell me how to get to the IT department.

R: … The IT department?

A: Yes.

R: It's that way.

A: Thanks.

Conversation 2

W = Waitress, **H** = Horst

W: Can I help you?

H: Would you be so kind as to give me a chicken sandwich and an orange juice, please?

W: Excuse me?

H: Would you be so kind as to give me a chicken sandwich and an orange juice, please?

W: Yeah, OK. I heard you the first time.

Conversation 3

T = Teacher, **P** = Pieter

T: OK, so we'll go by train. Pieter, do you think you could check the train times on the internet tonight?

P: No, I can't tonight. Sorry.

T: Oh, OK … Ana, would you mind checking the times?

9D, Page 94, Exercises 4 and 5

Situation 1

1

W = Woman, **Wa** = Waiter

W: A caffè latte, please.

Wa: One latte, coming up.

2

A: Do you mind if I help myself to coffee?

B: Sure. Go ahead. The kitchen is the first door on the right.

Situation 2

1

A: Would it be OK to use the Canon projector for my presentation?

B: I'm afraid not. The thing is, it's being repaired at the moment.

A: Oh, OK. I'll just use my laptop then.

2

A: I'd like to speak to somebody in technical support, please.

B: Press *one* for technical assistance. Press *two* for all other services.

Situation 3

1

A: Do you mind leaving at four?

B: Actually four is a bit early. I thought we could leave at about four thirty if that's all right with you.

A: Of course. That'll be fine.

2

A: Let's leave around four, OK?

B: Is that four o'clock real time or your time?

A: Four my time, of course. Cheeky!

Situation 4

1

A: Do you think you could send me those pdf files?

B: Certainly. I'll do that right away.

2

A: Oh no, my computer's crashed. Can I use yours?

B: Actually, I have to send an urgent email. Sorry. Try Liz.

9E, Page 97, Exercise 6

Tanya

I spend a lot of time writing emails and using Skype and I sometimes organize teleconferences. But they're difficult to set up because of the time differences. And then I have to confirm everything and put any verbal agreements in writing. I think I'm developing a bit of a 'Superwoman syndrome'. You know, you think you can do everything yourself and it's difficult to know when to stop, but I'm really excited about the project!

Lauren

My supervisor is busy all the time, so I don't get to speak to her on the phone that much. But she trusts me to get on with the job. She's also really good at giving me regular positive feedback and she always replies within 24 hours. But we usually meet up face-to-face with the team once a month, which is good fun. I think it's important to have that social contact. The downside is I've got to be connected to the intranet most of the time and sometimes at weekends, but I enjoy the autonomy. That's cool.

Lidia

The thing I find challenging is that I feel quite isolated. The time differences are a problem, too. We usually start talking about work straightaway and there's no time to make small talk. I think remote managers have a difficult time managing people in different locations. I know travel budgets are being cut these days, but I think the team should meet more often face-to-face.

7

9E, Page 97, Exercises 8 and 9

E = Erik, L = Lidia

E: Hi, Lidia.

L: Hello, Erik.

E: What's up?

L: I'm just phoning to check if you got the user manual for the new software because it's been updated …

E: Listen, Lidia, I'm between meetings, so this will have to be quick. Before I forget, can you send me those pdf files with the new project proposals? It's urgent.

L: The thing is, I haven't received all the proposals yet. There are two missing …

E: … I'm sorry, this line's bad. It would be great if you could email them to me today.

L: Today? I'm really sorry, Erik. Do you mind if I send them on Friday? For the weekend …

E: The weekend? No, no, that's too late.

L: The thing is all the project managers have been very busy with this new software.

E: I know. I know. But I've got meetings all day today and tomorrow. Look, can you do me a favour?

L: Sure. What is it?

E: Do you think you could phone the project managers?

L: Uh, OK. I'll do that straightaway. Actually, Erik, I think the team should meet to, er …

E: No problem. It's already been set up.

L: Er, I don't mean another videoconference. I mean a face-to-face …

E: Lidia, is it OK if I call you this evening? About nine?

L: Is that Oslo time?

E: … Sorry, got to go now, Lidia.

L: I'll speak to you later then.

E: Oh, by the way, I'm having trouble using this new software.

L: I've already sent you the manual, Erik.

E: Thanks. Bye.

L: Bye.

10A, Page 101, Exercise 8

1
If I'd been in Karl's position, I'd've done the same.

2
If he'd known nothing about the software, he'd've had problems doing his job.

3
My sister wouldn't've got her first job in radio if she hadn't claimed that she already had some experience.

4
Would the company've fired him if he hadn't been the boss?

10A, Page 101, Exercise 10

Then I went into my new boss's office and told her that she'd be getting a call from Human Resources in a moment. I explained exactly what I'd done. She thanked me for my honesty and told me that there was more on my resume that recommended me besides my degree. She said that I seemed to be doing OK – although I'd only been working there for two weeks or so. And she let me stay on. I did very well there, but I learnt my lesson and I've never lied on my resume since.

10B, Page 103, Exercises 5 and 6

Dan

It was a dream house. Just what I'd always wanted – in a quiet suburb, perfect for writing. I've been a good friend to Kumar. I've helped him move, and I've also lent him my car. I didn't want to ask him for the money, but, hey, house prices are so high these days. … Yeah, I guess I should have waited another year.

… Sure, if Kumar had had financial difficulties, I would've done the same for him. I mean, we've known each other since we were at college. Anyway, he agreed, I paid the down payment and moved in and spent loads of time writing on weekends and during my vacation. The thing is, I couldn't find a publisher for the book. It was really frustrating. So, after six months of this, I explained the situation to Kumar, saying that I was really sorry but I didn't have enough money to pay him back. Actually, I was a bit surprised when he looked annoyed and asked me to pay it back by the end of the year. He knows I have the mortgage to pay and that I don't earn much money at the bookstore. And he earns much more than me.

… Yeah, of course I plan to pay back two thousand dollars by the New Year.

I'm going to save up and if it doesn't work out, I suppose I'll get some extra work in the evenings. … I dunno, as a waiter, or something.

… No, I can't ask my mom for the money. No way.

She can't afford it on her pension. I just think Kumar could've been a bit more understanding about my financial situation. After all, that's what friends are for, right?

10B, Page 103, Exercises 7 and 8

Kumar

Dan and me used to get on really well until this business with the money. We'd been to college together and I'd always been able to talk to him about everything. But we'd never discussed personal finances. I mean, I knew he earned less than me, but he'd never asked me for money before. … Sure, when he asked for five thousand dollars for the down payment for the house, I was surprised.

It was a lot of money. But I thought, hey, he's a great guy, so I gave it to him.

… Yeah, I felt a bit uncomfortable about the situation 'cos I wasn't sure how he planned to repay it.

He said he didn't wanna ask his mom because she was retired and all that. What was I supposed to do? I couldn't say no, could I? Dan promised to pay me back and I believed him, although my other friends say I shouldn't have lent him the money.

Anyway, six months later, he *still* hadn't paid me back. We'd never agreed on an exact date or anything. He hadn't been able to find a publisher for his book and I thought, well, that's not my problem. So I just asked him to pay it back by the end of the year. I wasn't charging interest, was I? And he looked kind of offended, but I thought, five thousand dollars is five thousand dollars. I mean, we've always been close but he's not family, or anything.

… No, I don't see much of him these days.

It seems as if he's avoiding me. He's not answering my calls – stuff like that. If he doesn't have enough money to pay me back, he should ask for a bank loan. But the worst thing is the money has changed things between us. It shouldn't have affected our friendship.

Audio scripts

10D, Page 106, Exercise 3

Companies often resort to the public apology when things go wrong. Take the disastrous opening of Heathrow Airport's terminal 5. The day the terminal went into full operation in 2008, thousands of passengers suffered long delays and lost their luggage. British Airways quickly apologized and promised immediate action. The company even organized four hundred volunteers to help sort out the mess and reunite passengers with their luggage.

In another famous example in 2007, US toy company Mattel apologized publicly to Chinese manufacturers and political officials for the recall of nearly 20 million toys made in China. Executive Vice President Thomas Debrowski said at the time, 'Mattel takes full responsibility for these recalls and apologizes personally to you, the Chinese people, and all of our customers who received the toys.'

Mr Debrowski added that a majority of the problems were associated with design problems, not Chinese manufacturers. Experts said this public apology by Mattel in China was important to maintain good relationships with suppliers there. It was all about saving face and a private apology wouldn't have done that for China.

10D, Page 106, Exercises 6 and 7

Conversation 1

E = Employee, **A** = Alicia.

E: I'm really sorry, Alicia. You know that progress report you wanted today? I'm afraid I haven't had time to finish it. There's just been so much to do and a few people are off sick. I'll get on to it first thing tomorrow.

A: Well, thanks for letting me know. Don't worry about it. Tomorrow will be fine.

Conversation 2

A: I'm sorry. I didn't see you there. Are you all right?

B: Yes, yes. Fine thanks.

Conversation 3

J = Jin, **W** = Werner

J: I'm sorry, Werner. I did something silly and accidentally deleted that match you were recording.

W: What?

J: I feel really bad about it. I know you love your tennis.

W: Jin! It was the Shanghai Open final. I really wanted to watch that later.

J: I know, I know. I'm sorry. Look, I'll make us something special for dinner.

W: Oh, go on then.

Conversation 4

A: Next, please.

B: Yes. Can I have …?

C: Excuse me, I was here before you.

B: Oh, so sorry. I didn't mean to push in.

C: That's OK.

10E, Page 108, Exercise 4

S = Susan, **T** = Tom

S: How was your day, Tom?

T: Not bad, not bad, nothing special.

S: How's that friend of yours, Raul?

T: Hey, he found a fantastic cellphone in the park on the way home from school.

S: Yeah? What did he do with it?

T: He's gonna keep it. It's much better than his old phone. He threw away the chip and put in his.

S: Oh!

10E, Page 108, Exercise 6

T = Tom, **S** = Susan, **J** = John

T: He's going to keep it. It's much better than his old phone. He threw away the chip and put in his.

S: Oh! Do you think he should've done that, Tom? Kept the phone?

T: Well, no. I guess not.

J: Why not?

T: Well, it's not exactly stealing, but it's kind of dishonest.

J: What did you say to him?

T: I said he was lucky. I'd really like a cellphone like that.

S: You know, you could've told him to use the phone to call the owner or given it to a teacher to find the owner.

T: Yeah, I know. I'm really sorry. But, hey, you found twenty dollars the other day and kept it.

S: That's not the same!

10E, Page 109, Exercises 10 and 11

S = Susan, **J** = John, **D** = Driver

S: Well, we've finished all the shopping.

J: What'll we have for dinner?

S: I don't know. How about pizza? It's nice and quick.

J: OK, sounds good to me. Hey, isn't that Michelle's new boyfriend over there? Who's he with?

S: I don't know. Look! They're holding hands!

J: I knew there was something I didn't like about him.

S: So, are you going to tell Michelle?

J: Tell her? Would that be a good idea?

S: And if she finds out you knew something, but didn't tell her?

J: Oh! But what if she hates me for telling her? Why don't you talk to her?

S: She's your sister. I think it's better if you do it.

J: I'll have to think about it. Hey, I wanna go to the bookstore. Let's cross here.

S: Wait for the light! …

D: Get out of the road!

J: Watch where you're going!

D: Are you blind? The light was red!

J: The light was changing! I had the right of way.

S: Come on, John, let's go.

8

11C, Page 114, Exercise 2

J = Jasmine, **D** = Daniel

J: So, what have we got lined up for next month, Daniel?

D: Well, there's an interview with dental nurse Sandra Harzog for our *Spotlight On* column. I spoke to her last week. She's Australian, you know. She's been working at the hospital for two years now. And we haven't done an article about anyone from that department recently.

J: Have we got a photo to go with the article about her?

D: Not yet, she's going to email one.

J: OK. And Alan Murray has sent his annual message about future plans for the hospital. We'll have to include that somewhere.

D: Do you think we could put that on page two, Jasmine, and keep the front page a bit light and fun for the staff?

J: Yes, he's a good sort. I don't think he'll mind.

D: And I've got a nice little piece about the new public park. Hospital staff have been helping to raise funds for improvements to the park and they've collected £5,000 already. The mayor has agreed to attend the official opening.

J: Yes, that sounds great.

D: Now what about something on a big public event? What's on the calendar for next month?

J: Not much. January and February is kind of a quiet time. Ah! There is the Lunar New Year, but we did something on that last year.

D: It doesn't matter. Nobody will mind. Anyway, there's a big Chinese community locally and it's colourful. We can include images of the Chinese horoscope as well. It'll look good on the page.

J: OK, I'll go along with that.

11C, Page 114, Exercise 3

D = Daniel, **S** = Sandra

D: So, how long have you been working at the hospital, Sandra?

S: I've been working at Barkington for almost two years now.

D: Is that an Australian accent I hear?

S: Yes, that's right. I'm originally from Melbourne.

D: Have you been living in the UK long?

S: Not very. I've only been living here since 2007. I miss the sun but I love it here.

D: Tell us about the project you're working on.

S: I've been working on the new digital records scheme for six months. It's making a huge difference to the way we work.

D: What do you like doing in your free time?

S: Well, I never learnt to play a musical instrument when I was young and I've always wanted to. My partner surprised me and bought me a piano for my birthday in September. And I've been learning to play since then. But I'm terrible at it!

11D, Page 117, Exercises 7, 9 and 10

M = Michaela, **D** = Dev

M: Hi, I don't think we've met before. I'm Michaela Perry.

D: Nice to meet you, Michaela. I'm Dev Sharma.

M: So, tell me about yourself Dev. Which department are you in?

D: PR. I'm the Assistant to the Events Coordinator, Amrita Krishen.

M: Really? That's cool! How's it going?

D: Things are pretty quiet at the moment. It's going to be hectic next month though. And Amrita's going to be away.

M: Oh yes, I hear she's expecting.

D: That's right. Twins!

M: Oh terrific. So who will be in charge when she goes on maternity leave?

D: Me, I'm taking over from her next month.

M: Are you? Congratulations!

…

D: So, how about you Michaela? What do you do?

M: Well, I work in IT. I've just become Head of Special Projects, and I'm still finding my feet.

D: Wow! Sounds interesting! Doesn't Massimo work in your department?

M: Well, yes, he did. Actually, he left under a cloud.

D: No! I'm sorry to hear that.

M: It's probably best not to talk about it.

D: I see. So, Michaela perhaps you could help me sort out a new database for the PR department.

M: I'd be very happy to. Hey! Maybe at the same time you could give me some ideas for some team-building activities for my new staff.

D: Um. It's not my area, I'm afraid, but I know just the man to help you. Let me introduce you to Stefan. He's just over there.

11E, Page 119, Exercise 7

A = Aidan, **M** = Marama

A: Marama, I've been thinking about the annual barbecue.

M: Yeah. I've been thinking about that myself. Summer's fast approaching, so we'll have to start working on it.

A: Well, I was wondering if we should do something different this year.

M: What did you have in mind?

A: Well, I get bored sitting around all day eating. I'd like to do something more active for a change. How about we cancel the barbecue with the staff and their families? I've been reading up on team-building events. We could organize one of these instead.

M: Would we invite the partners and the kids to it?

A: No, I'd like it to be more of a work event this year, but we'd have fun, of course. What do you think?

M: It could work. I mean, if you've involved staff in planning the activities, it will motivate them more. You know, find out what they enjoy doing and learning.

A: Good point. Can you ask around then?

M: OK, will do.

Audio scripts

11E, Page 119, Exercise 8

1

Yeah, we've been having a summer barbecue for years now. I think it's time for a change. I'm only 25, so it isn't of much interest to young people like me in the company. It would be different if they organized some team sports or something on the day, for those who want to do something more active.

2

To tell you the truth, I'm really not keen on team-building events. It seems like it's just for the sporty types and I don't see how being competitive helps to develop a team spirit. The winners go away happy and the losers feel miserable. I know there are a lot of sporty types among the engineers, but I think team-building events are a waste of time.

3

I've got a suggestion. I think it would be good if we do some volunteer work as a team-building exercise for the day. You know, we could plant some trees somewhere or do something more useful than hang off ropes. Let's make the event something that brings the team together and is worthwhile at the same time.

4

Most of us have young families in the company. And my husband and kiddies love coming to the barbecue every year. They'll miss it if we don't do it this year, and I'm going to feel guilty if I have to go off somewhere without them.

5

A friend of mine told me about a great event she attended. She said that each group had to plan and put on a show together. She said it was fun and non-competitive and everyone was able to draw on their creativity. They discovered all sorts of hidden talents. At the end of the day, it was entertaining to see the shows.

12B, Page 122, Exercises 4 and 5

P = Presenter, **T** = Tim

P: So now we're going over to South London to speak to Tim Gordon, our correspondent there. Good morning, Tim.

T: Good morning.

P: Could you tell us how she is this morning?

T: Well I heard from the hospital just half an hour ago. It seems she's a little better this morning. She's had breakfast and was talking to the hospital staff.

P: Do you know why she was taken ill like this?

T: The hospital hasn't made any official statement. It's possible that it was mainly stress. People are saying that the latest tour was a mistake so soon after her recent operation, and of course there's been her divorce as well.

P: But it was very dramatic, the way it suddenly happened during the interval of the concert. There has been speculation in the press that this was a heart attack. Is that still a possibility?

T: Well, like I said, the hospital hasn't confirmed anything.

P: Have you spoken to her daughter yet?

T: No, but she's staying nearby. We're expecting her to visit later this morning.

P: So we can't rule out the possibility that this was a heart attack?

T: No. It could have been.

12C, Page 124, Exercises 1, 2, 3 and 4

1

Well, I've often paid for flights and holidays on the internet and felt safe about giving my credit card details. But this one time I was nearly ripped off. You see, I hired a car through this cheap online car hire company, but when my credit card bill arrived, they'd overcharged me by 500 euros. So, you know, I email the company and they say the 500 euros is just being held as a deposit and they'd refund my money within 15 days. Well, it didn't happen, and so I keep phoning and emailing but I just get an answerphone message or no reply at all. It was really frustrating. Anyway, in the end, I reported them to the trading standards people. They were absolutely great. They found out this car hire company was still operating, got the address and wrote to them. And, you know, I got my money back. Needless to say, I've learnt my lesson. I'll only give my details online to well-known, reputable companies now. I mean, there are a lot of internet scams about these days.

2

Results from a survey reveal that 60% of UK homeowners prefer cash-in-hand builders. The survey commissioned by the National Federation of Builders claims that over half of Britons would risk hiring a cowboy builder to carry out work on their home.

Sixty-one per cent of the 2,000 UK adults surveyed are tempted by a tax-free deal on their building work because of the high costs.

Many people are victim to cowboy tradesmen in order to save money, but then find they have no legal protection when things go wrong. There are over 100,000 complaints made about rogue tradesmen each year, according to figures from the Trading Standards.

3

So, yesterday I was at work – I work in a chemist's – this guy comes up and we were really busy for a Monday. And, so anyway, he drops off a prescription and I told him that it'd be about half an hour, because we were, you know, really busy. And so anyway, I passed his prescription to the pharmacist and continued to serve the other customers in the shop. Well, he comes back about forty minutes later. In the meantime, the pharmacist had given the prescription back to me 'cos we didn't have any in stock. Well, he got really angry about it at all. He started screaming and yelling, 'Ah, this service is terrible! Blah, blah, blah. Let me talk to your manager'. I mean this guy was really shouting. And, so you know, my manager comes over and she tries to talk to him and, you know, he keeps shouting and insulting her. I mean, just, we didn't do anything wrong, we didn't make any mistakes. I didn't know we wouldn't have any of that medicine when I told him to come back in half an hour. Well, as you can imagine, we're not going to serve that man again.

4

Overcharged bills! Low quality goods! Poor customer service! Just when bad business thought it was safe to rip people off, there's a new consumer site that's hit the internet: www.iripoff.com. A site designed by consumers for consumers. By filling out an anonymous complaint, it's like putting up your very own website. Users can upload images and attach voice audio to their complaints. Complaints which are then visible to millions worldwide on www.iripoff.com.

12D, Page 126, Exercise 4

Call 1, Part 1

N = Neil, **R** = Recorded message, **C** = Customer Service rep

N: Hello, I'd like to speak to customer services, please.

R: If you would like to place an order, press 1.

N: Here we go again.

R: … If you wish to talk to one of our customer service representatives, press 2.

N: Two. …

C: Ritchie's Customer Services. How may I help you?

N: Hello, I'd like to make a complaint about the delivery charges on my last order.

C: Could I have your name, please, sir?

N: Yes, it's Neil Jackson, that's N-E-I-L Jackson.

C: And your order number?

N: Let me see … Um, it starts with a hash sign, then five, two, eight, oh sorry, that's five, eight, two, slash, one, O, seven, hyphen nine, four, O, three, six.

C: So that's hash, 582, slash, 107, hyphen, 94036.

N: That's right.

Call 2

C = Customer Service rep, **T** = Tara

C: Ritchie's.

T: Hello, is that customer services?

C: Yes, how can I help you?

T: I'm phoning about a delivery you sent me.

C: I see. Can you give me your name, please?

T: Tara Jackson.

C: Is that T-A-R-A?

T: Yeah. The thing is, you've sent me the wrong stuff. I didn't order a blue top. I ordered a brown one. Blue's not my colour …

C: Just one moment. Can I have the order number, please, Ms Jackson?

T: What? Oh yeah, it's somewhere here. … Dad, have you seen the piece of paper with the order number? … On the table? Wait a minute, it's here somewhere. … Got it. It's, er … one of those funny signs.

C: You mean a hash?

T: Yeah, hash, then five, eight, two, slash, four, one, two, hyphen, eight, seven … oh sorry, that's a nine, seven, double two, seven.

C: Can I read that back to you? Hash, 582, slash, 412, hyphen, 97227. And you say that you've received the wrong colour top?

T: Yeah, I've already told you. I wanted brown, not blue.

12D, Page 126, Exercises 6 and 7

Call 1, Part 2

C = Customer Service rep, **N** = Neil

C: And what seems to be the problem, Mr Jackson?

N: The thing is, on your website it says all deliveries are free but I see from my bill that I have been charged for delivery.

C: Just one moment … I see your order came to 48 Euros, Mr Jackson. But the offer only applies to deliveries of over 50 Euros, not for orders of less than 50 Euros.

N: Well, I think your promotion is misleading because it doesn't say that.

C: If you look at our website, sir …

N: Hold on a minute. … Right, I have it here on my screen.

C: … and scroll right down to our terms and conditions, you will see that they refer to deliveries over 50 Euros only. It's the last part.

N: Oh, I didn't see that. The terms and conditions are at the bottom of the screen.

C: I'm afraid your bill is correct, sir. Do you require any more assistance?

N: No, but I don't think that's right.

C: I'm sorry to hear that, but you have been charged correctly. Would you like another service, Mr Jackson?

N: No. It's just that your website is confusing. If I'd known, I would have bought another item because my order only came to 48 Euros.

C: I understand, sir. That must be annoying for you. I'll pass on your complaint and you could also complete our online customer service questionnaire.

N: Oh, all right then. Where's that?

Grammar reference

Present tenses

Present simple

Use

We use the present simple to talk about regular activities, long-term situations and things that are always true.

> I often **listen** to my mp3 player on my way to work.
>
> She **works** as a life coach.

Form

Affirmative sentences	
Use the base form of the verb. Add s to third person forms.	I/You/We/They **work** long hours. He/She/It **watches** a lot of TV.
Negative sentences	
Use don't (do not). Use doesn't (does not) with third person forms.	You **don't do** much exercise. It **doesn't take** long to walk to the office.

Frequency adverbs

1 We usually place frequency adverbs before the main verb.

> I **often work** at weekends.
>
> He **usually remembers** my name.

2 Frequency adverbs usually come after the verb be.

> She **is often** out of the office.

Present continuous

Use

We use the present continuous to talk about current activities or short-term activities.

> She**'s talking** on the phone at the moment.
>
> I**'m taking** an MBA course.

> ⚠️ There are some verbs that we do not usually use in their continuous form because they describe states, not activities, e.g. want, need, believe, know and have (in the sense of own or possess).
>
> He ~~is wanting~~ **wants** to spend more time with his family.
>
> She ~~is having~~ **has** a lot of responsibility at work.
>
> We can use think in the present simple and present continuous, but there is a change in meaning.
>
> What do you **think**? (What's your opinion?)
>
> I**'m thinking** of hiring an assistant. (I'd like to hire an assistant but it's just an idea at the moment.)

Form

Affirmative sentences	
Use the verb be + the -ing form of the verb.	I am **working**. You/We/They **are working**. He/She/It **is working**.
Negative sentences	
Use the negative form of the verb be.	I**'m not studying** any more today. You **aren't working**. He **isn't working**.

Present tense question forms

Use

We use open questions when we want more information from someone or we want to keep the conversation going. We start these with a question word or question words.

How often do you cycle to work?

How long does the journey take?

What do you suggest I do?

Which activity do you prefer?

Where are you going now?

What kinds of things do you like doing in your free time?

Form

Present simple Use *do* or *does* and a question word if necessary.	*Do you* have many hobbies? *Does he/she* work long hours? *Where do you* live?
Present continuous Change the word order and use a question word if necessary.	*Are you* trying to find a new job? *What is he* doing now?
Subject questions These are questions where the first word is the subject. Don't use *do* or *does* and don't change the word order.	*Who likes doing* adventure sports? *Which machine isn't working* today?
Short answers There are no question words in *yes/no* questions. These types of questions start with an auxiliary verb. In the present simple, use *do/ does* or *don't/doesn't* in short answers and in the present continuous use the verb *be*.	*Does* he know Nancy? *No, he doesn't.* *Are* you prioritizing your work? *Yes, I am.*

Present perfect simple

Use

We use the present perfect simple to speak about the past and the present together. We use it to talk about:

1 Present results – past actions with results that are important in the present:

I've finished the report. (You can have it now.)

We often use the present perfect to give news:

He's just got a new job.

2 Unfinished actions – actions or states that began in the past and are still continuing now:

She's worked as a journalist for a long time.

He's played professionally since 2001.

The time expressions **for** and **since** are often used to connect the past and present. We use **for** with a period of time and we use **since** with a point of time.

She's lived here for five years.

He's worked here since 2008.

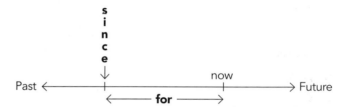

When we speak about 'unfinished time' we often use the adverbs *already* and *yet* to describe things which are happening or expected to happen around the present. The adverb *already* may express some surprise, e.g. because something has happened sooner than expected.

She's only 28 but she's already written three novels.

We use *not yet* to describe something that hasn't happened so far but is expected to happen in the future.

He hasn't found the right business partner yet.

3 Experience – finished actions that happened at an indefinite time in the past:

I love that film. I've seen it three times. (three times in my life before now)

She has won several business awards. (it's part of her life's experience)

Have you ever been to Paris? (at any time up to now)

I've never seen that before. (not at any time in my life)

For information on the present perfect and the past simple, see page 164.

Form

Affirmative sentences Use *have/has* + past participle. Irregular verbs sometimes have a special past participle form. For a list of irregular verbs see page 176.	*He/She/It has worked* here for five years. *I/You/We/They have been* to Italy. *He/She/It has been* to Italy.
Negative sentences Use *has/hasn't* + past participle.	*I/You/We/They haven't seen* this before. *He/She/It hasn't done* this before.
Questions Change the word order.	*Has he/she/it* ever won an Oscar? *Where have you* been?
Short answers Use *has/have* or *hasn't/haven't*.	Have they seen the report? *Yes, they have.* / *No, they haven't.*

Present perfect continuous

Use

1 We use the present perfect continuous with *for* and *since* to talk about unfinished activities.

> **A:** How long **have** you **been learning** to play the piano?
>
> **B: For** a few years now.

2 We use the present perfect continuous to talk about or explain the present consequences of an activity.

> You**'ve been running**, haven't you? You're out of breath.
>
> He's tired because he**'s been working** a lot lately.

3 We often use the adverbs *lately*, *recently*, *always*, *only*, *never*, *ever*, *still* and *just* with the present perfect continuous. The adverbs *always*, *only*, *never*, *ever*, *still* and *just* are put between the auxiliary and main verb. *Lately* and *recently* are usually at the start or end of the phrase.

> I've **just** been talking to the supplier.
>
> We've **only** been working on this project for a few months.
>
> I've been travelling a lot for work **lately**.
>
> **Recently**, he's been working very hard.

Form

Affirmative sentences Use *have/has* + *been* + verb + *ing*.	*I/You/We/They* **have been living** here for three years. *He/She/It* **has been living** here since 2008.
Negative sentences Use *have/has* + *not* + *been* + verb + *ing*.	*I/You/We/They* **haven't been feeling** well lately. *He/She/It* **hasn't been feeling** well lately.
Questions Change the word order.	**Have** *I/you/we/they* **been talking** too loudly? **Has** *he/she/it* **been working** today? What **have** you **been eating**?
Short answers Use *has/have* or *hasn't/haven't*.	Have they been working hard? **Yes, they have. / No, they haven't.**

Present perfect simple vs present perfect continuous

Use

We use the present perfect continuous with 'active' verbs (e.g. *learn*, *run*, *study*). With 'state' verbs (e.g. *be*, *know*, *have*, *like*) we generally use the present perfect simple.

> I **have had** my flat for ten years now.
>
> We **have known** each other since we were at primary school.

When we talk about unfinished actions, the present perfect simple and present perfect continuous have the same meaning.

> I**'ve worked** here for two years. = I**'ve been working** here for two years.
>
> How long **have** you **lived** in Rome? = How long **have** you **been living** in Rome?

However, when we're using the present perfect continuous to talk about recent activities, there can be differences in meaning. Compare these sentences:

> He's been travelling a lot for work lately. (a situation that continues today)
>
> He's travelled to a lot of countries. (life experiences and completed actions)
>
> We've been packing all morning. (this activity is probably not finished)
>
> We've bought some new furniture. (this is a completed activity)

2

Past tenses

Past simple

Use

We use the past simple to talk about finished actions and situations in the past. They may have happened recently or in the distant past.

> I **saw** the film a few days ago.
>
> The first modern Olympic Games **were** in April 1896.

One common use is to tell stories.

> I **went** to a conference last month and met an old colleague.
>
> A funny thing **happened** to me on my commute to work yesterday.

Form

Affirmative sentences Add -ed to the base form of the verb. There is no special third person form. Irregular verbs have a special past form. See page 176 for a list of irregular verbs. The past forms of be are was and were.	I/You/He/She/It/We/They **worked** in a jazz club. He **became** a professional player in 2001. She **began** her career 30 years ago. He/She/It **was** in Hong Kong last year. We/You/They **were** in Australia in March.
Negative sentences Use didn't (did not) + the base form of the verb. With the verb be, use wasn't (was not) and weren't (were not). For modal verbs, e.g. could, would, add not to the end of the modal verb.	We **didn't** understand the question. He **wasn't** good at sports at school. They **weren't** happy about their team's result. I **could** understand French but I **couldn't** speak it.
Questions Use did + the base form of the verb. With the verb be, change the word order.	**Did** you **get** my email? When **did** he **win** a gold medal? **Was he** good at sports at school?
Short answers Use did/didn't. With the verb be, use was/were or were/weren't.	Did you get my email? **Yes**, I **did**. / **No**, I **didn't**. Was he an author? **Yes** he **was**. / **No**, he **wasn't**. Were they late? **Yes**, they **were**. / **No**, they **weren't**.

Pronunciation of regular verbs

The pronunciation of regular verbs depends on whether the verb ending is voiced or unvoiced.

Some unvoiced sounds are: f, k, p, t, sh

Some voiced sounds are: b, d, g, n, v

Verbs ending in voiced sounds: End with a /d/ sound, e.g. clean<u>ed</u>	cleaned, retired, planned, earned, received, changed, discovered, happened, trained, opened
Verbs ending in unvoiced sounds: End with a /t/ sound, e.g. wash<u>ed</u>	washed, asked, focused, talked, worked, based, placed, looked, stopped, missed, promised
Verbs ending with a /d/ or /t/ sound: Add an extra syllable: /ɪd/, e.g. want<u>ed</u>	wanted, needed, created, exceeded, depended, contacted, decided, visited, mended
⚠ Make sure you pronounce the extra syllable with verbs ending with a /t/ or /d/ sound. The extra syllable is pronounced /ɪd/, not /ed/. want (one syllable) wanted (two syllables) need (one syllable) needed (two syllables)	

Past simple vs present perfect simple

Use

1 We use both these tenses to describe actions that started or ended in the past. Which tense we select depends on whether:

a we're referring to a definite or indefinite time.

b the action is finished or unfinished.

2 We often use adverbs like *recently, already, yet, ever, never* and *just* and the time expressions *for* and *since* with the present perfect.

3 We often use time expressions like *yesterday, ago, last night/week/month*, etc. with the past tense.

Form

Indefinite time	Definite time
Have you **seen** a good film **recently**?	**Did** you **see** a film **yesterday**?
We'**ve already met**.	We **met** at the conference **last year**.
Has the meeting finished **yet**?	The meeting **finished an hour ago**.
Have you **ever been** to India?	I **went** to India **in 2006**.
I'**ve never read** any of his books.	She **read** the book **last month**.
I'**ve just bought** a new car.	The show **started at 7.30**.

Unfinished actions	Finished actions
She'**s been** an actress **since she was 18**. (She is still an actress.)	She **was** an actress **during the 90s**. (She isn't now.)
I'**ve had** this car **for five years**. (I still have it.)	I **had** that car for five years but then I got a new one. (I don't have it any more.)

⚠ British speakers use the present perfect simple slightly more in conversation than American speakers. American speakers sometimes use a past tense where only the present perfect simple is possible in British English.

British and American speakers both use *yet, already* and *just* with the present perfect simple.

Have you done it yet?

I've already done it.

I've just finished. (BrE and AmE)

American speakers might also use a past tense with *yet* and *already*.

Did you do it yet?

I already did it. (AmE)

British and American speakers both use *just* with the past tense to describe something that happened a moment ago.

Did you just call me?

British speakers generally use *just* with the present perfect simple to give news.

I've just passed my driving test!

American speakers might say this, too, but they also use the past tense to give news.

I just passed my driving test!

used to

Use

Past habits

1 We use *used to* when we talk about things we did in the past but which we don't do any more, and to describe past states that are no longer true.

*He **used to spend** weekends skiing in the Alps.*

*I **didn't use to enjoy** my work but I do now.*

2 We use *used to* when we want to compare the past with the present.

*Marcus **used to earn** £500,000 a year but now he earns £60,000.*

3 We often just use the past simple, instead of *used to* in negative and question forms.

*He **didn't like** sports very much when he was younger.*

*Which sports **did you play** when you were at school?*

Present habits

We don't use *used to* to talk about present habits. We use the present simple with an adverb of frequency such as *usually/normally/often*, etc.

*Marcus **is normally** at home for only six months of the year.*

*I **often watch** my favourite TV programme on Sunday nights.*

Form

Affirmative sentences used to + base form of the verb	I **used to buy** the newspaper every day. He **used to be** a football player.
Negative sentences Use *didn't* + *use to* + base form of the verb.	We **didn't use to read** free newspapers. She **didn't use to have** much money.
Questions In *yes/no* questions use *did* + subject + *use to* + base form of the verb. In open questions use question word(s) + *did* + subject + *use to* + base form of the verb.	**Did** he **use to work** as a waiter? **Did** they **use to make** solar panels? **What did** you **use to do** in your previous job? **How much did** he **use to earn**?
Short answers Use *did/didn't*.	**Did** he **use to like** cities? Yes, he **did**. / No, he **didn't**.

⚠ **used to**
In the negative form and in questions, remember to use the base form.

*She **didn't use to travel** much, but she does now.*

NOT *She didn't ~~used~~ to travel much, but she does now.*

*Did you **use to travel** a lot for work?*

NOT *Did you ~~used~~ to travel a lot for work?*

Past continuous

Use

1 We use the past continuous to talk about the background situation in a story. We often use the past continuous together with the past simple.

*It **was raining** so I offered him a lift.*

*She **was working** as a model when she got her first part in a film.*

2 We use the past continuous to describe past actions or situations which were in progress at a particular time in the past.

*We **were living** in Paris at the time.*

*By the age of four, he **was singing** in a band with his brothers.*

3 We can also use the past continuous to show two or more actions were in progress at the same time.

*While he **was taking** acting lessons, he **was** also **working** part-time.*

Form

Affirmative sentences Use *was/were* + the *-ing* form of the verb.	He **was studying**. We **were wearing** security badges.
Negative sentences Use *wasn't* (*was not*) and *weren't* (*were not*).	He **wasn't studying**. They **weren't wearing** security badges.
Questions Change the word order.	**Was he** studying? What **were you** doing?
Short answers Use *was/wasn't/were/weren't*.	*Was he studying?* **Yes**, he **was**. / **No**, he **wasn't**. *Were they working?* **Yes**, they **were**. / **No**, they **weren't**.

Past perfect

Use

1 We use the past perfect to talk about actions or events that happened before another in the past. We can use it to talk about something which continued up to a point of time in the past, or ended a short time before. It is often used with the past simple.

Past ← —————×————————×————— → Present
              had turned 30   *got fired*

*Steve **had turned** 30 when he **got fired**.*

*Ben didn't know he **had bought** a girl's mountain bike when he **went cycling**.*

2 We can use the past perfect to talk about life experience before a point of time in the past. We often use the adverbs *ever*, *never*, *already*, *yet* and *just* with the past perfect.

*It was the best thing that **had ever happened** to me.*

*The film **had already started** when we arrived.*

3 We often use the past perfect for reporting events in the past and with certain time expressions such as *by (the age of)*, *by the time*, etc.

*She had set up her own company **by the age of** 19.*

Form

Affirmative sentences Use *had* + past participle of the main verb.	In ten years it **had grown** into a $2 billion company.
Negative sentences Use *hadn't* (*had not*) + past participle of the verb.	She **hadn't worked** as a waitress before. Ben **hadn't seen** the tree because it was dark.
Questions Change the word order.	**Had** you **ever been** to Paris before? **Had** the film **already started**?
Short answers Use *had/hadn't*.	*Had she **recognized** him from TV? Yes, she **had**. / No, she **hadn't**.*

⚠️ In spoken English *had* often contracts to *'d*. *It was the first time she**'d** visited the US.*

Future forms and modal verbs

There are many different ways to talk about the future in English. The form we choose depends on the situation and how certain we feel.

1 Sometimes there are no important differences in meaning:

I'm going to be forty next year.

I'll be forty next year.

I'm going to come to the meeting on Friday. (I intend to be there.)

I'm coming to the meeting on Friday. (It's a planned arrangement.)

2 Sometimes the forms indicate different meanings:

Er ... OK, I'll come to the meeting. (I'm deciding now.)

I'm going to come to the meeting. (I've already decided.)

I'm coming to the meeting. / I'm going to come to the meeting. (It's definite.)

I might come to the meeting. / I may come to the meeting. (It's not certain.)

The modal verb *will*

Use

We often use *will*:

1 when we're making predictions:

*In the future, people **will retire** at seventy.*

*Chinese **will become** an important language for business.*

2 when we're deciding something at the moment of speaking:

*A: It's raining.   B: Then I**'ll take** an umbrella.*

*I think I**'ll get** some perfume in the duty free shop.*

3 to make offers and promises:

*I**'ll do** it for you.*

*We**'ll give** you a lift.*

4 in sentences with *if* (See notes on conditionals page169):

*If you walk more, you**'ll feel** refreshed.*

Form

Affirmative sentences Use *will* (or *'ll*) + the base form of the verb. There is no special *he/she/it* form.	*I**'ll see** you on Friday.* *She**'ll take** questions at the end of her speech.*
Negative sentences Use *won't* (*will* + *not*).	*He **won't be** here for at least half an hour.*
Questions Change the word order.	*What time **will he get** here?*
Short answers Use *will/won't*.	*Will it work?* **Yes**, *it* **will.** / **No**, *it* **won't.**

going to

Use

1 We often use the expression *going to* when we talk about intentions and future plans:

*I**'m going to visit** my sister tomorrow.* (I've bought my ticket and she's expecting me.)

*They**'re going to open** a new office in Shanghai.* (They've already made the decision.)

2 We also use *going to* when we can see now that something will happen in the future:

*There are black clouds. It**'s going to rain**.*

*The train's delayed. We**'re going to be** late.*

Form

Affirmative sentences Use *be going to* + the base form of the verb.	*They**'re going to reorganize** the office.* *I**'m** only **going to stay** there for a week.*
Negative sentences Use the negative form of the verb *be*.	*We**'re not going to clean up**.* *He **isn't going to arrive** in time.*
Questions Change the word order of the verb *be*.	*Are **you going to employ** an assistant?* *What**'s he going to do**?*
Short answers Use the verb *be*.	*Is he going to come?* **Yes**, *he* **is.** / **No** *he* **isn't**.

⚠ We don't usually use *going to* with the verb *go*. We prefer other future forms like the present continuous or *will*.

I'm going to Paris.

I'll go to Paris.

~~I'm going to go to Paris.~~

Present continuous

Use

We often use the present continuous to talk about future plans and arrangements.

*We**'re meeting** at 3.30 on Thursday.* (It's in my diary.)

*I**'m not seeing** him on Friday.* (It's not planned.)

*What time **are you arriving**?* (What's the schedule?)

Form

For information on the form of the present continuous, see page 160.

4

Future possibility modals

Use

1 We use *may*, *might* and *could* to talk about future possibilities. They indicate actions are possible but not certain:

*I **may** be late. / I **might** be late. / I **could** be late. (It's a possibility.)*

2 We also use *could* to say things are possible and we often use it to make suggestions:

*We **could** call his mobile and see if he answers.*

3 We generally use *might* in negative sentences and questions about future possibilities.

*She **might not** get here on time.*

*What problems **might** we have?*

Form

May/might/could have no special third person form.	*I **may** need some help.* *She **might** not get here in time.* *We **could** ask Sally if she's free.*

Ability modals

Use

can, could and be able to

1 When we talk about abilities people have now, we generally use *can*.

*He **can speak** French very well.*

*I **can't remember** a lot about my school days.*

2 *Be able to* and *can* sometimes have the same meaning.

*You **can/will be able to integrate** this into your life fairly easily.*

3 When we talk about abilities people will have in the future, we use *will be able to*.

*You **will be able to improve** your memory with these exercises.*

4 We use *could* and *was able to* to describe abilities people had in the past.

*I **could/was able to learn** things a lot faster when I was younger.*

Form

The modal verbs *can*, *can't*, *could*, *couldn't* have no special third person form. Use *can*, *can't*, *could*, *couldn't* + the base form.	*They **can** sing very well.* *I **can't** speak French.* ***Could** you do the homework?*
When a base form or an *-ing* form is needed use *be able to*.	*I'd like to **be able to** swim better.* ***Being able to** type is a useful skill.* *Will you **be able to** do this work yourself?*

Obligation and permission modals

Use

1 can and can't

We can use *can* and *can't* to talk about things that are or aren't allowed or permitted.

*You **can't** park here during the daytime.*

*You **can** park here after six o'clock at night.*

2 must, have to and need to

We use *must*, *have to* and *need to* to describe things that are necessary or obligatory.

*We **must** / **have to** / **need to** turn left here.*

Must is the strongest verb. We rarely use *must* to give orders to other people, but we might use *must*:

a to say what I oblige myself (not another person) to do.

*I really **must phone** the suppliers today.*

b to say something is a rule, regulation or law.

*Fire exits **must be kept** clear.*

c to suggest something that you think another person will like.

*You **must visit** the Prado Museum. It's wonderful!*

Have to and *need to* are more common ways to describe what is necessary or obligatory.

*I **have to** log on to the computer system.*
*You **need to** give me a password.*

In spoken English, people also use *want to* when they're giving instructions.

*Don't tell anyone your password. You **want to** keep it secret.*

3 mustn't, don't have to and don't need to

The positive forms of *must*, *have to* and *need to* have similar meanings. But the negative forms are different.

Mustn't describes things that are forbidden or not allowed.

*Employees **must not** accept valuable gifts from clients.*

Don't have to and *don't need to* describe things that are not necessary.

*It's only a small gift. You **don't need to** report it.*

*We have plenty of time. You **don't have to** hurry.*

We can also say *needn't* instead of *don't need to*. The meanings are the same.

*It's OK. You **needn't** tell anyone.*

> ⚠ American speakers use *must* less frequently than British speakers and they do not use the contraction *mustn't*. Instead of *must*, they might say *have to* or *required to*. Instead of *mustn't* they might say *not allowed to*.
> *We **have to** meet the targets.*
> *We're **required to** meet the targets.*
> *We're **not allowed to** tell anyone our password.*

4 should and shouldn't

Should and *shouldn't* are weaker forms of *must* and *mustn't*.

*You **should** read the documents. (It's a good idea – the correct thing to do.)*

*You **shouldn't** tell anyone your password. (It's not a good idea.)*

We often use *should* with *think* to exchange opinions.

*I **think** we **should** stick to the agenda in meetings.*

*I don't **think** people **should** take mobile phone calls in meetings.*

*Do you **think** we **should** hold meetings standing up? Yes, I **do**. / No, I **don't**.*

Grammar reference

Form

Modal verbs: *can, must, should*	
Affirmative sentences Use *can/must/should* + the base form of the verb. There is no special third person form.	You **can park** here for as long as you want. I **must remember** to switch off the lights. She **shouldn't agree** to that.
Negative sentences Add *not*	We **cannot agree** to that. I **mustn't forget**. We **shouldn't worry** about it.
Questions Change the word order.	**Can** I **wear** jeans? **Must** I **report** this? **Should** I **wear** a suit and tie?

Semi-modals: *have to, need to*	
Affirmative sentences Add *s* to third person forms.	He **has to tell** his customers about it right away. She **needs to ask** her boss if it's OK.
Negative sentences Use *don't* (do not) / *doesn't* (does not).	You **don't have to report** it. He **doesn't need to report** it.
Questions Use *do* or *does*.	**Do** I **have to attend** the meeting?

had to and need to

There are no past forms of the modal verbs of obligation *must* and *should*. Instead we use the past forms of *have to* and *need to*.

1 We use *had to* and *needed to* when something was necessary in the past.

   I **had to** wear a uniform in my last job.

   We **needed to** work until 10 p.m. yesterday.

2 We use *didn't have to* and *didn't need to* when something was not necessary in the past.

   She **didn't have to** give a presentation in the end.

   We **didn't need to** keep a record of the hours we worked.

3 We use *wasn't/weren't allowed to* when something was not permitted in the past.

   Nobody **was allowed to** make personal phone calls.

make / let / allow

1 We use *let / allow … to* when you have permission to do something.

   He **allows** his staff to vote on most major decisions.

   He **lets** his staff vote on most major decisions.

2 We use *not allow to* when you don't have permission.

   They **don't allow** staff to use the internet.

3 We use *make (someone)* when you force someone into doing something.

   They **made** all their staff work at the weekend.

4 We use *not make (someone)* when you don't force someone to do something.

   We **don't make** our staff work overtime.

5

Conditional sentences

Conditional sentences have two or more clauses joined with *if*. We use them in two kinds of situations.

1 Normal situations where we use normal verb forms.

*If we **charge** for parking, more employees **will** cycle to work.*

*Life **is** more interesting **if** you **have** a lot of friends.*

*If it's **not** the right size, **bring** it back.*

*If you're **going to buy** a new car, you should get a fuel-efficient one.*

See the notes on the right on first conditionals for more examples.

2 Imaginary or unreal situations where we don't use normal verb forms.

*If I **had** a problem, my boss **would** help me.* (imaginary because I don't have a problem)

*If I **were** you, I'd tell the truth.* (unreal because I'm not you)

See the notes on page 170 on second conditionals for more examples.

Punctuation

The *if*-clause can be the first or the second part of the sentence. When it comes at the beginning, we usually put a comma between the two clauses.

*You'll feel better **if** you **do** some exercise.*

*If you **do** some exercise, you'll feel better.*

The zero conditional

Use

We use the zero conditional to talk about situations and events that are generally true. The *if*-clause talks about the cause and the other clause talks about the effect. We can use *when* or *whenever* in the main clause instead of *if*.

*Employees tend to be happier **if/when** they are able to contribute their ideas to plans.*

Form

Zero conditional	
Use *if/unless* + present simple, present simple.	*If I **go** shopping, I **use** recyclable plastic bags.* *I **use** recyclable plastic bags **if** I **go** shopping.* ***Unless** someone **is** in the room, I **switch off** the lights.*

The first conditional

Use

1 We use the first conditional to talk about a possibility in the future. The *if*-clause contains the condition and the other clause contains the result.

*If you **take** more exercise, you'll **feel** fitter.*

*You'll **save** money **if** you **use** energy-efficient light bulbs.*

2 We can use other modal verbs in conditional sentences instead of *will*:

a to talk about something which is only a possible result of the *if*-clause, we use *may/might/can/could*.

*If you replace your old light bulbs for low energy ones, it **can** reduce your electricity bills.*

b to give advice, talk about the correct thing to do or make a strong recommendation, we use *should, need to* or *have to*.

*We **need to** replace these old light bulbs if we want to reduce our electricity bills.*

*If you use a lot of electricity, you **should** consider using renewable sources of energy.*

Form

First conditional	
Use *if /unless* + present simple, *will/ won't* (do).	*If you **cycle** to work, it'll **save** you money.* *If the price **is** too high, she **won't buy** it.* *I'll **take** the job unless I **get** a better offer.*
Similar conditionals	
Use *if/unless* + verb forms that are normal for the situation.	*If you **need** any help, you **can ask** me.* *If it's too expensive, we **shouldn't buy** it.* *If shoppers **don't have** a carrier bag, they **have to pay** for one.*

The second conditional

Use

1 We use the second conditional to talk about imaginary or unreal situations.

> **If** I **had** the time, I**'d have** a long holiday. (I don't have the time.)

> **If** I **were** the mayor, I would ban cars in the city centre. (I'm not the mayor.)

2 We can also use other modal verbs like *could* and *might* in second conditional sentences to talk about possibilities.

> **If** you **wanted** to be eco-friendly, you **could stop** using plastic bags.

> **If** you **cycled** to work, you **might get** fit.

3 We can sometimes use either the first or second conditional, depending on our perception of the situation, and if we think something is likely or unlikely.

> If we **have** enough money, we**'ll** go on a cruise. (likely)

> If we **had** enough money, we**'d** go on a cruise. (unlikely)

Form

Use *if* + past simple, *would/ wouldn't* + base form of the verb.	**If** we **didn't have** a car, we **would take** the bus. **If** I **was** rich, I **wouldn't work**.
In spoken English, *would* often contracts to *'d*. In formal English, we use *were* instead of *was* in all persons in the second conditional.	**If** I **were** in your situation, I**'d resign**.

The third conditional

Use

1 We use the third conditional to imagine a different past from the reality.

> **If** he**'d had** more money, he**'d have bought** the house. (In reality he didn't have the money to buy the house.)

2 We can use other modal verbs in conditional sentences instead of *would have*. To criticize our past actions and the past actions of other people we use *should/shouldn't have*.

> He **should have come** to me if he needed money. (criticism)

> If I **had thought** about it, I **shouldn't have done** a Sociology degree. (regret)

Form

Affirmative sentences *If* + past perfect + *would have* + past participle. The *if*-clause can come first or second.	If **you'd asked** me, I **would have helped** you. I **would have helped** you if **you'd asked** me.
Negative sentences One, or both clauses, can be in the negative form.	If **she hadn't fallen**, she **would have won** the race. She **wouldn't have lost** the race if she **hadn't fallen**.
Questions Change the word order.	**Would** you **have got** the job if **you hadn't lied**?

Passives

Use

1 We use the passive when we are interested in the action, not who does it.

> Mobile novels **are read** by many people on the metro. (We are interested in the mobile novels, not the people who read them.)

2 We often use the passive when we don't know who did an action.

> Japan's first Pocket Films Festival **has recently been launched** in Yokohama. (We don't know who launched the festival.)

> The novel **was written** by an Italian I think. (We don't know exactly who wrote the book.)

3 When we want to say who did an action, we use the preposition *by*.

> The first cellphone call **was made by** Dr Martin Cooper in 1973.

4 We can use different modal verbs in the passive form.

> Professional information **can be stolen** on the web. (It's a possibility.)

> Your manager **must be informed** of any incidences. (It's an obligation.)

> Employees **should be encouraged** to use web tools. (It's a recommendation.)

Passives are more common in written than spoken English. They are also more common when we are writing or speaking in a formal style.

Form

The passive	
Affirmative sentences Use *be* + past participle.	A billion text messages **are sent** each day. The book **was written** by Jhumpa Lahiri.
Negative sentences Use *be* + *not* + past participle.	It **isn't made** of gold. The goods **weren't delivered** on time.
Questions Change the word order.	**Are** everybody's seat belts **fastened**? Where **was** the movie **shot**?
Short answers Use *was/were* or *were/ weren't*.	Was it made in China? **Yes**, it **was**. / **No**, it **wasn't**.

Present simple	Using mobile phones **is forbidden** on this train.
Present continuous	The book **is being made** into a film.
Past simple	The first ring tones **were sold** in Finland.
Past continuous	Her novel **was being promoted** in August.
Present perfect	Her new film **has been released**.
Future	The film **will be shown** all over the country.
Modal passives	It **cannot be done** in two weeks. We **should be allowed to send** personal emails.

6

Nouns and adjectives

Compound nouns

1 A compound noun is a noun that is made up of two or more words. Compound nouns can be formed in different ways.

noun + noun: *toothbrush, suitcase, weekend, room service, business class, tour guide, etc.*

adjective + noun: *single/double room, executive suite, weekly ticket, guided tour, etc.*

verb + noun: *swimming pool, skiing instructor, waiting room, walking tour, etc.*

adjective + verb: *dry-cleaning, multi-tasking*

noun + verb: *car hire, hotel catering, sightseeing, etc.*

2 The two words can be joined together.

air + port = airport, seat + belt = seatbelt, suit + case = suitcase, news + paper = newspaper, camp + site = campsite, etc.

3 The two words can be joined using a hyphen.

check-in, three-star (hotel), *five-day* (cruise), *wake-up call, low-cost* (airline), etc.

4 Compound nouns can also appear as two or more separate words.

hotel reception, window seat, summer holiday, security guard, seafood restaurant, tourist information office, etc.

Quantifiers

Countable and uncountable nouns

Countable nouns	Uncountable nouns
They can be singular or plural. *pizza* → *pizzas* *egg* → *eggs*	They cannot be plural. *food* → ~~foods~~ *salt* → ~~salts~~
They are used with singular or plural verb forms. **Pizza is** my favourite fast food. **These pizzas don't contain** any meat.	They are only used with singular verb forms. **Processed food has** a lot of added salt.

Some nouns have more than one meaning, and they can be countable in one context and uncountable in another.

There was **some chicken** in the salad.

We bought **a chicken** for Sunday lunch.

1 *much*

We use *much* with uncountable nouns, mainly in negative sentences, questions and with *too*.

*I've got **too much food**. I can't eat it all.*

*There isn't **much milk** in this tea.*

*How **much salt** do you put in that?*

2 *many*

We use *many* with countable nouns, mainly in negative sentences, questions and with *too*.

*I've got **too many bags**. I can't carry them all.*

*There aren't **many eggs** in the fridge.*

*How **many grams** of rice do we need?*

3 *a lot of / lots of*

We use *a lot of* and *lots of* with countable and uncountable nouns to talk about large quantities.

*I bought **lots of fruit**.*

*We don't have **a lot of time**.*

A lot of is a very common expression in informal spoken English. In more formal English we prefer other expressions like *a great deal of* + uncountable noun and *a great many* + countable noun.

4 *a little / a few*

We use *a little* with uncountable nouns and *a few* with countable nouns. *A little* and *a few* mean a small quantity.

*I've put **a little chicken** in the salad.*

*There are **a few eggs** in the fridge.*

5 *(very) little / (very) few*

We use *(very) little* and *(very) few* to suggest that there is not as much, or many, of something as we would like.

*I have **little time** to cook these days.*

*There are **few healthy dishes** in a fast food restaurant.*

6 *too / too much / too many*

We use *too, too much* and *too many* when there's more of something than we want or need. We use *too* before adjectives, *too much* before uncountable nouns and *too many* before plural nouns.

*This curry is **too spicy** for me.*

*I can't eat all this food. It's **too much**.*

*He ate **too many cakes** and now he doesn't feel well.*

7 *(not) enough*

We use *(not) enough* when there is less of something than we need or want. We put *enough* before a noun and after an adjective.

*There aren't **enough tables** in the staff dining room.*

*Are you getting **enough vitamins** in your diet?*

*Do you think this dish is **big enough**?*

8 *any / no / none*

We use *any, no* and *none* to express no quantity. We use *any* in negative sentences, *no* in positive sentences and *none* in short answers.

*He doesn't eat **any vegetables**. = He eats **no vegetables**.*

*A: How much pasta is there? B: **None**.*

*A: How many apples are there? B: **None**.*

-ing forms

Use

1 We use -ing to form part of the continuous tenses.

*Young Europeans **are** still **reading** books.*

*She **was waiting** for 20 minutes before her coffee arrived.*

2 Some adjectives end in -ing.

*It's **surprising**, isn't it?*

We use the adjective ending -ed to talk about how the person feels. We use the adjective ending -ing to describe the person or thing that causes the feeling.

*He gave a very **interesting** talk. (Interesting describes the talk.)*

*I was **interested** to hear his talk. (Interested describes the reaction to the talk.)*

3 -ing forms can also be used as nouns. We can use them when an activity is the subject of a sentence.

***Thanking** your host is considered to be polite.*

Comparative and superlative adjectives

	Moscow	Mexico City	Beijing
Population	10.4 million	19.2 million	17.4 million
Cost of living	$$$$$	$$$	$$$$

Use

1 We use comparative adjectives to compare two things:

*Beijing is **larger** than Moscow.*

*Beijing is **more expensive** than Mexico City but it is **less expensive** than Moscow.*

2 We use superlative adjectives to compare three or more things:

*Mexico City is **the largest** city in the world.*

*Mexico City is **the least expensive** of the three cities and Moscow is **the most expensive**.*

Form

Short adjectives Add -er /-est.	Beijing is **cheaper than** Moscow, but Mexico City is **the cheapest**.
Long adjectives Use *more / the most* or *less / the least*.	Beijing is **more expensive than** Mexico City but Moscow's **the most expensive**. Beijing is **less expensive than** Moscow, but Mexico City is **the least expensive**.
Irregular adjectives good　better　best bad　worse　worst far　further　furthest much/many　more　most	The weather in Beijing is **better than** the weather in Moscow, but Mexico City has **the best** weather. The traffic in Beijing is **worse than** in Moscow, but Mexico City probably has **the worst** traffic in the world. Mexico City is **further than** Moscow. Beijing is **the furthest**. Moscow has **many** traffic jams but Beijing has **more**. Mexico City has **the most** traffic jams.
Other cases	
With many two-syllable adjectives, we use *more/most*: *more/most modern, recent, famous, correct, normal, frequent*	
With some two-syllable adjectives, we use either -er/-est or *more/most*: *more clever / cleverer, more simple / simpler, more quiet / quieter,* etc.	

1 For small and big differences, use *a lot, much* and *far* to indicate a big difference in a comparison.

*Studying online is **much more flexible** than attending full-time classes.*

We use *slightly, a little* and *a bit* to indicate a small difference in a comparison.

*It's also **a bit cheaper** than a traditional course.*

2 We use *the same as* to say two thing are equivalent.

*Doing a course abroad costs **the same as** staying here this summer.*

We use *as* + adjective/adverb + *as* to say that things are similar in some way.

*Tokyo can sometimes be **as cold as** Oslo in winter.*

3 To make the expression negative, we use *not as/so* + adjective/adverb + *as*.

*Malta is **not as expensive as** Sardinia.*

Comparative and superlative adverbs

Use

1 We use comparative adverbs to compare two actions.

*I'm progressing **more slowly** than him.*

2 Use superlative adverbs to compare three or more actions.

*She tries (**the**) **hardest**.*

Form

We form the comparative of adverbs ending in -ly with *more*, e.g. *more slowly*.

We form the superlative of adverbs ending in -ly with *most*, e.g. *the most carefully*.

With adverbs which keep the same form as the adjective, we add -er to form the comparative and -est to form the superlative, e.g. *hard, harder, hardest, fast, faster, fastest*.

There are a few irregular adverbs that change their form completely.

good → well, better, best
bad → hadly, worse, worst

(to) + base form or -ing form

Use

1 We use *to* + the base form after *It is* + adjective.

It's **polite to compliment** the cooking and your host.

It's **important to give** people gifts in my country.

2 We use the base form without *to* after modal verbs.

You **should try** some of this. It's delicious.

I'm sorry. I really **must go** now.

3 Some verbs are followed by *to* + the base form, e.g. *would like, want, plan, need, hope, offer*, etc.

Would you **like to have** a coffee break now?

I didn't **want to eat** the bird's nest soup, but I tried a little.

4 A few verbs can be followed by *to* + the base form or *-ing*, e.g. *begin, start, like, love, prefer*, etc.

Do you **prefer having / like to have** lunch at 1 or 2 p.m.?

I don't **like going / to go** out on my own late at night.

5 We use the *-ing* form when the verb is the subject of the sentence.

Understanding different cultures can positively influence your business.

Asking for more food is a compliment.

6 We use the *-ing* form after a preposition.

We honour our guests **by serving** them local specialities.

They had a coffee **after finishing** their meal.

7 Some verbs are followed by the *-ing* form, e.g. *enjoy, mind, suggest, insist on*, etc.

Do you **mind picking** me up from the airport?

Our host **insisted on paying** for everything.

8 We use *to* + the base form to express purpose and explain why you do something.

We're eating out tonight **to celebrate** my birthday.

They wanted to book an expensive restaurant **to entertain** their Mexican guests.

9 There are some verbs that can be followed by either *to* + the base form or *-ing*, but with a change in meaning, e.g. *stop, try* and *remember*, etc.

We **stopped to have** lunch. (pause an activity to do something else)

Could you please **stop sending** me joke emails? (not continue)

Try eating with your hand. It's much easier. (experiment something)

Try to be on time for the meeting. (make an effort to do something)

Remember to take your toothbrush! (don't forget to do something)

Do you **remember visiting** Shanghai? (have a memory of doing something in the past)

Relative pronouns

Use

1 We can use relative pronouns, e.g. *who/that, which/that, where, when* and *whose*, to define people, places or things.

That's the woman **who/that** took the photographs at my wedding.

This is the café **where** we first met.

It's a kind of team-building activity **which/that** you do with ropes.

Trust is **when** you believe in the goodness of other people.

2 We also use relative pronouns when we want to give more information about people, places or things.

David, **who I've known since I was a kid**, is a close friend of mine.

The hotel, **which has fantastic views of the beach**, is ideal for a weekend break.

3 We use relative pronouns to combine two shorter sentences or ideas.

My company always organizes an away day. It isn't doing anything this year.

My company, **which always organizes an away day**, isn't doing anything this year.

4 We use *whose* when you want to say 'of which' or 'of who'.

My wife, **whose parents come from Poland**, was born in Germany.

Do you know that French car manufacturer **whose CEO is a woman**?

5 We don't use commas in defining relative clauses or before *that*.

That's the house **where I grew up.**

6 We use commas in non-defining relative clauses when giving extra information about someone or something.

Abseiling, **which is a kind of adventure sport,** is only for people who are fit.

7 We can use *that* instead of *who* or *which* in defining relative clauses, but we cannot use *that* in non-defining relative clauses when we are giving additional information.

Sandra, ~~that~~ **who** is as old as me, is having a birthday party on Saturday.

New Zealand, ~~that~~ **which** has spectacular scenery, is great for outdoor sports.

8 In defining relative clauses where the main clause and the relative clause have different subjects we can leave out *who/which* or *that*.

That's **the man** (who/that) **I've** been talking about.

Compare these sentences:

That's the girl whose motorbike was stolen.

That's the girl they've just recruited.

It's a national dish we only eat on special occasions.

It's a national dish that is made with seafood and rice.

> ⚠ whose v. who is
> That's the man whose ~~who's~~ wife is a multi-millionaire.
> Who's ~~whose~~ been drinking coffee at my desk? It's very messy.

Grammar reference

Reported speech

Use

1 We use reported speech to say what someone has said and the verb usually goes back one tense.

Direct speech: *'I'm arriving in LA on Thursday.'* →

Reported speech: *She said she **was arriving** in LA on Thursday.*

2 We don't change the verb tense in reported speech when we talk about facts or if something is still true, or if it happened recently.

*'Hollywood **is** the home of the stars.'* → *He says Hollywood **is** the home of the stars.*

*'I **phoned** this morning.'* → *He says **he phoned** this morning.* (It's still morning.)

'I've never been to New York.' → *Lauren said she **has never been / had never been** to New York.*

3 *Tell* is followed by a pronoun. We don't use a pronoun with *say*.

*She **told me** she was arriving in LA on Thursday.* →

*She **said** she was arriving in LA on Thursday.*

4 Modal verbs also change in reported speech. But *might*, *would* and *should* do not.

*'I'**ll** write a letter of complaint.'* → *The customer said she **would** write a letter of complaint.*

*'You **can** complete a questionnaire.'* → *They told me I **could** complete a questionnaire.*

*'You **should** phone to complain.'* → *He said I **should** phone to complain.*

5 We often have to make other changes such as time expressions, pronouns and words like *this* or *here*.

*'The builders are coming **next week**.'* → *He said the builders were coming **the following week**.*

*'The technician was meant to come **last week**.'* → *She said the technician was meant to come **the previous week**.*

*'I'll give **you my** mobile phone number.'* → ***He** said **he** would give **me his** mobile phone number.*

*'We've lived **here** for nine years.'* → *They told us they'd lived **there** for nine years.*

*'We want **this** done by tomorrow.'* → *They said they wanted **it/that** done by the following day.*

6 We can report a statement word for word, or we can summarize what has been said.

'The manager is busy. Could you phone back later?'

*The secretary **asked me to phone** back later.*

7 *That* after the reporting verb is optional.

*She told me (**that**) she was arriving in LA on Thursday.*

*She promised (**that**) she would write.*

Form

Tense changes in reported speech
Present simple → Present simple / Past simple
Present continuous → Present continuous / Past continuous
Past simple → Past simple / Past perfect
Present perfect → Present perfect / Past perfect
Past perfect → Past perfect

Other changes:

Modal verbs
We'll do it. → *They said they **would** do it.*   *I can't start until Monday.* → *He said he **couldn't** start until Monday.*   *I must/have to call them.* → *She said she **had** to call them.*

Time expressions
I'll fix it tomorrow. → *She told me she would fix it **the following day**.*   *I called twice yesterday.* → *He said he **had called** twice the day before.*   *We need the order for next week.* → *They said they **needed** the order for the following week.*

Pronouns
I'm going to complain to your manager. → ***He** said **he** was going to complain to my manager.*

 Reported negative requests

We say *not to* + verb when we report negative requests.

*The customer asked me **not to call** again.*

say vs **tell**

We mention the person, or use an object pronoun, after *tell* but not with *say*.

She said she didn't agree.

*She told **the teacher/him** she didn't agree.*

Embedded questions

Use

1 Sometimes we do not ask questions directly. Instead we start with phrases like *Do you know …?, Could you tell me/us …? I'd like to know …,* or, *I'd be interested to know …*

> *What time does the film start?*
>> **Do you know** *what time the film starts?*
>> **Could you tell me/us** *what time the film starts?*

> *What did you think of the film?*
>> **I'd like to know** *what you thought of the film.*
>> **I'd be interested to know** *what you thought of the film.*

2 After one or two embedded questions, we generally change to direct question forms.

> **Do you know** *when they're getting married?* (embedded question)
> **Could you tell me** *if it's going to be a big wedding?* (embedded question)
> *So, how many guests are coming?* (direct question)

3 We can also use expressions like *Did you say …?* or *Are you saying …?* in embedded questions. We use these expressions to check hearing and understanding, but also to signal a challenge, for example, to express surprise, or when we want to say, *I don't believe you.*

> **Did you say** *15 or 50?* (checking hearing)
> **Are you saying** *the meeting's been cancelled?* (checking understanding)
> **Are you saying** *they haven't separated?* (I don't believe you!)

Form

Direct question	Embedded question
Change the word order in a direct question. *Why **did he quit** the show?*	Use the expression + question word(s)+ the usual word order. **Could you tell me why he quit** *the show?*
Are they planning *to get married?*	Use *if* when there isn't a question word. **Do you know if they're planning** *to get married?*
Be careful with word order in questions that start with *Could you tell me …? Do you know ..?* etc. *Could you tell me where ~~do they live~~ **they live**?* *Do you know if ~~has the concert been cancelled~~ **the concert has been cancelled**?*	

Irregular verb list ~~WITHDRAWN~~

Verb	Past simple	Past participle	Verb	Past simple	Past participle
be	was/were	been	lend	lent	lent
beat	beat	beaten	let	let	let
become	became	become	lie	lay	lain
begin	began	begun	light	lit	lit
bend	bent	bent	lose	lost	lost
break	broke	broken	make	made	made
bring	brought	brought	mean	meant	meant
build	built	built	meet	met	met
buy	bought	bought	pay	paid	paid
burn	burnt/burned	burnt/burned	put	put	put
burst	burst	burst	quit	quit	quit
catch	caught	caught	read (ri:d)	read (red)	read (red)
choose	chose	chosen	ride	rode	ridden
come	came	come	ring	rang	rung
cost	cost	cost	rise	rose	risen
cut	cut	cut	run	ran	run
deal	dealt	dealt	say	said	said
do	did	done	see	saw	seen
draw	drew	drawn	sell	sold	sold
dream	dreamt/dreamed	dreamt/dreamed	send	sent	sent
drink	drank	drunk	set	set	set
drive	drove	driven	shoot	shot	shot
eat	ate	eaten	show	showed	shown
fall	fell	fallen	shut	shut	shut
feel	felt	felt	sit	sat	sat
fight	fought	fought	sink	sank	sunk
find	found	found	sleep	slept	slept
fly	flew	flown	speak	spoke	spoken
forget	forgot	forgotten	spend	spent	spent
freeze	froze	frozen	spill	spilt/spilled	spilt/spilled
get	got	got (BrE) / gotten (AmE)	spoil	spoilt	spoilt
give	gave	given	spread	spread	spread
go	went	gone/been	stand	stood	stood
grow	grew	grown	steal	stole	stolen
have	had	had	stick	stuck	stuck
hear (hiər)	heard (hɜːrd)	heard (hɜːrd)	swim	swam	swum
hide	hid	hidden	take	took	taken
hit	hit	hit	teach	taught	taught
hold	held	hold	tell	told	told
hurt	hurt	hurt	think	thought	thought
keep	kept	kept	throw	threw	thrown
know	knew	known	understand	understood	understood
lay	laid	laid	wake	woke	woken
lead	led	led	wear	wore	worn
learn	learnt/learned	learnt/learned	win	won	won
leave	left	left	write	wrote	written

Costume History

CLOTHES OF THE ANCIENT WORLD

Christine Hatt

Illustrated by Jane Tattersfield

Chrysalis Children's Books

First published in the UK in 2001 by

Chrysalis Children's Books

The Chrysalis Building, Bramley Rd, London, W10 6SP

Paperback edition first published in 2003

ISBN 1 84138 138 1 (hb)

ISBN 1 84138 858 0 (pb)

British Library Cataloguing in Publication Data for this book is available from the British Library.

A BELITHA BOOK

Series editor: Claire Edwards

Series designer: Angie Allison

Cover design: Keren-Orr Greenfeld

Illustrator: Jane Tattersfield

Picture researcher: Diana Morris

Consultant clothing historian: Dr Jane Bridgeman

Education consultant: Anne Washtell

Printed in Hong Kong

10 9 8 7 6 5 4 3 2 1 (hb)

10 9 8 7 6 5 4 3 2 1 (pb)

Picture acknowledgements:

Acropolis Museum, Athens/Werner Forman Archive: 6b. David Bernstein Fine Art, NY/Werner Forman Archive: 7r. British Museum/Werner Forman Archive: 6t. V&A Picture Library: 7t.

The artwork of the High Priest on page 16 is based on a drawing by Barbara Phillipson, copied with permission from Alfred Rubens, *A History of Jewish Costume*, published by Weidenfeld and Nicolson 1967.

CONTENTS

Words in **bold** are explained in the glossary.

INTRODUCTION

This book will show you the clothes that people from many different lands wore in the ancient world. This period began thousands of years ago in prehistoric times. It continued through the rise, rule and fall of the first great civilizations around the world. It ended in about 500 AD, as the **Roman Empire** collapsed in the West.

Why wear clothes?

No one knows exactly why or when people began to wear clothes. The most obvious reason for covering the body is to protect it from the weather. Early humans probably started to cover themselves in furs to keep out the cold of the **Ice Age**. But even in hot places, such as Africa, **prehistoric** people often wore some clothing. This may have been to protect themselves from insects, thorny plants, or rough rocks. But many experts believe that men and women of the distant past did not dress for practical purposes alone.

This prehistoric man is wearing an animal fur 'skirt'. The animal's tail can be seen at the front. The skirt is held up at the waist by leather strips.

Early prehistoric people dressed in furs and skins. This archer's skirt-like loincloth is made from a single fur. The fur's ragged ends show that it has not been cut to fit, but left in its natural shape.

Looking good

People who study the history of clothing have suggested three other main reasons why the earliest humans wore clothes – status, religion and appearance. Garments may have shown a person's status, for example as a member of a group or tribe. During religious ceremonies, people may have worn special clothes. They probably believed these clothes would give them magical powers (see page 9). Then as now, humans may simply have wanted to look good, either for their own pleasure or to attract a partner.

The *toga picta*, made of gold-embroidered purple cloth, was worn in Roman times. At first it was the costume of victorious generals. Later it was worn by emperors (above) and consuls.

4

Robes of rank

As civilizations developed, clothing became a common way of showing someone's **rank** and wealth. Rulers wore splendid robes in fabrics that ordinary people could not afford. Members of important professions, such as priests, dressed in special costumes to make their status clear. Most civilizations also had armies, which led to the development of uniforms. Soldiers could be instantly recognized in a uniform and this also helped them to bond with one another to create strong fighting units.

About this book

The next two pages will show you how experts have discovered what ancient people wore. Each double page that follows describes the clothing of a particular place and time. Material Matters boxes give more information on types of material from which clothes were made. Other boxes give information on special subjects, such as military or religious costumes. There is a brief timeline at the top of each page, and maps on pages 44–45 will help you find some of the places mentioned in this book.

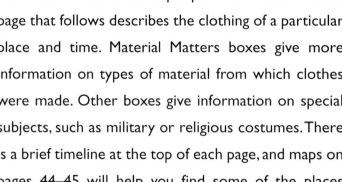

The royal bodyguards of the ancient Persian Empire were known as the Immortal Archers. They wore loose, embroidered tunics with flared sleeves, and probably close-fitting tunics underneath.

What is a costume?
A garment is an individual item of clothing. A costume is a set of clothes designed to be worn together.

Date fact
Some of the dates in this book have a c. in front of them. This stands for the Latin word *circa* and means 'about'.

A Matter of Modesty

Today, one of the main reasons for wearing clothes is modesty. Even on the beach in hot weather most people still wear swimming costumes. But many ancient people did not worry about nudity. For example, Greek athletes did not wear clothes, even when taking part in public events such as the Olympic Games. Modesty became more important after the rise of Christianity in the first century AD and of Islam in the seventh century.

HOW WE KNOW

The study of early clothing is very difficult, because so few garments have survived from the ancient world. But experts look at those that do exist, as well as other evidence such as paintings, sculptures and written descriptions. In this way they can gradually build up fairly accurate pictures of what humans wore many thousands of years ago.

This Ancient Egyptian tomb painting is more than 3500 years old. It shows the fine linen garments and jewelled collars worn by a man called Nebamun, his wife and their daughter (the small figure at the front of the picture).

Ancient garments

Clothing materials usually fall to pieces as time passes. However, extremely dry, cold or wet conditions can preserve them. **Archaeologists** have found fragments of ancient textiles and even whole garments in hot, dry deserts, frozen **steppes** and wet bogs. Among them are linen clothes from Egypt, cotton clothes from Peru and woollen clothes from Denmark. Often these clothes had been buried in graves alongside their owners.

Ancient art

Ancient art of all sorts can give us valuable information about clothing. Experts can study Egyptian tomb paintings, Greek vases, Roman sculptures and Maya pots. Tiny wooden statues from Ancient Chinese tombs are often clothed in miniature silk costumes. Small **terracotta** statues from Ancient Greece may also show the shape and detail of clothing, but not the colours. Coins and **seals** may carry pictures of richly dressed rulers.

Greek statues were often very detailed. This one was made in the sixth century BC. You can see the folds in the woman's *peplos* dress and the curls in her hairstyle. Objects like this help experts find out what people wore in the past.

Looking at the evidence

This museum conservator is carefully repairing a child's dress.

Costume experts have to be careful when they study art evidence. There are several reasons for this. First, ancient art usually shows rich people, so it may tell us little about what ordinary people wore. Second, early artists often drew an ideal world. For example, many Egyptian tomb paintings show people dressed for the afterlife, not daily life. Lastly, some civilizations had strict, unchanging rules about how to draw humans. So artists may have shown them in clothes that were in fact long out of date.

MATERIAL MATTERS

Experts in the USA examined the wrappings around a 2000-year-old Egyptian mummy. They discovered that the inner wrappings were linen and the outer wrappings ramie, a fabric made from nettles. It is difficult for insects to eat through ramie, so this material was ideal for protecting the mummy.

Written sources

Costume experts also learn about what people wore by studying books and other written sources. But records from the ancient world are patchy. For example, the historians, novelists and poets of Ancient Greece and Ancient Rome often mention clothes, but they rarely describe them in much detail.

Costume Care

Ancient costumes are precious. After archaeologists have studied them under microscopes and carried out chemical tests, they are cared for by **conservators**. Their job is to make sure that the clothes do not crumble or fade. They may add backing material to textiles to hold them together. They may treat them with chemicals to stop insects from eating them. They also make sure that the heating, lighting and air-conditioning in museum rooms do not damage the garments.

This piece of cloth was made by people of the Paracas culture, who lived in Peru between about 600 and 200 BC. They embroidered garments with brightly dyed llama and alpaca wool.

PREHISTORIC CLOTHING

Early humans spread across the world during the last **Ice Age**, when ice sheets covered much of Northern Europe, North America and other areas. **Prehistoric** people in cold places may have begun to dress in furs over 40 000 years ago.

To prepare animal hides for clothing, prehistoric people first pegged them firmly out on the ground. This stretched the hides and stopped them moving around while the fur and flesh were removed.

First furs

In Europe, people often wore bear and reindeer furs. They tied them on or held them in place with thorn shoulder pins and leather waist thongs. In North America, people dressed in the furs of buffalo, and later deer and beaver.

This picture shows an 8000-year-old pair of moccasins. They are made of antelope hide and were found in Danger Cave, Utah, USA.

Preparing hides

Humans slowly invented ways to make the hard animal **hides** soft and waterproof, such as by rubbing them with fish oil or egg yolk, or a solution of oak-tree bark. They removed the fur by scraping it off with **flints** or by dissolving it with **alkaline** substances such as ashes.

Successful sewing

Humans also learned how to cut the hides into shapes to fit the body, and to sew the pieces together into garments. In Northern Europe, they sewed with needles made of bone, horn or **ivory**, while in North America, bone **awls** were used. For thread they used leather thongs, animal **sinews** or tough plant fibres.

People used bone awls to punch holes in animal hides, so they could thread strips of leather or other material through to sew garments together. With needles (above), they could make the holes and pull the strips through at the same time.

Textile traditions

Farming first developed in the Middle East, and people soon began to make fabrics from farmed plants and animal hair. Linen, made from **flax**, may be the oldest fabric. Pieces more than 8000 years old have been found in Israel. **Archaeologist**s have also found 5000-year-old woollen cloth in Egypt, and cotton fabric of a similar age in Pakistan.

This woollen shirt was made in Sweden during the Bronze Age. It has embroidery on the sleeves and around the neck.

MATERIAL MATTERS

The oldest known piece of felt was discovered in the village of Çatal Hüyük, Turkey. It is more than 7000 years old. Felt is made by pressing, heating and wetting tightly rolled fur so that the hairs tangle and weave together. Felt was made in Central Asia during the prehistoric era, and Mongolians who live there now still make it in the same way.

Ritual Dress

Ancient paintings on cave walls, for example in France and Spain, sometimes show people wearing antlers (see right), horses' tails and masks, as well as animal skins. These prehistoric humans may have dressed in special garments to take part in religious rituals. By wearing something taken from an animal, they may have hoped to gain its strength, or the ability to hunt the animal successfully. Such ceremonies have taken place for at least 35 000 years.

SKINS FOR ALL SEASONS   FROM c.40 000 BC

Many of the garments made in Ice Age Europe were similar to suits worn by **Inuit** people in Canada today. People wore thick fur boots, trousers and long-sleeved tunics, usually with a hood (see left). These were sewn together with reindeer sinews using needles made from reindeer horn. Some had bone buttons. In warmer parts of the world, people dressed in skin loincloths or skirts, or trousers and sleeveless tunics (see right). These garments were sometimes decorated with shells. People also wore necklaces and other jewellery made of animal teeth, ivory or **amber**.

c.4000 BC
Rise of Sumerian civilization.

c.2000 BC
Rise of Babylonian civilization in south Mesopotamia.
Rise of Assyrian civilization in north Mesopotamia.

c.1700 BC
Babylonian Empire at height of its power.

MESOPOTAMIA

Mesopotamia was the area of the Middle East between the Tigris and Euphrates rivers. This is where modern Iraq now lies. Several of the world's earliest civilizations grew up in the region, and their peoples gradually developed many distinctive styles of costume.

A Sumerian man wearing a wrap-around *kaunakès* skirt. These garments sometimes had long tails of fabric attached at the back.

Sumerian skins

The first of these civilizations was the Sumerian, which began in about 4000 BC. Its early people dressed in skirts made of sheepskins. They also wore short skin cloaks. In about 3000 BC the Sumerians began to weave wool into a cloth to which they attached tufts of animal hair. This cloth, called *kaunakès*, was made into skirts and full-length cloaks. Later in the Sumerian period, people wore long, draped wool and linen garments with tasselled edges.

The kings of Babylon sometimes wore this decorative style of headdress with feathers around the top.

Babylonian costumes

From about 1700 BC the **empire** of the Babylonians became the most important in Mesopotamia. The people wore two main items of clothing – a full-length, short-sleeved tunic and a fringed shawl draped over the top. These garments were often made of fine wool and dyed bright colours. Patterns were sometimes embroidered on to the cloth. In the late years of the empire, men wore tunics alone, with long sleeves and neck tassels.

This bracelet was found inside a royal tomb in a city called Kalhu, once the capital of Assyria. It is made of gold with pieces of turquoise-coloured **enamel set in it, and has an **agate** gemstone in the centre.**

The Babylonians usually wore leather sandals on their feet. Most styles covered the heel at the back and held the big toe in a ring.

Assyrian gold

The Mesopotamian empire of Assyria reached the height of its power in about 750 BC. Its people wore similar clothes to the Babylonians. Assyrians were very fond of jewellery – both men and women wore heavy gold earrings, bracelets and 'dog collar' necklaces. Slaves shielded rich women from the sun with parasols.

ASSYRIAN SPLENDOUR
C.EIGHTH CENTURY BC

The Assyrian king on the left is dressed in a short-sleeved tunic with a long shawl wound round his body to make a double-fringed skirt. Only the king was allowed to wear the shawl in this way. Like all Assyrian men, kings took great care of their hair and beards. They often darkened them with black dye and curled them with hot irons. Sometimes they also wore wigs. The king's tasselled headdress is called a mitre.

The Assyrian queen on the right wears a fringed robe with a circle pattern over a white linen tunic. Her accessories include a gold crown and large gold earrings.

Army Outfits

The uniforms of the Assyrian army developed over time. At first, soldiers on foot and horseback dressed in short fabric tunics, belted at the waist. Later, they wore breast- and backplates (see right) or knee-length tunics made of metal for extra protection. Archers in chariots or on horseback often wore full-length tunics covered in metal plates. Conical metal helmets with cheek-flaps protected soldiers' heads.

MATERIAL MATTERS

Kaunakès cloth (see page 10) was covered in tufts of animal hair. These were often arranged in decorative layers and combed to look neat. *Kaunakès* was sometimes also made by weaving loops into the cloth rather than sewing tufts on afterwards. The aim was to make a material that looked like sheep or goatskin, but that was easier to shape and wear.

ANCIENT EGYPT

Egypt became a powerful, united kingdom in about 3100 BC and its civilization lasted for almost 3000 years. The people of this hot, dry, desert land wore light garments. Clothing styles changed little during this long period of history.

This Old Kingdom noble is wearing a linen kilt with an overlapping pleated section. The end of this section is pulled through the linen belt around his waist to hold the kilt firmly in place.

Early styles

The history of Ancient Egypt is divided into three main periods, the Old, Middle and New Kingdoms. The Old Kingdom lasted from about 2686 to 2181 BC. At this time many working men wore very little. The main items of clothing were loincloths or short **kilts**, made of rough, unbleached linen. Nobles wore longer kilts of finer linen, some pleated at the front. Styles changed little in the Middle Kingdom (1991–1786 BC), but some nobles began to wear kilts with skirts over the top.

Rich Egyptians usually shaved their heads then put wigs made of human hair on the top. This New Kingdom woman wears a long lappet wig. It is decorated with a headband made of gemstones set in a wire frame.

New Kingdom novelties

Egyptian civilization reached its high point under the New Kingdom, from 1567 to 1085 BC. During this time, its rulers, called pharaohs, conquered nearby lands such as Phoenicia and Syria, and new clothing styles spread from there. Rich men began to wear long tunics and draped robes, either loose or belted. Kilts remained the standard garment for working men.

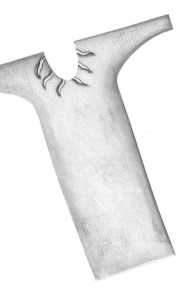

Women's wear

During the Old and Middle Kingdoms, women wore tight, straight sheath dresses and possibly also long-sleeved, V-necked dresses with tie fastenings at the neck. Sheath dresses remained popular in the New Kingdom. But many rich women began to wear robes made of two pieces of linen joined at the top, and **sari**-like garments made of a single piece of fabric draped in a variety of ways.

Linen tunics like this were found in an Egyptian woman's tomb. Egyptians believed in life after death, and the tunics were probably made for her to wear then. Experts are not sure if women wore such tunics in real life.

MATERIAL MATTERS

Most Ancient Egyptian clothes were made of linen, but animal hides were also popular for kilts, belts, shoes and sometimes gloves. In very early times, people wore raw skins. Then, gradually, they learned to make soft leather. At first, they spread salt and other minerals on the hides in a process called **tawing**. Later they buried the hides in pits with oak **galls**, oak bark and water. This **tanning** process took many months.

Priestly Costume

The priests of Ancient Egypt dressed in tunics and kilts of bleached white linen, which were sometimes pleated. Some important priests draped leopard skins over their linen garments (see left). The leopards' heads, paws and tails were usually left on the **hides**. The priests may also have worn fabric that was painted or woven to look like leopard skin instead.

MIDDLE KINGDOM MODES c.1990 BC

The woman on the right is wearing a full-length sheath dress with two shoulder straps. (Some dresses had just a single strap fastened over one shoulder.) The zigzags on her dress were a common fabric design, but a pattern of four-petalled flowers was also popular. Linen was very difficult to dye, so patterns were usually made by embroidering the cloth with coloured wool, by painting, or by sewing beads on to the bleached white fabric. Beaded collars were worn by both men and women.

The court official on the left is dressed in typical Middle-Kingdom style. He is wearing a transparent linen skirt over a short kilt. The cape was also a new fashion of the Middle Kingdom and was worn by women, too.

13

PHARAOHS AND QUEENS

Ancient Egypt was ruled by kings called pharaohs. The special styles and fine fabrics of their costumes showed that they were the most important people in the kingdom. Their wives looked equally splendid.

Early outfits

The earliest pharaohs wore short, sleeveless tunics. Belts with jewelled **pendants** were fastened around the waist and bulls' or lions' tails attached at the back as a sign of royal power. In the Old Kingdom, pharaohs often wore grander versions of nobles' kilts. One type was made of pleated linen wound around the body to form three sections at the front. Another had a triangular **apron** decorated with royal symbols such as serpents.

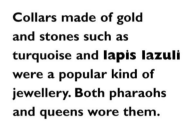

Collars made of gold and stones such as turquoise and **lapis lazuli** were a popular kind of jewellery. Both pharaohs and queens wore them.

The regions of Upper and Lower Egypt were united in about 3100 BC (see page 12). Afterwards, the pharaohs wore a double crown that combined Upper Egypt's white crown with Lower Egypt's red one.

New styles

Pharaohs' clothes changed little during the Middle Kingdom, but their garments became more elaborate in the New Kingdom. Pharaohs of this era often wore long robes of transparent, pleated linen with short kilts underneath and jewelled aprons on top. Robes were sometimes draped to look like three separate garments – a **kilt**, tunic and cloak. Long, pleated kilts with low waists also became fashionable.

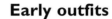

Pharaohs and queens often wore thonged sandals made of plaited leather or palm leaves. There were several different designs.

Queens' costumes

During the Old and Middle Kingdoms, queens often wore sheath dresses. In the New Kingdom, robes (see box right), **sari**-like garments and long skirts with short capes were popular. Egyptian queens decorated their costumes with jewels, gold and embroidery. They also wore special royal headdresses, including one shaped like a vulture with its wings spreading down over the hair.

This early tunic is sleeveless and has a strip at the top that fastens over the left shoulder. The animal's tail at the back was a sign of the pharaoh's power. The pendants at the front were made of leather and precious stones.

ROYAL ROBES C.1320 BC

This couple are the New Kingdom pharaoh
Tutankhamun and his wife Ankhesenamun.
Tutankhamun is wearing a pleated linen kilt in the
low-waistline style. A decorative belt with pendant
apron and streamers holds the kilt in place.
He has a large, jewelled collar around his neck,
and on his head he wears a ceremonial
headdress and a curled wig.

Ankhesenamun's robe is made from two pieces of
fabric joined at the top. The piece at the back is
pulled forwards and tied in a knot over the piece at
the front. Decorated streamers fall from the knot. Like
her husband, the queen also wears a collar, wig and
elaborate headdress. Her eyes are outlined with
black paint and coloured with eye shadow.

Into Battle

Pharaohs often wore tight-fitting
armoured coats (see right) when
they rode into battle on their
war chariots. The coats were
made of leather with protective
metal or bone panels. On their
heads they usually wore a crown known
as a *khepresh*. This was decorated with
a serpent at the front. The *khepresh* was
often blue, but could also be red or white.

MATERIAL MATTERS

Pharaohs, queens and their
people liked to wear linen
garments for several reasons.
First, it comes from **flax**, which
is a plant. This meant that it
was not considered unclean like
wool, which comes from an
animal. Second, it was white, a
colour that Egyptians believed
to be sacred. Also, linen was
cool to wear and easy to wash.

THE HEBREWS

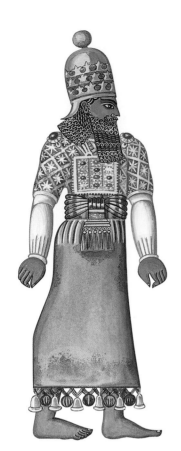

The clothes worn by the High Priest of the Hebrews are described in the Bible. They included a long tunic, and a chest panel decorated with 12 gemstones. Each stone represented one of the tribes of Israel.

The Hebrews were an ancient people of the Middle East. Their early history is told in the **Old Testament** of the Bible, but many details are unclear. Experts do know that by the eleventh century BC, they were living in a kingdom called Israel and were later conquered by the Assyrians. Early Hebrew dress was influenced by Assyrian and also Egyptian styles.

Problems of evidence

It is not easy to find out what the Hebrews wore. Costume descriptions in the Bible are difficult to understand. Religious laws did not allow people to make carvings of humans, and no other art has survived. Experts must look at images made by other peoples, such as the Egyptians and Assyrians. None survives from early times.

Early garments

The earliest Hebrews probably wore loincloths, skirts and shawls made from the **hides** of their sheep and goats. Gradually, they learned to spin and weave a kind of rough clothing fabric. By about 4000 years ago, men and women were probably wearing long woollen tunics decorated with stripes or zigzags. They may have been woven from or embroidered with dyed wools from nearby Phoenicia.

Tunics and tassels

By about the eighth century BC, important men and women wore a full-length, sleeved tunic (*kethoneth*) with a fringed hem. A fringed cloak (*simla*) was wrapped over the top. Men may also have worn tasselled waist **girdles**. According to the Bible, the tassels (*tsitsith*) were to help the Hebrews remember God's commandments. In fact Assyrians and others also wore tassels on their hems.

Hebrew men often attached *tsitsith* tassels to their garments. By about the fifth century AD, cloaks with *tsitsith* on the corners had become special Jewish garments known as *talliths* (prayer shawls). Today, Jewish men still wear prayer shawls during religious services.

This mother-of-pearl shell from the Red Sea was once used to hold make-up. It was found in the Jewish royal palace and fortress of Masada, near the Dead Sea. It dates from the first century AD.

A pair of leather sandals was also discovered at Masada (see left). They were found near a female skeleton, so were probably worn by a Jewish woman nearly 2000 years ago.

MATERIAL MATTERS

The Hebrews usually made their clothes from wool and linen. Religious laws did not allow them to weave the two into a single fabric, but they could be worn together in separate garments. Fabrics coloured with bright dyes were very popular. Red dye was made from a type of plant called henna, and yellow was made from safflowers. The Hebrews also used wools that had been coloured red, blue or purple using dyes from a type of shellfish called murex.

Greek Garments

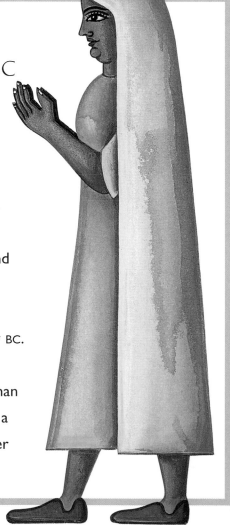

By the first century AD, the kingdom of Israel had long ceased to exist, but Judaea had survived Persian and Greek rule to become part of the **Roman Empire**. Its people, now known as Jews, sometimes wore items of Persian clothing, such as trousers, but experts think that their everyday costume was based on Greek dress. Evidence for this comes from **frescoes** painted in a **synagogue** in Syria in the third century AD (see left). They show Jewish men wearing the Greek **chiton** tunic (see page 22). People also wore **himation** cloaks – Jesus wore one edged with *tsitsith* tassels.

CARVED IN STONE
NINTH TO EIGHTH CENTURY BC

The picture on the left is based on the earliest surviving image of an ancient Hebrew. The man is probably a king and appears on an Assyrian **obelisk** that dates from the ninth century BC. He is wearing a short-sleeved, full-length *kethoneth* tunic with fringing along the bottom. He has a girdle around his waist and a soft, pointed cap on his head.

The Assyrians conquered Israel in the eighth century BC. The image on the right is taken from a carving that shows Israelites captured by the Assyrians. The woman is wearing a long-sleeved, calf-length *kethoneth* with a *simla* cloak over the top. The cloak is pulled up over her head and covers her hair.

PERSIA

Persian men often wore a type of hat known as a Phrygian cap. The caps were made of felt or leather and had a point at the top that drooped over to the front, back or side.

Ancient Persia covered roughly the area of the modern country, Iran. In the sixth century BC, the Persians defeated the Babylonians to create a huge **empire** stretching from India in the east to Turkey in the west. Unlike earlier peoples in the region, the Persians mainly wore sewn, fitted clothes, rather than loose, draped robes.

Trousers and tunics

The Persians' ancestors had been horse-riding **nomads** in the icy Asian **steppes**. They developed clothing that was warm and easy to wear in the saddle. Men wore trousers and knee-length tunics, often with a coat over the top. At first these garments were made from animal skins, but in Persia, people began to use wool, linen and, later, silk.

Flowing robes

The Persians adopted another item of clothing from the Medes, who lived in the same region. Many high-ranking Medes wore a long, draped garment similar to the Egyptian robe (see page 12). In Persia this garment was worn by the king. Trousers were often worn underneath.

The Persians wore various types of leather shoe. Some were tied tightly to the foot with laces (above). Others were fastened with buttons (see right).

Female fashions

Persian carvings and other art forms show mainly men, so it is difficult for experts to work out what women wore. In the early years of the empire, women probably dressed in short-sleeved tunics, large veils that covered their heads and shoulders, and perhaps also trousers. As time passed, women probably began to wear Assyrian-style clothing with their veils. Assyrian styles included fuller tunics with fringed shawls draped over the shoulder, around the waist or both. The most common fabric was linen.

Experts believe that Persian women often wore large, plain veils that covered their heads, shoulders and mouths.

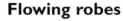

A KING AND A RICH MAN
c.500 BC

The picture on the left shows King Darius I, who ruled the Persian Empire from 521 to 486 BC. His full, brightly coloured robe is patterned with rosettes and pulled tight around the waist with a jewelled belt. He wears tight, legging-style trousers underneath his robe and has buttoned leather shoes on his feet. Darius' crown is made of gold **inlaid** with jewels. It is perched on top of dark hair that has been curled into ringlets.

The man on the right is a rich Persian. His woollen trousers are close-fitting like leggings at the foot, but wider at the top. His short tunic is made of patterned wool and is belted around the waist. The coat reaches almost to the ground. The man's cap is made of felt and has streamers at the back.

War Wear

There were many types of Persian military uniform. **Cavalry** often wore plumed helmets with metal-plated tunics and fabric trousers. Foot soldiers wore colourful tunics with waist sashes and felt caps or fabric hats (see above). The best royal archers, called the Immortals, dressed in long, gold-embroidered tunics (see page 5). There are pictures of the Immortals on the walls of Emperor Darius' palace at Susa, once the capital of the Persian Empire.

MATERIAL MATTERS
Silk was originally produced in China, but knowledge of how to make it gradually spread along the **Silk Roads** (see page 37) to Persia. Brightly coloured and patterned silks were woven by the Sassanians, who ruled Persia from the third century AD. These materials were highly valued in the West and fragments of them have survived.

c.3000 BC
Minoan civilization grows up on Crete.

c.2000 BC
Palace of Knossos built.

c.1600 BC
The Mycenaeans of eastern Greece come into contact with the Minoans.

CRETE AND MYCENAE

The first civilization in Europe was the Minoan civilization. It grew up on the Mediterranean island of Crete from about 3000 BC. The Minoans developed a unique, decorated style of costume. From about 1600 BC, Greeks living in Mycenae on the nearby mainland came into contact with the Minoans and adopted their styles of dress.

Palace pictures

The best evidence for Minoan costume comes from **frescoes** and **terracotta** figurines. These have been discovered in the ruins of Cretan palaces such as Knossos. Most of the people shown are high-ranking members of society, priests or gods, so experts know more about their garments than the clothing of ordinary people.

Skirts and bodices

In the early years of Minoan civilization, women dressed in loincloths. As time passed these developed into long skirts, often with flounces, that curved out from belted waists. The skirts were made of linen, or from wool or leather dyed in bright colours such as purple and red. The fabric was often embroidered with patterns. Above their skirts, women wore tightly laced, short-sleeved **bodices**.

Minoan men

Minoan men dressed in loincloths made of wool, linen or leather. Some loincloths were in a **kilt** style – short at the back with a tasselled point at the front. Others were in a shorter **apron** style, which finished in a point at the back, or at the back and the front. Men wore cloth or leather belts decorated with gold, silver and other metals, often beaten into shapes such as spirals. The belts were pulled tight to emphasize the men's broad, muscular chests.

This Minoan man wears an apron-style loincloth with a point at the back and the front. He has a dagger tucked into the leather belt around his waist. The man is barefoot but has cloth strips wound round his legs.

This picture of a woman is based on a small statue of a Minoan goddess. Her skirt has six layers and a decorative apron over the top. Above the waist she wears a tight bodice.

Minoan men's sandals often had leather strips wound round the ankles. The rich sometimes decorated these with beads. In cold weather, men generally wore short leather boots instead.

c.1400 BC
Eruption of a volcano on the island of Thera destroys
the Minoan and probably the Mycenaean civilization.

c.1400–800 BC
The Dark Age – Greece recovers from the volcanic eruption.

MATERIAL MATTERS

The Cretans were expert wool weavers. A flock of about 80 000 sheep supplied fleeces for use in a major workshop at the palace of Knossos. There the wool was spun and coloured with plant and animal dyes. It was then woven into fine fabrics for rich people's clothing.

Mycenaean Dress

Mycenaean Greek women often dressed in Minoan-style skirts and bodices. They also wore long tunics with short sleeves and belts around the waist. Mycenaean men often wore short tunics with leggings. Another popular fashion was for shorts with a matching vest top. Both shorts and top were decorated with tassels, tufts of animal hair or perhaps felt (see left).

CRETAN FINERY   c.1500 BC

The man on the left is dressed in a kilt-style loincloth made of embroidered linen. The leather belt is trimmed with gold and the triangular tassel at the front is made of beads. The man's long, fringed hair and the **lapis lazuli** bracelets around his arm and ankles are all typically Minoan. Both men and women loved to adorn themselves with jewellery.

The woman on the right wears a flounced dress from the Late Minoan period. At this time a piece of light, see-through linen joined the two sides of the bodice at the front. This style was also popular in Mycenae. The woman's dark hair is very long and covered with a delicate pearl headdress.

21

800–500 BC
Archaic Greece – the first
city states are founded.

500–300 BC
Classical Greece.
Greek civilization reaches its height.

499 BC
Beginning of wars with Persia.

479 BC
Greeks defeat Persians
and end their threat to Greece.

ANCIENT GREECE

The Minoan civilization (see pages 20–21) was destroyed by a volcanic eruption in about 1400 BC. The Mycenaeans probably perished, too. But by about 900 BC Greece was slowly recovering, and in the early fifth century BC the Classical Period began. During this era, most people wore graceful, draped clothing.

The Doric *chiton*

The main item of clothing was the **chiton** (tunic). The simplest type was the Doric *chiton*. It was made of one or two lengths of woollen fabric pinned at the shoulder and belted at the waist. The men's tunic was short. The women's tunic, known as the *peplos*, was worn in various lengths, often on top of an Ionic *chiton* (see below). A special style of *peplos* was made by folding a piece of cloth to create a double layer at the top.

The Ionic *chiton*

The Ionic *chiton* became fashionable later than the Doric. It was made from a rectangle of linen or fine wool folded in half and sewn together down the long side. The fabric was pinned together on the shoulders and folds of fabric were joined along the arms to create elbow-length sleeves. Women's Ionic *chitons* were full-length, men's usually knee-length. A single or double **girdle** held the *chiton* at the waist.

Classical cloaks

Men and women wore long, loose **himation** cloaks. Men often wound their cloaks over one shoulder and under the other. Women sometimes draped them over both shoulders and pulled up the back to cover their heads. Some people wore a short cloak called a *chlamys*.

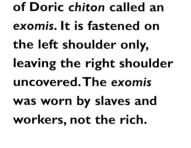

This man is wearing a type of Doric *chiton* called an *exomis*. It is fastened on the left shoulder only, leaving the right shoulder uncovered. The *exomis* was worn by slaves and workers, not the rich.

Greeks pinned their tunics and cloaks together with brooches called *fibulae*. Only a rich person could have afforded a *fibula* like this one, made of decorated gold.

Many Greek women kept themselves cool by waving small feathered fans (above) in front of their faces. Other women employed slaves to wave much larger fans for them. These fans were attached to long poles.

Turning Heads

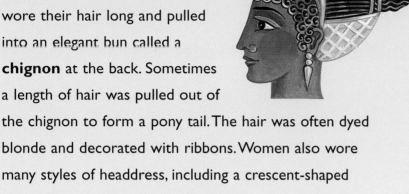

Women in Classical Greece usually wore their hair long and pulled into an elegant bun called a **chignon** at the back. Sometimes a length of hair was pulled out of the chignon to form a pony tail. The hair was often dyed blonde and decorated with ribbons. Women also wore many styles of headdress, including a crescent-shaped tiara called a *stephane* (see above). It was often joined to a linen bag that supported the chignon.

MATERIAL MATTERS

Classical Greek garments were made of wool, linen and, sometimes, cotton. Starch was used to produce fashionable, crinkled linen, or the crinkles were woven into the fabric itself. A shiny version of this material was made by working oil into the weave. Silk clothing was sometimes worn in this era (wild silk was made on the Greek island of Kos), but became more common later.

GRACEFUL GREEKS c.450 BC

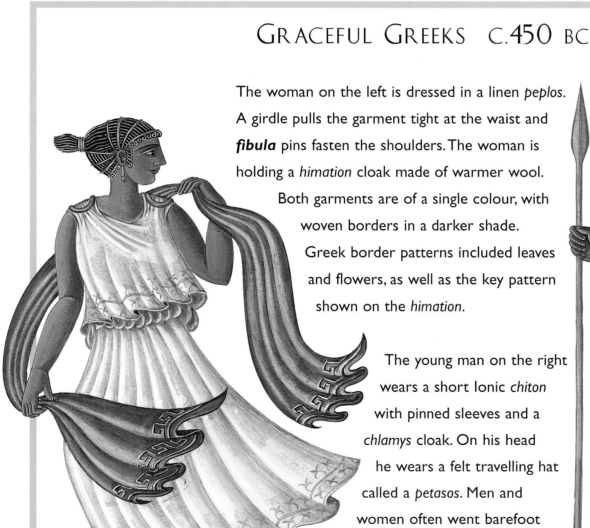

The woman on the left is dressed in a linen *peplos*. A girdle pulls the garment tight at the waist and **fibula** pins fasten the shoulders. The woman is holding a *himation* cloak made of warmer wool. Both garments are of a single colour, with woven borders in a darker shade. Greek border patterns included leaves and flowers, as well as the key pattern shown on the *himation*.

The young man on the right wears a short Ionic *chiton* with pinned sleeves and a *chlamys* cloak. On his head he wears a felt travelling hat called a *petasos*. Men and women often went barefoot at home and outside, but sometimes wore strapped leather sandals.

ANCIENT GREEK ACTORS AND SOLDIERS

In Ancient Greece, as in the modern world, people with special jobs often had special clothing. Soldiers dressed in armour, while actors wore costumes and masks that showed the type of character that they were playing.

Foot-soldier fashions

Greek foot soldiers of the Classical Period were called *hoplites*. They wore short **chitons** with armour on top. The armour had three main parts – a **cuirass** (breastplate and backplate), **greaves** (leg guards) and a helmet. The cuirass was made of shaped bronze, metal scales, leather or linen. The greaves and helmets were also made of bronze. Hoplites were named after the shields they carried, which were called *hoplons*.

Cavalry costume

The Greek **cavalry** dressed in *chitons* and cuirasses. They also had brimmed metal helmets and knee-length leather boots. They usually wore a bronze arm guard on one arm to fend off blows and carried a sword or spear with the other. Stone-throwers called *psiloi* also formed part of Greek armies. They held animal skins in front of themselves for protection.

Theatrical costume

The Greeks enjoyed going to the theatre. All actors were men but they played male and female parts, changing character several times in a single play. Men who acted in tragedies often wore long, padded *chitons* in dark colours, and thick-soled boots to make themselves tall. Comic actors wore short *chitons* in bright colours or dressed up as animals. All actors wore masks. The masks showed who the characters were and what they felt.

Stone-throwers called *psiloi* fought with the Greek army, but were not proper soldiers. They wore ordinary clothes and used animal furs as shields. *Psiloi* sometimes carried clubs as well as stones.

This actor is dressed as a soldier in a *chiton*, short *chlamys* cloak and mask. Even in tragedies, actors playing soldiers wore short *chitons*.

A group of actors known as the Chorus took part in most Greek plays. They all spoke together to comment on what the main actors were doing. This chorus member is dressed as a bird for a comedy play.

24

DRESSED FOR ACTION C.450 BC

The hoplite on the left is wearing a bronze cuirass shaped to look like a man's chest muscles. Leather strips hang from the bottom and partly cover the skirt of the *chiton* underneath. Bronze greaves, also shaped like muscles, protect the hoplite's legs. His helmet has cheek guards and a horsehair crest. He carries a short iron sword and is holding a round, bronze and leather shield called a *hoplon*.

The cavalryman on the right is wearing a *chiton*, metal cuirass, one full arm guard and a helmet. His *chlamys* cloak could be rolled up to give his arm extra protection. He is carrying a spear and has his sword in a **baldric**.

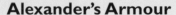

MATERIAL MATTERS

Greek actors' masks were usually made of cork or stiffened linen. Before masks were invented, the actors probably made up their faces with wine dregs or dangerous substances such as white lead.

Alexander's Armour

In 338 BC the Greek city states were defeated by King Philip II, who ruled the nearby state of Macedonia. His son Alexander the Great went on to conquer the Persian Empire. During one battle against the Persians, Alexander wore a linen cuirass instead of his usual bronze one. The layers of linen were glued together to make the cloth stiff, so that it protected him from weapons. The cuirass was also light and allowed him to move easily. He decided never to wear a metal cuirass again. In battle, Alexander also always wore a Phrygian-style helmet (see left).

ANCIENT ROME

The ankle-length *tunica talaris* had long, fitted sleeves and was often brightly decorated. It was worn by both men and women.

The Roman **republic** was founded in the sixth century BC. Its armies gradually conquered the rest of Italy, Greece, Egypt and other lands. In 27 BC, the republic became an **empire**, which lasted until 476 AD. Many Roman clothes copied Greek styles, but new fashions were often influenced by costumes from conquered regions.

Tunic styles

During the republic, men of all **ranks** wore tunics like Greek *chitons*. They were usually short, and did not have sleeves. In the empire, men generally wore short, T-shaped tunics with sleeves. They were often made of linen and decorated with two vertical stripes, or with **tapestry** panels. Later, the full-length *tunica talaris* (see left) and long, wide-sleeved *dalmatica* came into fashion.

Toga types

Men often wore togas over their tunics. A toga was made by draping a large semicircle of woollen cloth round the body. In imperial times, only Roman citizens were allowed to wear togas. There were several types of toga. The plain *toga virilis* was woven from undyed wool and was worn by adult men. The *toga praetexta*, which had a purple border along the straight edge, was worn by boys under 16 years and some officials.

Roman boys wore a necklace called a *bulla* to protect them from evil. Sometimes it was made of a golden ball with a charm inside. Poor boys made *bullas* from a long strip of leather tied in a knot.

Stolas and pallas

The main item of female clothing during the republic was the **stola**. This was a robe like a long *chiton*, with or without sleeves. A rectangular cloak called a **palla** was draped over it. Both garments were still worn under the empire and long tunics also became popular. During this period, women's clothing became more richly decorated.

This simple type of Roman shoe is called a *carbatina*. It was made from one piece of leather wrapped around the foot. The shoe was held in place with a leather tie around the ankle.

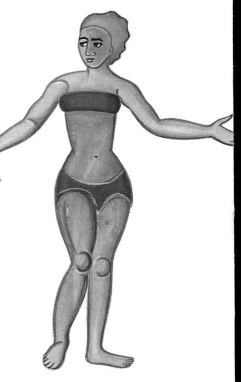

This drawing is based on a Roman **mosaic**. The woman is wearing a breast band and a short, fitted loincloth made of linen or leather. These garments were probably the underclothes worn by most Roman women.

From Tebenna to Toga

The Etruscans lived in central Italy from about the eighth century BC and were eventually conquered by the Romans. They may have originally come from Turkey and their clothing was influenced by both Asian and Greek styles. The Etruscans often wore a draped garment called a *tebenna* over a tunic (see right). The *tebenna* was the ancestor of the Roman toga.

MATERIAL MATTERS

The Romans wove wool and linen to make their garments, and brought cotton from India and silk from China. They also made a special fabric called *cilicium* from goats' hair. It was waterproof, so fishermen often wore *cilicium* clothing when they went out in their boats.

IMPERIAL STYLE   C.100 AD

The man on the right is wearing a short-sleeved tunic called a *tunica laticlavia*. This special type of tunic was worn only by **senators**. The tunic has two vertical tapestry stripes running from shoulder to hem, back and front. They have been coloured using a dye from a shellfish called murex. Over the top of the tunic the man wears a *toga virilis*, made of undyed wool. The fabric is draped simply, over the left shoulder, around the back and under the right arm, finishing at the shoulder again. In later years, togas were draped in more complex ways. From about the third century AD, togas were usually worn only for grand ceremonies.

The woman on the left is dressed in a *stola* with sleeves. It is made of fine linen. Her woollen *palla* is draped over one shoulder and pulled up over her head. The woman's hair is pulled into a **chignon** at the back, and at the front she has three rows of artificial curls.

SOLDIERS IN ANCIENT ROME

The Romans conquered a huge empire thanks to their large, disciplined army. During the rule of the first emperor, Augustus, the army became a permanent, professional fighting force. Imperial soldiers, called legionaries, went to war dressed in metal armour and carrying short swords, spears and shields.

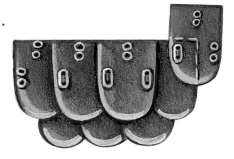

The small metal plates that made up Roman scale armour were joined together one by one. Then they were attached to a fabric lining. This was probably made of roughly woven linen.

Body armour

Legionaries protected their chests and backs with various forms of body armour – **chain mail** made of linked metal rings, **scale armour** made of overlapping metal plates, or the *lorica segmentata* (see far right). Leather straps protected shoulders, necks and thighs. Underneath their armour legionaries wore short tunics made of wool with short sleeves. In cold regions, they also wore half-length or full-length trousers called *braccae*, and often a thick, red woollen cloak called a *sagum*. Men tucked scarves into their armour at the neck to stop it rubbing the skin.

Roman army officers called centurions wore helmets with crests running from side to side rather than front to back.

Helmet styles

The earliest helmets were made of leather, but this was later replaced by metal, often decorated with feathers or horsehair crests. By the time of the **empire**, plain bronze or iron helmets were more common, although some officers wore helmets with crests. Imperial helmets had cheek and neck flaps to protect these areas.

Centurions carried special staffs (sticks) made of vine wood. They used them to beat legionaries as part of their training or to punish disobedience.

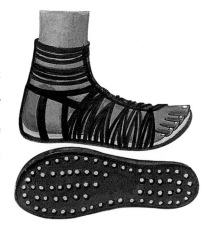

Both foot and **cavalry** soldiers wore sandals like this, known as *caligae*. They were made of leather and had nails in the soles.

Soldiers' shoes

Marching and fighting were hard on the feet, so Roman legionaries wore strong leather sandals called *caligae* or short, lace-up boots, some with animal-skin linings. The soles had nails in them to make them more hardwearing. Officers protected their lower legs with metal **greaves**.

FIGHTING FASHIONS c.150 AD.

The legionary shown here is wearing the *lorica segmentata* over his tunic and short *braccae* trousers. This type of armour was made of steel strips attached to a leather lining and fastened with buckles and leather ties. It allowed soldiers to move more freely than other types of back- and breastplate. An apron of metal-plated leather strips hangs from the soldier's belt. On his right is a wooden shield, painted blue and decorated with a thunderbolt. He carries a throwing spear called a *pilum* in his left hand.

The other soldier is a standard-bearer. His job was to carry the standard (emblem) of a century (a group of 80 legionaries) into battle. He is holding a standard and wearing chain-mail armour over his woollen tunic. He has an animal skin draped over his helmet.

MATERIAL MATTERS

The army used so much material for its uniforms that in the third century AD, the government set up mills to produce all the wool that it needed. The mills also supplied fabric for government officials' clothes.

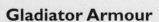

Gladiator Armour

A gladiator was someone trained to fight in public to entertain an audience. There were four types of gladiator. Each type had its own style of armour. Samnite gladiators (see left) wore metal helmets with **visors** and short wool or linen **kilts** that were cut high at the side of the legs. The lower halves of their legs were protected by metal greaves, and their right arms and left thighs were also armoured.

THE CELTS

Experts are unsure when the people known as the Celts arrived in central Europe, but they were settled there by about 800 BC. Slowly they spread into Spain, Portugal, Britain and Ireland. The Romans defeated the Celts of mainland Europe and Britain in the first centuries BC and AD. From then on, the two peoples greatly influenced each other's costume styles.

This bronze helmet with pointed horns was probably made in the first century BC. It belonged to a Celtic chieftain, but he may have worn it for special ceremonies rather than for battle.

From woad to wool

The early Celts wore little except furs. They also painted a blue dye called woad on their skin. Later, they learned to weave wool and to make simple clothes. Men wore short tunics, with short or long sleeves, and trousers. Women dressed in long gowns. The tunics and gowns were often belted at the waist. Both men and women wore large cloaks, which they also used as blankets.

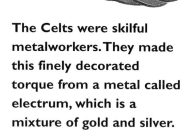

Military dress

While fighting for themselves and later as part of the Roman armies, Celtic warriors dressed in a variety of garments. These included tunics, cloaks, **chain mail** armour and horned helmets. They wore neck rings called torques, made of metals such as gold, and carried decorated metal shields. Some warriors tattooed woad patterns on their faces, arms and legs.

The Celts were skilful metalworkers. They made this finely decorated torque from a metal called electrum, which is a mixture of gold and silver.

The Celts knew how to make glass. They made rings of different colours by adding minerals to the glass mixture.

Celtic colours

The Celts loved bright colours and often dyed wool before it was made into clothing. Many plants and fruits were used to make the dyes. The wools were then used to weave patterns. Checks were popular, but circles, stripes and other designs were also common. Patchwork bands were sometimes added to finished garments.

c.3rd century BC
Celts spread into Greece
and Anatolia (modern Turkey).

2nd century BC
Romans defeat Celts in Italy.

1st century BC
Romans defeat Celts
in France and Germany.

1st century AD
Romans defeat Celts in Britain.

Roman Influence

Romans sometimes wore Celtic-style trousers and cloaks. In the same way, rich Celts in Roman Britain often wore Roman-style tunics and cloaks, though not togas. A hooded cloak called a *birrus* (see right) was especially popular among Celts under Roman rule in both Britain and France. The cloak was made of thick, coarse, undyed wool and eventually developed into the hooded habit worn by many Christian monks.

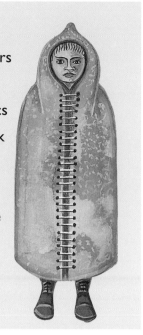

MATERIAL MATTERS

Poor Celts continued to wear tunics and trousers made of goatskin long after weaving was invented. The rich, both men and women, sometimes put simple fur waistcoats over woven garments and men sometimes draped animal skin capes around their shoulders for warmth.

CELTIC CHECKS c.100 AD

This family group is dressed in typical Celtic style. The man wears trousers made of checked wool. They are held up around the waist by a cord and tied tight around the ankles. His shoes are made of leather with the fur still attached and worn on the inside. Most Celtic men had long hair and a drooping moustache as shown here.

The woman in the group is wearing an ankle-length belted gown. She has a cloak of checked wool fastened around her shoulders with a bronze clasp called a **fibula**. Her hair is long and plaited, and her eyebrows are dyed black with berry juice. Her child wears a short tunic belted at the waist.

31

THE MIGRATING TRIBES

The Romans brought the Celts (see pages 30–31) under their control, but by the fourth century AD other peoples threatened their **empire**. They included Asiatic tribes from the east, such as the Huns, and Germanic tribes from the north, such as the Franks. All these peoples wore some form of trousers and short tunics.

Hun style

The Huns came from the cold **steppes** of central Asia. They were skilled horsemen who wore close-fitting trousers and short-sleeved tunics of rough linen, belted at the waist. They had cloaks, of fur or cloth, fastened around the neck, sometimes with brooches. The Huns were a fierce people who cared little for how they looked. They wore their garments until they fell apart.

This Hun is wearing a leather skullcap with a fur border. Hats like this were ideal for the cold climate of Central Asia.

Members of many tribes sometimes fought with the Roman armies instead of against them. They often wore simple tunics and trousers instead of metal armour. Their main weapons were shields, swords and spears.

The Franks

Early Frankish warriors, from western Germany, often wore legging-style trousers bound on with strips of cloth. These were sometimes worn with a short-sleeved fitted top, but could also be joined to a vest, forming a kind of all-in-one suit. Like the Celts, the Franks wore simple leather shoes with the fur on the inside.

The Goths

The Germanic Goths lived around the Black Sea until the Huns pushed them west. At first they wore trousers and long-sleeved linen tunics with fur borders, but later they also dressed in the **chain mail** armour and metal helmets of the Romans. On their feet they wore short leather boots. A group of Goths called the Visigoths captured and sacked Rome in 410 AD.

The Lombards were a Germanic tribe that invaded Italy during the sixth century AD. This engraved figure shows a Lombard horseman wearing a decorated tunic and plain leggings.

GERMANIC GARMENTS c.400 AD

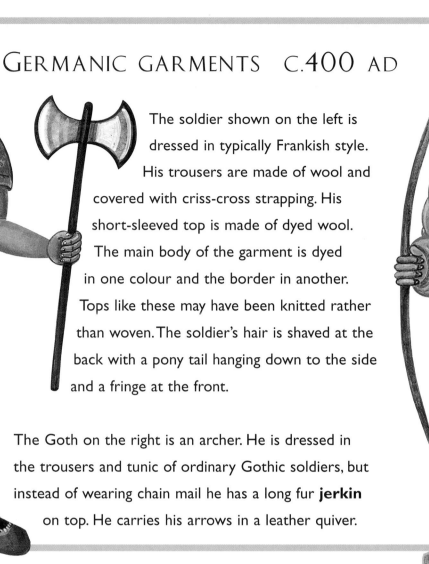

The soldier shown on the left is dressed in typically Frankish style. His trousers are made of wool and covered with criss-cross strapping. His short-sleeved top is made of dyed wool. The main body of the garment is dyed in one colour and the border in another. Tops like these may have been knitted rather than woven. The soldier's hair is shaved at the back with a pony tail hanging down to the side and a fringe at the front.

The Goth on the right is an archer. He is dressed in the trousers and tunic of ordinary Gothic soldiers, but instead of wearing chain mail he has a long fur **jerkin** on top. He carries his arrows in a leather quiver.

MATERIAL MATTERS

Some Germanic tribes, including the Teutons, made many of their clothes from the plant called **hemp**. They wove its fibres into a cloth. Hemp is a material used to produce rope, so the garments were probably rough and scratchy.

Gothic Jewels

The Goths made beautiful jewellery from precious metals, pearls and jewels such as garnets. The Visigoths continued this tradition when they set up a kingdom in Spain during the sixth century. This beautiful cross was discovered in their capital city, Toledo.

ANCIENT INDIA AND PAKISTAN

One of the world's first civilizations grew up in Pakistan's Indus Valley in about 2500 BC. The people who lived there dressed in loincloths. Similar, simple garments were worn in the Indian **sub-continent** for the whole ancient period.

This statue was found in the Indus Valley city of Mohenjo-daro. It is more than 4000 years old and shows a bearded priest-king. The man's shawl is patterned and draped over his left shoulder.

Clothes in the Indus Valley

There is little evidence to show what Indus Valley people wore. One surviving statue is of a man wearing a shawl, armlet and headband. He was probably a priest-king, so his garments are not typical. Ancient figurines suggest that ordinary men and women wore cotton loincloths. Women may have worn **girdles** around their waists, too.

Aryan attire

In about 1500 BC, the people known as Aryans settled in northern India. No images of their clothing have survived, but many items are mentioned in the Hindu scriptures, called the Vedas. Experts believe that people of this era wore a long, skirt-like garment that hung down from the waist in pleats. They probably also draped a piece of cloth over the upper body in various ways. Gold and silver jewellery were common.

Women probably began to wear the *bindi* mark on their foreheads in Gupta times. It may have been a sign that they were married.

Mauryan modes

The Mauryan dynasty ruled India from the fourth to the second century BC, and statues from the end of this era have survived. They show men in long *dhoti* (loincloths) with **kamarband** waistbands. Women are shown in similar garments draped lower on the waist. This style of clothing was worn over the following centuries, altering slightly under new dynasties such as the Guptas (see right). There were no major changes in costume until Muslims conquered parts of India in the eleventh century.

This necklace and bracelet were also discovered at Mohenjo-daro. The beads are made of **carnelian**, gold, baked clay and **soapstone**.

34

Tying Turbans

Turbans are mentioned in the Hindu scriptures and in very ancient times both men and women wore them. By the second century BC they were a standard part of men's dress. They were fastened with a large knot at the front. A lock of hair was usually tied into the knot.

MATERIAL MATTERS

The people of the Indus Valley were the first in the world to grow cotton and to turn it into fabric. They made dyes from the plants of the region and used them to dye the fabric many bright colours before making their garments.

CHANGING STYLES c.200 BC–1400 AD

The man shown on the left is wearing clothes from about 200 BC, during the Mauryan era. His loincloth has been pulled up at the overlap to create a V shape between the legs. A strip of embroidered cloth known as a *patka* hangs down the centre of the garment and a wide *kamarband* is tied in a bow round the man's waist. He has a scarf tied around his chest.

The woman above right is from the same period. Her loincloth sits on the hips, held by a jewellery girdle. A *patka* hangs from her waist. The second woman dates from the Gupta era (c.320–495 AD). You can see that the ends of her loincloth are raised to the waist to make legs in the fabric. The material is striped red and black in the style of the time. Women usually wore only jewellery on their upper bodies.

ANCIENT CHINA

The people of Ancient China discovered how to make silk more than 4000 years ago. China's first civilization, the Shang, grew up in the seventeenth century BC and its rich men and women often wore clothes woven from silk. But experts know little about Chinese costume before the time of the Han dynasty (206 BC–220 AD).

This ancient Chinese emperor is wearing a special style of flat hat that was probably made of stiffened black silk. It has rows of beads hanging down in front of the eyes and behind the head.

Flowing robes

In the Han era, wealthy people often wore a flowing, floor-length **p'ao robe**. The two sides of the robe crossed over at the front and were tied with a **girdle** at the waist. The robes were usually made of plain or patterned silk, sometimes embroidered in gold or trimmed with fur.

Trousers and jackets

Trousers were also common garments for men and women, especially the poor. A knee-length jacket was often worn on top, tied at the waist. These items were made of rough **hemp**, cotton or other fabrics, depending on the wearer's wealth and the climate. Padding was added for warmth. Poor people sometimes wore shoes made of cloth or straw, but usually they went barefoot.

Military costume

In the period just before the Han dynasty, China was united by Emperor Shi Huang Di. When he died in 210 BC, the emperor was buried in a tomb protected by an army of 7000 life-size clay warriors. They are modelled to look as if they are dressed in armour, or in cloth trousers and tunics. Like Roman soldiers, they have scarves around their necks to prevent their armour from rubbing. This **Terracotta** Army gives experts plenty of evidence for military costume in ancient China.

A pair of shoes like these were found in a Han dynasty tomb. They are made of silk and were held on the feet with silk ties.

The warriors of the Terracotta Army are very detailed. On many of them you can even see the rivets that held the iron squares of their armour together.

MATERIAL MATTERS

According to legend, a silkworm cocoon (see below) once dropped into hot tea that the ancient Chinese empress Hsi-Ling was drinking. At once the cocoon's long, shiny fibres unravelled and the empress realized that a fabric could be made from them. This story is probably not true, but the Chinese did develop a silk industry in the far-distant past. They grew orchards of mulberry trees for the silkworms to feed on, waited until they made their cocoons, then unwound, reeled and wove the fibres.

The Silk Roads

The Chinese kept the process of silk-making secret for thousands of years. So Romans and other foreigners who wanted silk **yarn** or fabric had to buy it from them. Trade routes from China through Central Asia to the West reached the **Roman Empire** by the first century AD. They were called the **Silk Roads**, although camel caravans also carried other goods along them. The secret of cultivating the silkworm was finally discovered in the West by about the fifth century AD.

RICH AND POOR c.100 AD

The wealthy man on the left is wearing a full *p'ao* robe made of red silk with a design in the weave. His sleeves are wide and hang in loose folds from his wrists. The man's silk slippers, tied on with ribbons, can just be seen under the hem of the *p'ao*. He has a cap made from cleverly folded black silk perched on his head.

The poor man on the right is dressed in a short, padded jacket with elbow-length sleeves. His wide trousers finish below the knee. He has cloth shoes tied around his ankles and a rough cloth hat on his head.

THE ANCIENT AMERICAS

During the last **Ice Age** a land bridge linked North America to Asia. Humans crossed over it into the Americas between 40 000 and 12 000 years ago. By 300 AD, the Maya civilization was at its height in Guatemala and Mexico. Many peoples also settled further north.

A backstrap loom had a strap at one end that was worn around the weaver's back. Another strap at the front of the loom was tied around a post or tree. Weavers sat back so that the cloth they were making was pulled tight.

Colourful cloth

The Maya made clothing of light materials suitable for their hot climate. Important members of society dressed in cotton, woven on backstrap **looms**. Feathers or rabbit fur were sometimes woven into the cotton for warmth. Poor people made clothes from tree bark. Woven sisal (see far right) was also used. The Maya loved colour and decoration. They stained cloth with plant dyes and decorated clothing with embroidery, shells and beads.

Maya costume

Maya men usually wore a loincloth. Women wore a long, wrapround skirt with a **poncho** (*quechquemitl*) or a tunic (*huipil*) over the top. Ordinary men and women wore cloaks made of cloth. The rich wore feather or jaguar skin cloaks. The Maya decorated themselves with **jade**, shell and other jewellery. They also wore feather headdresses. Maya soldiers wore tunics made of tough **tapir hide**.

North American variety

Many peoples made their homes in North America. Their clothing depended on local materials and climate. In the far north, they dressed in furs, as well as sealskin boots. Peoples of the north-west Pacific coast probably wore capes of woven cedar bark and blankets of goat hair. In the woodlands of the north-east, men and women dressed in deerskin decorated with porcupine quills.

This **Maya man** is wearing a jaguar skin. The jaguar's head is perched on top of his head and jaguar-skin bands decorate his feet.

The **Adena people** lived in south-east North America from about 1000 BC. They made burial mounds for the dead, and put carvings in them like this one. It shows a man wearing a patterned loincloth. He also has huge disks in his ears.

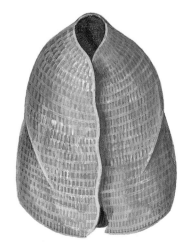

A **cedar bark cape** of the type made on the north-west coast of North America. These garments were often trimmed with the fur of sea otters.

FEATHERY FASHIONS c.400 AD

The Maya woman on the left is wearing a plain wrapround skirt made of loosely woven cotton. Her fringed *quechquemitl* has been coloured using natural dyes. The woman also wears a feathered headdress and decorated leather arm bands.

The Maya man on the right is wearing a loincloth. The fabric is pulled up between the legs, tucked in at the waist and left to hang in loops. Around his neck he wears shell beads. The man's headdress includes the tail feathers of tropical birds. On his feet he is wearing leather sandals that are closed at the back and open at the front. He also has leather bands on his legs.

Dressed for Success

Pacal was a seventh-century ruler of the Maya city of Palenque in Mexico. He wore water lilies in his hair and tied it up to look like the crest feathers of a macaw. His head was pointed because it had been bound when he was a baby to show that he was a member of Maya royalty.

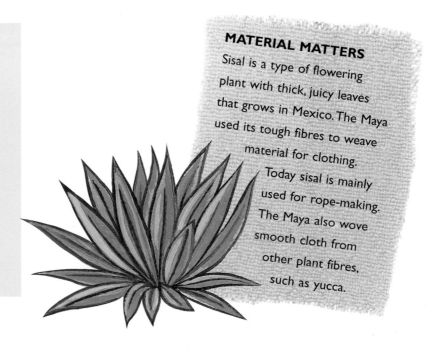

MATERIAL MATTERS

Sisal is a type of flowering plant with thick, juicy leaves that grows in Mexico. The Maya used its tough fibres to weave material for clothing. Today sisal is mainly used for rope-making. The Maya also wove smooth cloth from other plant fibres, such as yucca.

39

MATERIAL MATTERS

Here you can find out more about the most important clothing materials featured on earlier pages. They are animal furs and skins, and the four most widely used ancient textiles – linen, wool, cotton and silk.

A flax plant in full flower. The plants grow almost a metre high.

Animal furs and skins

Furs and skins were used to make the first garments in many parts of the world. Many animals, such as reindeer and caribou in Europe and jaguars in South America, were hunted for their fur coats. Often the hair was removed and the skins were **tanned** to make leather. This could then be turned into clothes and shoes. **Archaeologists** have discovered ancient robes in Asia that are made of squirrel fur and **sable hides**.

Early peoples often stretched and dried animal skins by attaching them to frames made of wooden sticks.

Linen

Linen was probably the first ever textile (see page 8). It was made from the stems of **flax** plants. The stems were dried, then soaked (retted) to separate the hard parts from the fibres suitable for spinning. The spun fibres were then woven into cloth. The whole process is shown in Ancient Egyptian tomb paintings. Linen clothing was especially popular in Egypt, where strips of linen were used to wrap mummies too. Linen was also worn in the Middle East, Turkey and parts of Europe.

Harvested stalks of flax

Wool

Wool is probably the second oldest fabric (see page 8). Woollen cloth was first produced when people in Mesopotamia and Egypt started to herd flocks of sheep. At first, the sheep's fleeces were plucked out, but later metal cutting tools were invented, and farmers sheared their flocks. The fleeces were combed, cleaned and spun

A Soay sheep. Some of the earliest woollen clothes in Europe were probably made from the fleeces of sheep like this. Their coats have several different colours in them and are made up of hair as well as wool.

Flax stalks before (top) and after retting. This process causes bacteria to break down the hard parts of the flax. The soft fibres suitable for cloth-making can then be removed.

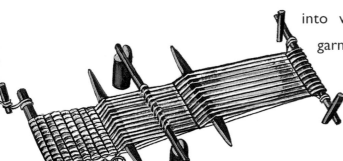

The early Ancient Egyptians used ground looms (above) for weaving. Later, they developed upright looms. These were also used in ancient Europe. The peoples of South and Central America often wove their textiles on backstrap looms (see page 38).

into wool thread, which was woven into garments. Goat wool was used in the Middle East, and in South America, llama wool was common. The Greeks and Romans wore fine sheep's wool clothing.

Cotton

Cotton was first planted and harvested in India and Pakistan (see page 8), but it was also grown in ancient China, Mesopotamia, Egypt and the Americas. Alexander the Great (see page 25) brought cotton plants to Europe from India in the fourth century BC, but the Greeks and Romans continued to wear wool and linen far more than cotton. The textile is produced by picking fluffy, white **bolls** off the plants (see right), carefully removing the seeds, then spinning and weaving the boll fibres.

Silk

Silk is made from silkworm cocoons (see below). It was first made in China between 4000 and perhaps as many as 7000 years ago (see page 37). The secret of silk-making spread to Korea and Japan in about the third century AD. Then it moved west along the **Silk Roads** to Central Asia, Persia, Syria and finally Europe in the first to fourth centuries AD. Before this date, the Greeks and Romans imported silk from China as silk fibre, or as clothing, which they unpicked and wove into their own fashions.

Cotton plants grow up to 2.5 metres tall. They produce flowers like this.

After the cotton flowers have fallen off, seed pods called bolls develop.

The bolls grow to about the size of eggs, then burst open to show their seeds. The seeds are surrounded by fluffy white cotton fibres known as lint (above). Before the fibres can be spun, the seeds have to be removed.

A Silkworms are the caterpillars of silk moths. Each worm feeds on mulberry leaves before settling on a twig to build a cocoon.

B The sticky silk threads come out of a hole in the silkworm's head. The worm surrounds itself with more and more of them.

C After about three days, the cocoon is complete. The worm is now surrounded by about 275 metres of glossy fibres ready to be unravelled.

A   B   C

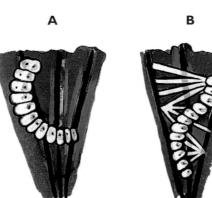

ANCIENT ACCESSORIES

To complete their costumes, ancient people wore all sorts of accessories. Some, for example glittering necklaces, were mainly for decoration. Others, for example hard-wearing army boots, had a practical purpose. You have already read about some of these items earlier in this book. This chart tells you more, and makes it easy to compare the jewellery, footwear and headwear worn at many times and in many places.

	JEWELLERY	FOOTWEAR	HEADWEAR
PREHISTORIC TIMES	30 000 years ago – the first jewellery is made of bone, stone and **ivory**. 10 000 years ago – **amber** is popular. 6000 years ago – **jade** and gold (from gold nuggets found in rivers) is introduced.	First humans go barefoot. In cold regions shoes are made from animal furs tied round the feet. People learn to sew, and make shoes and boots. **Moccasins** are made from skins with the fur removed.	People go bareheaded in hot regions. Fur caps are worn in cold areas. Some tunics have fur hoods. People sometimes wear special headdresses for religious rituals.
MESOPOTAMIA	Sumerians make jewellery from gold, pearls and gems such as **carnelian** and **lapis lazuli**. Babylonians and Assyrians use gold for heavy armbands and earrings, and delicate hair **fillets** often set with gems.	Mesopotamian peoples generally wear leather sandals with straps at the front, and a covered heel at the back. Soldiers usually wear knee-length leather boots tied with laces.	Women pull shawls over their heads. Babylonian and Assyrian kings wear high headdresses. Babylonian men have skullcaps with brims or (like the Assyrians) tall hats.
ANCIENT EGYPT	Egyptians make gold and silver jewellery set with stones such as lapis lazuli and turquoise. Collars, **pectorals** and bracelets are popular. Decorative patterns include **lotus flowers** and **scarab beetles**.	Ancient Egyptians often go barefoot, but sandals are also common. These are made of woven palm leaves, **papyrus** or leather. Most have a thong that separates the big toe and the second toe.	Pharaohs wear a red and white double crown, a striped linen headcloth called a *nemes*, or a headdress. Queens wear headdresses – one style is shaped like a bird. Ordinary women wear headbands.
HEBREWS	Hebrews often wear gold jewellery, including bracelets and chain necklaces. Some sprinkle gold dust on their hair. Women wear earrings and some wear veils with coins or jewels along the edges.	Strapped leather sandals are common. Some people may wear shoes with upturned toes. Women in cities sometimes put **pattens** over their shoes to protect them from mud in the streets.	Hebrew men wear soft caps or turbans. From the early centuries AD, men drape cloaks over their heads for prayer. Early Hebrew women pull cloaks over their hair. By the early centuries AD they wear veils.
PERSIA	Persians copy Assyrian jewellery styles. Pieces are made of gold and often carved with animal designs. Some include mythical creatures such as griffins, which have the head of an eagle and body of a lion.	Persians wear leather shoes fastened with ties or buttons (styles developed from horse-riding ancestors). Baggy leather boots with small heels are also worn, especially by **cavalry** soldiers.	There is a wide range of Persian headwear. Phrygian caps are popular among ordinary men. Kings usually wear gold and jewelled crowns. Soldiers wear hats and helmets. Women are often veiled.

	JEWELLERY	FOOTWEAR	HEADWEAR	
CRETE AND MYCENAE	Minoans wear elaborate bracelets and necklaces of gold, silver or bronze. Women wear spiral-shaped metal earrings and pearl hair decorations. Mycenaeans use gold for **diadem** crowns and other items.	Minoans and Mycenaeans often go barefoot. Leather sandals, often with straps winding up the leg, are also common. Men sometimes wear leather boots or wind strips of cloth around their lower legs.	Men in Crete and Mycenae usually go bareheaded. Sometimes they wear simple, beret-style caps. Women have a variety of ornate tall hats, but probably for ceremonial wear only.	
ANCIENT GREECE	Women wear delicate jewellery. Many items are decorated with twisted gold wire or set with **enamel**. People fasten clothing with *fibula* pins. Men wear little jewellery, apart from rings.	Men and women usually go barefoot. There are also boots, shoes and strapped sandals made of soft calf or tough cow leather. Sandals often have nails in the soles. Some spell out words such as 'Follow me'.	Men wear felt hats, such as the *petasos*. Women pull cloaks over their heads. In later years women wear brimmed, pointed hats called *tholia*, probably made of straw. Soldiers wear various types of helmet.	
ANCIENT ROME	Women wear several pieces of jewellery, including necklaces, bracelets and earrings. The finest are made of gems set in gold. **Cameos** are popular. Men wear rings only. Boys wear protective *bulla* necklaces.	Men and women wear a variety of leather sandals, shoes and boots. The *crepida* closes like a shoe over the heel, but has straps on top. Soldiers wear sandals called *caligae* or closed-in boots.	Men and women usually go bareheaded. Women also pull up their cloaks over their heads. Some cloaks have hoods. Women also wear veils and tie ribbons around their hair or cover it with pearl-decorated nets.	
CELTS	Celts make jewellery from gold, silver, other metals and glass. The torque neck ring is worn by important men and women. People fasten their clothing with decorated *fibula* pins.	Celts in Britain wear leather shoes with fur left on the inside for warmth. Celts in France, known as Gauls, wear leather sandals. Under Roman rule, many Celts wear Roman styles of footwear.	Celts generally use cloaks to cover their heads. In France, women may wear broad-brimmed hats made of felt. Men also own horned battle helmets, but these may be for ceremonial use only.	
MIGRATING TRIBES	Goths and other peoples who migrate into the **Roman Empire** often wear Roman jewellery styles. Later, the Visigoths in Spain make new styles of jewellery, buckles and other items from gold and gems.	Migrating tribes have a variety of simple leather shoes with fur left on the inside. Short leather boots are worn, especially by fighting men. Boots are sometimes pulled tight around the ankles with laces.	Many people go bare-headed. Hunnish men wear warm, fur-trimmed skullcaps. In battle, Goths and others begin to wear strong metal helmets, copied from those worn by Roman soldiers.	
ANCIENT INDIA AND PAKISTAN	Women of the Indus Valley wear metal bracelets and necklaces, and **girdles** made of stones such as jade and carnelian. Guptas wear diamonds, cut into shape so that they sparkle in the light.	Men and women of India and Pakistan usually go barefoot. Women wear toe rings and chains or metal hoops round their ankles. Sometimes the hoops are so heavy women find it difficult to walk.	Until the 2nd century BC turbans are worn by men and women, but then become garments for men only. Women sometimes wear circlets with two ribbons hanging down at the back, or simple diadems.	
ANCIENT CHINA	The Chinese prefer silver jewellery to gold, but sometimes put a thin layer of gold on top to prevent the metal from discolouring (it goes black in the air). Jade is a favourite stone. It is imported from Central Asia.	Rich men and women wear silk or silk-lined leather slippers. Some are fastened on with ribbons. The poor make their footwear from natural materials such as straw and rushes, or from pieces of cloth.	Rich Chinese men wear hats made of folded silk or other cloth. Some are decorated with beads. The different hat styles of officials show their **rank**. Women wear jewelled combs in their hair.	
THE ANCIENT AMERICAS	Maya wear heavy earrings, arm bands and **pendants**. Jade is the most popular stone. Jewellery is also made of tropical bird feathers. The Adena people of North America make copper bracelets and rings.	Maya often go barefoot, but also wear simple leather sandals or moccasins. Many early North American peoples also go barefoot. In the cold Northeast and Northwest, moccasins are popular.	Maya often wear headdresses made of brightly coloured feathers. In north-west North America, people weave hats from tree roots or bark. In the south-east, eagle feathers are used as hair decorations.	

MAPS OF THE ANCIENT WORLD

Many of the empires, countries, regions and cities of the ancient world were known by names that we no longer use. The maps on these pages will help you to locate where they were. The world map shows the area that each of the three more detailed maps covers.

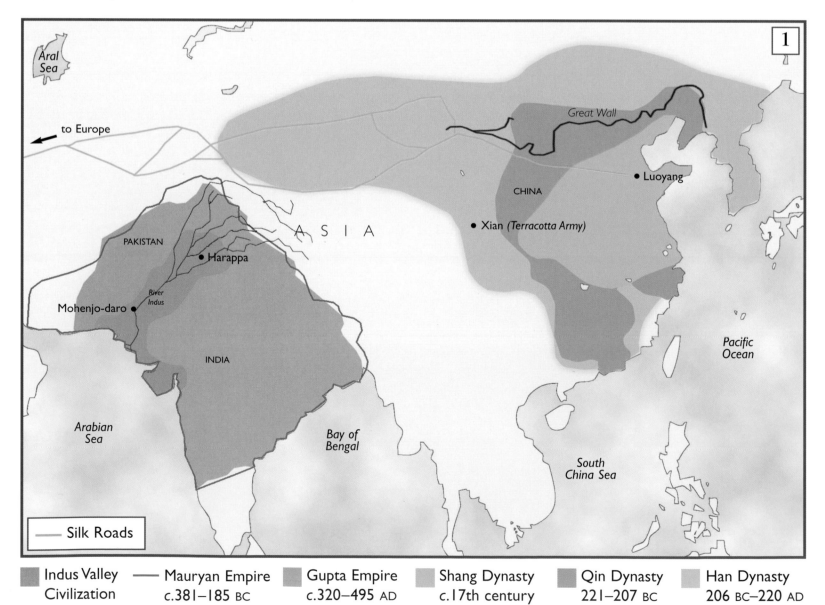

■ Indus Valley Civilization	— Mauryan Empire c.381–185 BC	■ Gupta Empire c.320–495 AD	■ Shang Dynasty c.17th century –1027 BC	■ Qin Dynasty 221–207 BC	■ Han Dynasty 206 BC–220 AD

The three detailed maps on these pages show:
1. Asia
2. North and Central America
3. Europe, the Middle East, North Africa and Western Asia.

They include places that existed at different times during the period covered by this book. Some modern country names have been included, to help you find your way around. The main pages of the book, and the time strips that run along the tops of the pages, will tell you exactly when each place played a major part in world history.

General key to place names

EUROPE	Continent name
GREECE	Country name
ASSYRIA	Region or empire name
Babylon	City name

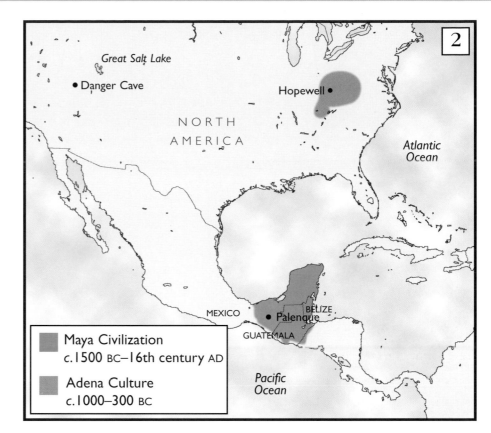

2

Great Salt Lake

• Danger Cave

Hopewell •

NORTH AMERICA

Atlantic Ocean

MEXICO

• Palenque
GUATEMALA
BELIZE

Pacific Ocean

▨ Maya Civilization
c.1500 BC–16th century AD

▨ Adena Culture
c.1000–300 BC

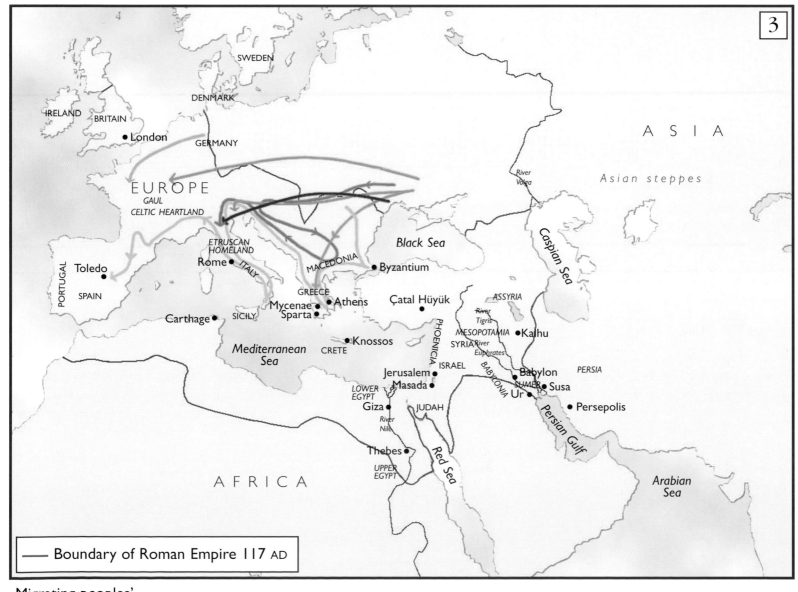

3

SWEDEN

DENMARK

IRELAND   BRITAIN

• London   GERMANY

EUROPE
GAUL
CELTIC HEARTLAND

ASIA

Asian steppes

River Volga

PORTUGAL
• Toledo
SPAIN

ETRUSCAN HOMELAND
Rome •   *ITALY*

MACEDONIA

Black Sea

• Byzantium

Caspian Sea

GREECE
Mycenae •   • Athens
Sparta •

Çatal Hüyük

ASSYRIA

Carthage •   SICILY

River Tigris

MESOPOTAMIA • Kalhu

Mediterranean Sea   CRETE

• Knossos

PHOENICIA
SYRIA *River Euphrates*

Jerusalem •   ISRAEL

PERSIA

LOWER EGYPT
Masada •

Babylon •
BABYLONIA
SUMER • Susa
Ur •

Giza •   JUDAH

• Persepolis

River Nile

Thebes •

Red Sea

Persian Gulf

AFRICA

UPPER EGYPT

Arabian Sea

—— Boundary of Roman Empire 117 AD

Migrating peoples' invasion of Europe   —— Visigoths   —— Ostrogoths   —— Huns   —— Lombards   —— Franks

45

GLOSSARY

agate A type of gemstone that comes in many colours, including blue and green. It is often striped.

alkaline A word describing an alkali – a substance that neutralizes acids. Some alkalis are so strong that they can dissolve materials such as fur.

alpaca A South American animal that belongs to the camel family. It has long, brown, silky fur.

amber Fossilized resin from extinct, cone-bearing trees. The resin is usually orange, brown or yellow.

apron A type of garment worn by men, for example in Egypt and Crete. Aprons hang down from the waist at the front and cover part of the legs. Some also cover the leg backs.

archaeologist A person who studies the past by digging up old sites and examining old objects.

awl A tool with a sharp point. It is used to make holes in leather and other strong materials.

baldric A sword belt worn across the upper body. The sword hangs down from the baldric at the side.

bodice A tight-fitting garment worn on the upper part of a woman's body. It may be sleeved or sleeveless and is often fastened with laces.

boll A seed pod on a cotton plant.

Bronze Age The period of prehistory during which people made tools from bronze. It followed the Stone Age, but its dates varied from place to place. In Scandinavia, it lasted from about 1800 to 500 BC.

cameo Jewellery made from two different gemstone layers. The top layer was often cut into a face shape.

carnelian A type of orange-red gemstone.

cavalry The part of an army whose soldiers ride horses into battle.

chain mail A type of armour made from linked metal rings.

chignon A hairstyle in which long hair is arranged in a roll or bun at the back of the head.

chiton A type of loose tunic worn in Ancient Greece.

conservator A person who looks after ancient fabrics and other objects, for example in a museum.

cuirass A piece of armour, usually made of metal or leather, that covers the wearer's chest and back.

diadem A large, open circle of precious metal worn as a crown.

empire A large area, often including many different countries, that is united under the rule of a single emperor or empress.

enamel A glasslike substance that is made in many colours. Pieces of enamel are often set into metal to make items of jewellery.

fibula A type of metal pin or brooch that was used by Greeks, Romans and others to fasten garments. Some *fibulae* were beautifully decorated.

fillet A ribbon or other band worn in a circle around the head.

flax A blue-flowered plant from whose stalks linen is made.

flint A type of grey-black rock. Prehistoric people often used sharp-edged pieces of flint as tools.

fresco A type of picture made by applying paints to wet plaster.

gall A growth on leaves or twigs caused by insects.

girdle A waist or hip belt, often with ends that hang loose.

greave A piece of armour, usually made of metal or leather, that covers the wearer's lower leg.

hemp An Asian plant from which people made rough cloth.

hide The skin of an animal.

himation A long cloak worn by Ancient Greek men and women.

Ice Age Any of several periods of history when much of the Earth was covered with ice. The most recent Ice Age lasted from about 1.6 million to 10 000 years ago.

inlaid Set into a surface, such as metal, wood or ivory.

Inuit A people descended from the first men and women to settle in Alaska and nearby areas thousands of years ago. Many still live there.

ivory The material animal tusks are made of. It was often carved into jewellery or precious objects.

jade A gemstone that occurs in many colours, but especially green.

jerkin A jacket with no collar and no sleeves.

kamarband A type of sash worn around the waist in Ancient India.

kilt A length of cloth that wraps round the waist to form a skirt.

lapis lazuli A bright blue gemstone.

lappet wig A style of Ancient Egyptian wig divided into separate hanging sections (lappets).

loom A machine used to weave yarn into cloth.

lotus flower The flower of a type of water lily that the Ancient Egyptians believed to be holy.

moccasins A simple leather shoe worn by some early American peoples.

mosaic A floor or wall decoration made of pieces of coloured glass or stone arranged into patterns.

nomad A person who moves from place to place in search of food.

obelisk A stone pillar that slopes inwards from the bottom to the top.

Old Testament The holy writings of the Hebrews that today make up the first part of the Christian Bible.

p'ao robe A long, loose, crossover robe worn in Ancient China.

palla A rectangular cloak worn by Roman women.

papyrus A tall, reedlike plant that grows by lakes and rivers in Africa.

patten An overshoe with a high sole, worn over an ordinary shoe to protect it from dirt and water.

pectoral An item of jewellery worn as a chest decoration.

pendants Strips that hang down from the waist of some Ancient Egyptian garments. Also objects that hang from a necklace.

poncho A sleeveless cloak that is pulled on over the head.

prehistoric The word that describes history before writing was invented.

rank A person's position in society. If a person was high-ranking, they were important.

republic A country or area with elected rulers and no king, queen or emperor.

Roman Empire The era (27 BC–476 AD) in which Ancient Rome was ruled by emperors. The term also refers to the area that they governed.

sable A small, weasel-like animal from northern Asia with a shiny, dark brown or black coat.

sari A garment formed by wrapping a long piece of cloth round the body. Saris are traditionally worn in India and Pakistan.

scale armour A type of armour made of overlapping plates of iron, bronze or other metal.

scarab beetle A beetle that the Ancient Egyptians believed to be holy.

seal A ring or stamp with a picture cut into it. In the past high-ranking people closed letters with a lump of hot wax or clay, then pressed their seal on it to prove it was from them.

senator An important official in the Roman republic and later the empire.

Silk Road One of the ancient trade routes along which silk was carried from China to the West.

sinew A band of strong white material in the body that joins a muscle to a bone.

soapstone A type of soft, grey-green, brown or white stone.

steppe A large, flat area of grass-covered land, usually without trees.

stola A long sleeved or sleeveless robe worn by Roman women.

sub-continent A land area that forms a large part of a continent.

synagogue A building where Jews hold religious services.

tan To treat animal hides with substances containing the chemical tannin. This process turns them into leather and stops them rotting.

tapestry A way of making textiles by weaving coloured threads into a fixed linen backing. Also fabric made using this technique.

tapir A type of animal. The South American tapir has a short, reddish-brown or black coat.

taw To spread salt and other minerals on animal hides. This ancient method of tanning turned hides into white leather.

terracotta A type of reddish clay.

visor A hinged metal flap on the front of a helmet. It can be raised so that the wearer can see clearly or lowered for protection.

yarn A length of twisted fibres ready to be woven or knitted into cloth.

INDEX

2ND EDITION
LEVEL 3
CONSTRUCTION
DIPLOMAS

Brickwork

NVQ and Technical
Certificate **Level 3**

£24.99

www.heinemann.co.uk

✓ Free online support
✓ Useful weblinks
✓ 24 hour online ordering

0845 630 44 44

Heinemann

Part of Pearson

Heinemann is an imprint of Harcourt Education Limited, a company incorporated in England and Wales, having its registered office: Halley Court, Jordan Hill, Oxford OX2 8EJ. Registered company number: 3099304

www.heinemann.co.uk

Heinemann is the registered trademark of Pearson Education Limited

Text © Carillion Construction Ltd 2007, 2009

First published 2007

12 11 10 09 08 07
10 9 8 7 6 5 4 3 2 1

British Library Cataloguing in Publication Data is available from the British Library on request.

ISBN 978 0 435 325 85 5

Edited by Sarah Christopher
Designed by HL Studios
Typeset by HL Studios
Printed in Italy

Illustrated by HL Studios
Original illustrations © Pearson Education Limited 2007, 2009

Cover design by GD Associates
Cover photo © Pearson Education / Ben Nicholson

Every effort has been made to contact copyright holders of material reproduced in this book. Any omissions will be rectified in subsequent printings if notice is given to the publishers.

Websites

The websites used in this book were correct and up to date at the time of publication. It is essential for tutors to preview each website before using it in class so as to ensure that the URL is still accurate, relevant and appropriate. We suggest that tutors bookmark useful websites and consider enabling students to access them through the school/college intranet.